Beginning Old English

D1289981

Beginning Old English

Carole Hough and John Corbett

First published 2007 by
PALGRAVE MACMILLAN
Houndmills, Basingstoke, Hampshire RG21 6XS and
175 Fifth Avenue, New York, N.Y. 10010
Companies and representatives throughout the world

PALGRAVE MACMILLAN is the global academic imprint of the Palgrave Macmillan division of St. Martin's Press, LLC and of Palgrave Macmillan Ltd. Macmillan® is a registered trademark in the United States, United Kingdom and other countries. Palgrave is a registered trademark in the European Union and other countries.

ISBN-13: 978–1–4039–9349–6   hardback
ISBN-10: 1–4039–9349–1   hardback
ISBN-13: 978–1–4039–9350–2   paperback
ISBN-10: 1–4039–9350–5   paperback

This book is printed on paper suitable for recycling and made from fully managed and sustained forest sources.

A catalogue record for this book is available from the British Library.

Library of Congress Cataloging-in-Publication Data
Hough, Carole.
    Beginning Old English / Carole Hough and John Corbett.
        p. cm.
    Includes bibliographical references and index.
    ISBN-13: 978–1–4039–9349–6 (cloth)
    ISBN-10: 1–4039–9349–1 (cloth)
    ISBN-13: 978–1–4039–9350–2 (pbk.)
    ISBN-10: 1–4039–9350–5 (pbk.)
        1. English language—Old English, ca. 450–100.   2. English language—Old English, ca. 450–1100—Grammar.   3. English language—Old English, ca. 450–1100—Readers.   I. Corbett, John, 1959–   II. Title.

PE135.H68 2007
429'.82421—dc22   2006048537

10   9   8   7   6   5   4   3   2   1
16 15 14 13 12 11 10 09 08 07

Printed and bound in China

To our parents

Contents

List of Illustrations

Preface

To understand who you are, you need to know where you are from. We construct our identities in many different ways – with reference to our ethnic heritage, family history, and religious upbringing or inherited system of beliefs. One of the most powerful ways of exploring our roots is by examining the evolution of our language – the very medium, after all, that binds our ethnic, family and religious communities together.

The English language now serves as the medium of communication for millions of people worldwide. However, its origins lie in a set of dialects spoken fifteen hundred years ago in the south-eastern lowlands of the British Isles, by bands of Germanic settlers, the Anglo-Saxons. Together, these dialects are known as Old English, and although they may look alien to us at first glance, on examination they quickly reveal their kinship to the English spoken and written today.

This book is intended to serve as a basic introduction to one of the dialects of Old English, that of the West Saxons. For reasons explained in the first chapter, West Saxon was the main written dialect of Old English, and is the medium of most of its surviving literature. It is not the purpose of this book to dwell in detail on the linguistic subtleties of Old English: it is designed as a 'taster' to introduce you to the character of the language and – crucially – to give you confidence first in reading simple and simplified West Saxon texts and then in tackling some original literature. The necessary explanation of Old English vocabulary and grammar is geared primarily towards your comprehension of these texts.

By the conclusion of this book, we hope you will be able – with the support of a glossary – to appreciate some of the glory of Old English literature in its original form. We hope that many of you will be encouraged to pursue your study of the language further, and to enter more fully the strange, yet strangely, familiar world of the Anglo-Saxons.

In writing this book, we have benefited from the support and enthusiasm of colleagues and students in the Department of English Language at the University of Glasgow, who have used and commented on earlier versions of the book. Our most particular thanks are due to Professor Mike MacMahon, for his help and encouragement in the early stages of planning. The faults that remain are naturally our own responsibility.

Acknowledgements

Where appropriate, every effort has been made to trace the copyright of literary texts and illustrations. The authors are grateful for permission to reproduce excerpts from *Beowulf*, translated by Seamus Heaney, copyright © 2000 by Seamus Heaney, used by permission of W. W. Norton and Company, and Faber and Faber Ltd; *Beowulf*, translated by Edwin Morgan, copyright © 1952, 1962, 2002 by Edwin Morgan, used by permission of Carcanet Press.

The authors are also grateful for permission to reproduce the following illustrations: Cathedral Library, Exeter, Manuscript 3501, fol. 110v detail, reproduced by permission of the Dean and Chapter of Exeter; Christopher Lee as Saruman in *The Lord of the Rings: The Two Towers*, copyright 2002, New Line Productions, Inc. ™ The Saul Zaentz Company d/b/a Tolkien Enterprises under licence to New Line Productions, Inc; all rights reserved, photo by Pierre Vinet, photo appears courtesy of New Line Productions, Inc.; Corpus Christi College, Cambridge, Manuscript 173, fol. 10r detail, reproduced by permission of the Master and Fellows of Corpus Christi College, Cambridge; Corpus Christi College, Cambridge, Manuscript 183, fol. 1^v, reproduced by permission of the Master and Fellows of Corpus Christi College, Cambridge; eighth-century helmet found at Coppergate, York, reproduced by permission of York Museums Trust (York Castle Museum); Franks Casket, front panel, © copyright The Trustees of The British Museum; MacLean's Cross, Iona, © Crown copyright, reproduced courtesy of the Royal Commission on the Ancient and Historical Monuments of Scotland; the Ruthwell Cross, Dumfriesshire, reproduced courtesy of RCAHMS (Erskine Beveridge Collection); the Annunciation Panel of the Ruthwell Cross, © Crown copyright, reproduced courtesy of Historic Scotland; Oxford, Bodleian Manuscripts Junius 27, fol. 118^r detail, and Hatton 20, fol. 1^r detail, reproduced by permission of the Bodleian Library, University of Oxford; St Columba's Bay, Iona, reproduced by permission of Alison Phipps. The maps are by Mike Shand, Department of Geographical and Earth Sciences, University of Glasgow.

Every effort has been made to trace the copyright holders but if any have been inadvertently overlooked the authors and publisher will be pleased to make the necessary arrangement at the first opportunity.

Part I

1 Origins

The Anglo-Saxon invasion

Early in the fifth century AD, the Roman Empire in northern Europe was in terminal decline. Gaul, now France, was conquered by tribes whose barbarian languages were Germanic in origin. As a result, Rome stopped sending its governors and administrators to its north-ernmost outposts in the British Isles. The Britons, who over almost 500 years had become Romanised in behaviour and attitude, but were still Celtic-speaking, now had to look after themselves.

The Britons were in a weak position. Germanic tribes had also started attacking the south-east coast of the British Isles even before Roman rule came to an end. They seem to have come mainly from what is now Denmark and the north-east of Germany. In the 50 years after Roman administration ceased, three groups of these Germanic-speaking tribes – Jutes, Angles and Saxons – invaded and settled the eastern lowlands of what is now England. According to the account given by the Anglo-Saxon monk and historian Bede (c.673–735), the Jutes settled in the area around present-day Kent, the Saxons occu-pied and gave their name to Essex, Sussex and the ancient kingdom of Wessex, and the Angles took land principally in Suffolk and Norfolk. In the settled territories, different kingdoms gradually emerged – what was later described as the Anglo-Saxon 'heptarchy' of Northumbria, Mercia, East Anglia, Essex, Sussex, Wessex and Kent (see Illustration 1).

The nature of these 'seven kingdoms' and the relationship between them are now debated amongst scholars. What is beyond dispute is that the dominant language spoken in these territories shifted from Celtic varieties to the Germanic dialects spoken by the invaders and settlers. Celtic-speaking tribes remained in control of the mountain-ous country to the west – now Wales – and the lands north of the abandoned Hadrian's Wall. In both areas, the Celtic-speaking natives

3

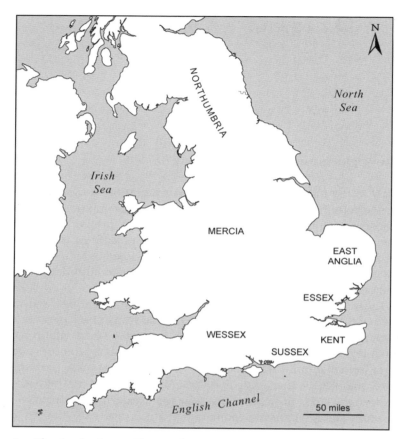

1   The Anglo-Saxon Heptarchy, *c.* 700

referred to the settlers indiscriminately as 'Saxons', or, in their own language, *sassenachs.* They still do.

The Germanic dialects spoken in the Anglo-Saxon kingdoms were distinct but mutually intelligible varieties that began to evolve from the tribal tongues spoken by the settlers' continental ancestors. The varieties can be grouped into four main types – Northumbrian, Kentish, Mercian and West Saxon. We refer to these dialects together as Old English. No-one, 1500 years ago, could have imagined that in these obscure Germanic dialects, spoken by warring tribes in the southern lowlands of an abandoned Roman colony on the very periphery of Europe, would lie the origins of today's global language.

From speech to writing

For several hundred years, little was written in any of the dialects of Old English. Although the Roman Empire had receded, the language of the Romans, Latin, remained the medium of scholarship and the Catholic Church throughout Europe. The Anglo-Saxon settlers in Britain were pagans, but were converted to Christianity by missionaries from Rome and Ireland. The process started in Kent, with the arrival in 597 of a group of monks sent by Pope Gregory the Great under the leadership of St Augustine. Missionaries and monks constituted a literate order in the Anglo-Saxon kingdoms, and they were primarily responsible for those valuable records of written Old English that survive in manuscript. Sometimes the monks interlaced their Latin texts with Old English, 'glossing' the Latin terms by giving their Old English equivalents, as in the tenth-century copy of the Psalms known as the 'Junius Psalter' (Illustration 2). In the first line, the Latin words for God are glossed by Old English *dryhten* and *hlaford*, both meaning 'lord'.

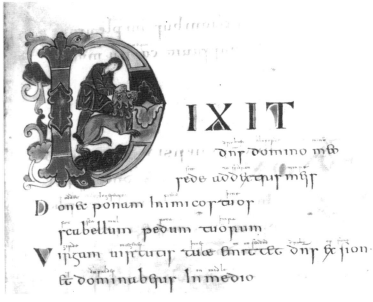

2   Oxford Bodleian MS, Junius 27, fol. 118^r (*detail*)

Most of the Old English texts that are known to us today date from or after the reign of Alfred the Great, who ruled Wessex from 871 to 899. Indeed, it is because of Alfred that most surviving Old English texts are in West Saxon, the variety that we shall be studying in this book.

Alfred's adoption of Old English as a written language was the result of a crisis. In the century before his reign, a series of events occurred that was to shape the future of the English language. The northern and eastern Anglo-Saxon kingdoms were threatened by a new wave of pirates, invaders and settlers – Vikings from what is now Denmark and Norway. The language of the Vikings was Old Norse, a close cousin of Old English and in many ways similar.

The Viking invasion

The Viking raids began in the late eighth century: the Norsemen attacked Ireland, around what is now Dublin, sacked the holy island of Iona in western Scotland, and raided the English east coast. Then they began to stay longer. In 851 they wintered on the island of Thanet, and in 865–9 they conquered the Anglo-Saxon kingdoms of East Anglia, Northumbria, and Mercia. However, Alfred led the men of Wessex to a famous victory in battle, and the Vikings retreated, settling mainly in Northumbria and East Anglia, in a territory called the Danelaw (see Illustration 3). In this area, the merging of Old English and Old Norse would eventually shape the essential character of later English.

Meanwhile, the Anglo-Saxon territories now centred on Wessex, where Alfred began a literary project that shifted the focus of activity from Latin towards English. The centres of learning in the Anglo-Saxon kingdoms had been the monasteries, where Latin still reigned supreme, but the raids of the heathen Vikings had disrupted their activities. By Alfred's time, even the monks' knowledge of Latin had declined. Alfred established a court school, imported scholars, and began a translation project to which he himself significantly contributed. Anglo-Saxon literature had truly begun. Alfred's project ensured that, today, we know what Old English looked like, and we can even work out what it must have sounded like.

3　Britain and the Danelaw

Old English literature

It is a considerable task to create a written form of a language that for 400 years had mainly been spoken. The scribes who occasionally glossed difficult Latin words in Old English had used a mixture of the roman alphabet used for Latin, and the ancient runic alphabet used by Germanic tribes on the continent. Runes were straight-sided characters, suitable for carving on hard surfaces such as wood, bone or stone. If you visit the small church at Ruthwell in Dumfriesshire, you will see a sandstone monument, some six metres high – the Ruthwell Cross (Illustration 4). On the Cross, in runes, are inscribed some lines from, or related to, the Old English religious poem *The Dream of the Rood*. The Ruthwell Cross dates from the late seventh or eighth century; originally it would have stood in the open air and would have been used as the focus for worship.

There are no surviving Old English manuscripts written entirely in runes, although occasionally Anglo-Saxon scribes made use of them for special purposes, for instance within riddles. By Alfred's time the Roman alphabet, with a few runic additions, had become adopted by most writers. Illustration 5, for instance, shows the opening lines of a letter sent by Alfred to each of his bishops in or soon after 890, announcing his educational project.

The heading reads ÐEOS BOC SCEAL TO WIGORA CEASTRE, 'This book shall (i.e. must go) to Worcester'. The runic letter 'wynn', shaped like an angular letter 'p', is used at the beginning of the place-name for the sound later represented by 'w'.

Using their extended alphabet and a spelling system that seems to have closely reflected pronunciation (unlike present-day English!), Alfred, his scholars and their successors began to produce both translations from Latin and original work in English. Due in large part to their efforts, we now have access to a rich variety of Old English literature, including religious prose (e.g. parts of the Bible, sermons, and saints' lives), histories (e.g. Bede's *Ecclesiastical History of the English People*, and the *Anglo-Saxon Chronicle*), philosophical works, medical writings, religious and secular poetry (see Chapter 6), and laws. This book introduces you to some of the most important of these works.

The authorship of many Anglo-Saxon texts is a mystery. Some, like *Beowulf*, clearly draw on earlier oral tradition, captured by scribes whose own contribution to the works is unclear. Other early authors are known to us – Alfred himself, Caedmon (see Chapter 6), Cynewulf

4   The Ruthwell Cross

5   Oxford Bodleian MS, Hatton 20, fol. 1ʳ (*detail*)

and Ælfric 'the Grammarian' (*c.*950–1010). Ælfric, typically for an Anglo-Saxon author, was educated in a monastery, the Benedictine monastery in Winchester, before becoming an abbot near Oxford. He wrote various religious works including sermons and saints' lives, and devised his *Colloquium* to teach his novice monks conversational Latin. We shall be looking at an adapted version of this in later chapters.

The Norman invasion

The literary activity sparked by Alfred the Great lasted for more than 200 years, until it was rudely curtailed and then entirely halted by the Norman Conquest of 1066 and its aftermath. The Norman French, themselves descendants of Vikings, led by William the Conqueror, over-ran the Anglo-Saxon kingdoms and extended their territory throughout the Danelaw as far as the northern kingdom of Scotland. In their vicious land-grab the Normans depopulated whole areas of Northumbria, carrying out an ethnic displacement later called 'the harrying of the north'. Refugees from the defeated Anglo-Saxon dynasty fled with their retainers and servants to the court of the Celtic-speaking Scots in Edinburgh. There the Anglo-Saxon Princess Margaret married the widower King Malcolm. The speech of Queen Margaret and the Northumbrian refugees would eventually spread out over the Scottish lowlands, and become the basis of the lowland Scots tongue. But south of the border, the language of the governing classes of England was now Norman French. English became the speech of peasants.

Even before the arrival of the Normans, Old English was changing. In the Danelaw, the Old Norse of the Viking settlers was combining with the Old English of the Anglo-Saxons in new and interesting ways. In the poem *The Battle of Maldon*, as we shall later see, grammatical confusion in the speech of one of the Viking characters has been interpreted by some commentators as an attempt to represent an Old Norse speaker struggling with Old English. The languages were closely related, and both relied very much on the endings of words – what we call 'inflexions' – to signal grammatical information. Often these grammatical inflexions were the main thing that distinguished other- wise similar words in Old English and Old Norse.[1] For example, the word 'worm' or 'serpent' used as the object of a sentence would have been *orminn* in Old Norse, and simply *wyrm* in Old English. The result was that as the two communities strove to communicate with each other, the inflexions became blurred and eventually disap- peared. The grammatical information that they signalled had to be expressed using different resources, and so the nature of the English language began to change. New reliance was put on the order of words, and on the meanings of little grammatical words, such as prepositions like *to, with, in, over* and *around*. Without the restraining influence of a written standard, based in Wessex, the pace of linguistic change began to accelerate.

The transformation of Old English

For around two centuries after the establishment of Norman rule in England, English was spoken but relatively seldom written. Even so, the influence of English continued to spread. Although Scotland was a separate kingdom, King David, the heir of Malcolm and Margaret, established peaceful relations with many powerful Norman barons, granting them land in the Scottish lowlands. These barons brought with them many English-speaking retainers, mainly from northern England, where there was a strong Norse influence. A distinct variety of the language, first known as 'Inglis' and much later as 'Scottis', evolved. Today, the pronunciation and vocabulary of the lowland Scots language is often very close to its Old English (OE) origins, as in 'hoose', 'moose' and 'coo' (OE *hūs, mūs, cū*). Sometimes the sounds of Scots and English developed in different directions, as in 'hame/home', and 'stane/stone' (OE *hām, stān*). At other times, the Scots term derives from Old Norse (ON), where the Old English form derives from the dialects of the Anglo-Saxons, as in Scots 'kirk' (ON *kirkja*) and English 'church' (OE *cirice*).

In the south, though, England and France embarked on a war that would last, on and off, for over a hundred years (1337–1453). By the time it concluded, the political and personal links between the Norman aristocracy and France had been eroded. It was considered unpatriotic for an Englishman to speak or write French, and slowly there was a re-emergence of English as a written language. The character of the 'Middle English' dialects was considerably different from their Old English predecessors, however. The complex nature of contact and interaction between Norman French, Old Norse and the dialects of Old English resulted in new varieties whose pronunciation, spelling, vocabulary and grammar were greatly changed. These varieties would continue to change – and a form that was especially designed for writing began to be developed. This written form, originally intended for use by clerks in the Treasury (and known, consequently, as Chancery English), was finally fixed by dictionary-makers and popular grammarians in the eighteenth century. Today we call it 'standard English'.

Sister languages

English continues to evolve, still incorporating new words from different languages around the world, still changing its pronunciation and grammar from region to region. At first sight, Old English may look different from today's English, but there is a continuous line that links the different varieties. For this reason, if no other, it is wrong to consider Old English a 'dead language', just as it is wrong to consider a butterfly a dead caterpillar. It has simply transformed. The echoes of Old English can still be heard in the speech and writing of millions of people around the globe. These echoes are also evident in other related modern languages – in German, Norwegian, Danish, and Frisian, a Germanic variety still spoken in the coastal areas of northeast Germany, where some of the original Anglo-Saxon invaders embarked.

One related, or 'cognate', modern language that still has some of the appearance of Old English is Icelandic, another Viking tongue, which, because of Iceland's geographical isolation, has changed little over the centuries. Like Old English, modern Icelandic employs an extended roman alphabet that includes symbols like <ð> and the runic symbol <þ>, both for 'th'. If the Norman Conquest had not occurred, tourist phrases in present-day English might have looked something like the following phrases in modern Icelandic!

I need to send a fax.	Ég þarf að senda fax.
I need to buy a map.	Ég þarf að kaupa kort.
Can you take us to the airport?	Geturðu farið með okkur á flugvöllinn?
Can you take us to our hotel?	Geturðu keyrt okkur á hótelið okkar?

The Icelandic phrases might seem incomprehensible at first glance. But a second look shows that English and Icelandic are indeed related. For example, *senda* is almost identical to 'send', and the two words translated here as 'take' – *farið* and *keyrt* – are not unlike 'ferry' and 'cart', which also have the sense of transporting something. Even the end of the expression *geturðu* ('can you'), when pronounced, is similar to the older English form for 'you', *thou*. A study of the oldest form of our language reveals the similarities between English and its closest relatives all the more clearly.

Old English scholarship

Old English studies were effectively begun during the sixteenth and early seventeenth centuries by Protestant reformers aiming to demonstrate the historical independence from Rome of the Anglo-

Saxon church. Leading churchmen and scholars such as Archbishop Matthew Parker (1504–75), Sir Robert Cotton (1571–1631), and Francis Junius (1591–1677) compiled important collections of early manuscripts now held respectively at Corpus Christi College, Cambridge (the 'Parker Library'), the British Library in London (the 'Cotton Collection'), and the Bodleian Library in Oxford (including the 'Junius Psalter' – see illustration 2). Interest in the origins of English grew with the rise of 'philology', or the evolutionary study of languages, in the nineteenth century. One of the most influential Victorian scholars of English was Henry Sweet (1845–1912), an Oxford academic whose name became synonymous with Old English studies for generations of learners. Sweet became an expert in the history of English and was particularly interested in its pronunciation. He shared with the playwright George Bernard Shaw an interest in spelling reform, and Shaw claimed to have used Sweet as his model for Professor Henry Higgins in his play *Pygmalion*, which was subsequently turned into a musical and film, *My Fair Lady*. Sweet wrote a number of books designed to teach Old English to undergraduates, principally *An Anglo-Saxon Primer* (1882) and *An Anglo-Saxon Reader* (1876). These have been frequently revised, and are still in print. A relatively neglected work, however, was his *First Steps in Anglo-Saxon* (1897), which included a number of simplified texts such as a prose version of the famous Old English poem *Beowulf*. We have borrowed from several of Henry Sweet's simplified texts in the early chapters of this book.

Much recent popular interest in Old English has been stimulated by the success of J. R. R. Tolkien's novels, and their film adaptations. As an undergraduate, Tolkien (1892–1973) studied Old English at Exeter College, Oxford. There, he was particularly struck by two lines from the poem *Christ A*:

Ēalā Ēarendel engla beorhtast   *Hail, Earendel, brightest of angels,*
Ofer middangeard monnum sended   *On Middle Earth sent to men*

'Middle Earth' – *middangeard* – in Old English poetry refers to the human world between Heaven above and Hell below. In Tolkien's own novels, most famously *The Hobbit* and *The Lord of the Rings*, Middle Earth became the site of struggles and quests involving creatures of his own imagination, inspired by the literature and languages of the Anglo-Saxons and Vikings.

Perhaps seeking to emulate the success of the screen versions of Tolkien's novels, producers and directors have returned to the most famous Old English poem, *Beowulf*, which has been adapted many times in many media (see Chapter 7). Recent film versions are *Beowulf and Grendel* (2005), which was shot in Iceland, and *Beowulf* (2007). Anglo-Saxon culture echoes down the centuries, in one form or another.

The study of Old English also remains strong today. It is sustained in part by the desire to engage directly with the oldest literary texts in English, partly by a desire to know how and why language changes, and partly by curiosity about the historical development of different aspects of the cultures of the people of Britain. Old English studies embrace topics such as the history of names and the development of English law. Above all, Old English invites us on a journey into a world that is both our own and unfamiliar. Like Henry Sweet's *First Steps in Anglo-Saxon*, this book is designed to start you off on your own quest.

We aim this book to appeal to those with an interest in Anglo-Saxon literature and culture, but with little background in language study. Chapter 2 focuses on the main initial obstacle to understanding – Old English spelling and vocabulary – and familiarises the reader with the look of Old English, giving guidance on how to learn sufficient words to become a reasonably fluent reader. Chapters 3–5 then explain how Old English grammar works, paying particular attention to how the grammatical resources of Old English communicate meanings. Throughout Chapters 2–5, we begin to look at simple and then gradually more sophisticated texts.

Chapters 6 and 7 turn from a language focus, to consider first the way our Anglo-Saxon ancestors composed poetry, and then how later writers have translated and adapted one of the greatest Old English poems, *Beowulf*, for page and screen. Chapter 7 also reflects on the role of translation in the teaching and learning of Old English. The book concludes with Part II, a selection of four key texts presented in unsimplified Old English, but with sufficient 'scaffolding' to allow the inexperienced reader to navigate his or her way through the texts. We believe that the richest experience of Old English literature is a direct and unmediated one. We hope that this book will help you on your way.

Note

1. A course on Old Norse for beginners is available at http://www.hi.is/ ~haukurth/norse.

2 Recognising Old English Words

It is likely that one of the biggest obstacles readers encounter when tackling Old English texts is the apparent unfamiliarity of the vocabulary. First of all, the spellings of many words have changed – so even if a word has survived from Old English into today's English, it might not be immediately recognisable. An example is *cwēn* 'queen'. A further issue to do with spelling is that some of the letters that are used in the Old English alphabet are no longer used in today's English, so 'forth', for example, is spelled *forþ* or *forð*, and 'was' is spelled *wæs*. A greater hindrance is that many Old English words have disappeared entirely from our active vocabulary, and simply have to be learnt as you would learn a word in a foreign language. Three words for 'spear', for instance, were *gār*, *ord* and *spere*. The third has survived, but the others have not. Finally, even if you do recognise a word and think you understand it, you might find that over the centuries the meaning of the word has shifted. An example of this is *dēor*, which in Old English means any wild animal, but in today's English means only one kind, a 'deer'.

This chapter aims to help you over the first hurdles by introducing you to some useful and quickly identifiable Old English words, and suggesting some strategies with which you can begin to build up your own 'word hoard' (Old English *wordhord*) of ancient expressions. With the minimum of effort, many Old English words are easy to recognise. They have not changed very much for over a thousand years. For instance, most if not all of the following words should be recognisable (their present-day equivalences are given at the end of this chapter). It often helps to say the words aloud.

and	*ēast*	*gold*	*help*	*blis*
god	*west*	*understandan*	*word*	*wundor*[1]

As you read through many of the texts given later in this book, there-fore, some phrases here and there will be relatively easy to under-stand. Here are some examples, adapted from texts we shall encounter:

Cyneheard wæs Sigebryhtes brōþor.	Cyneheard was Sigebryht's brother.
Crist wæs on rōde.	Christ was on the cross ('rood').
Þæt wæs God æl-mihtig.	That was God almighty.
Hē fēoll on eorþan.	He fell to the ground ('earth').
Hit wæs ne riht.	It was not right.
Ic hæfde twā honda and twēgen fēt.	I had two hands and two feet.
Mīn tunge is heard.	My tongue is harsh ('hard').

It is not surprising that words for such basic concepts as relationships and parts of the body remain fairly stable in the language. Our task as language learners is to build on this shared vocabulary and to try to internalise the vocabulary that has been lost.

The Old English alphabet

One of the most noticeable characteristics of the Old English alphabet is that not all of its letters have survived into today's English. There are two extra consonants, þ and ð, which both represent the sounds now shown as *th*, whether voiced as in '*th*is' or unvoiced as in '*th*ing'. Occasionally, voiced *th* becomes pronounced as *d*. Knowing this, then, can you recognise the following words?

dēað	*þing*	*þis*	*norþ*
morþor	*ōðer*	*brōðor*	*eorðe*[2]

In later chapters of this book, you will find some words spelled with both þ and ð in different texts, and even within a single text. This reflects the variation in spellings in manuscripts of Old English. In Chapters 2–5, we have standardised the spellings somewhat in order to ease the initial encounter with the language, so here occurrences of ð have been regularised to þ.

There is one extra vowel character in the Old English alphabet: *æ* was pronounced *a* as in *cat*. It can be found in the following words:

> *æfter*   *æt*   *wæter* (compare today's broad Scots pronunciation, 'watter')

Missing letters

Although the Old English alphabet contains a few extra letters, it does not use all the letters we are familiar with in today's English. There are some modern letters that are rarely if ever used in Old English:

Present-day English	Old English
k	c
v	f
z	s

Knowing this, the following Old English words should be a little more recognisable:

> *dēofol*   *drinc*   *dysig*   *folc*   *ofer*   *weorc*[3]

Switched sounds

A common change in English over a thousand years is caused by people's habit of changing sounds around, for example saying *modren* rather than *modern*. This switching of sounds, technically known as 'metathesis', often happens with *r* but occurs with other sounds too. This is why modern English has *third* and *thirty* alongside *three*: all originally began with *thr-*. Can you recognise the following words?

> *beorht*   *gærs*   *þrēo*   *þridda*   *þrītig*   *þurh*[4]

Changes in spelling and pronunciation

Over time, many Old English words changed their pronunciation (and spelling) in a regular way – so regular, in fact, that once you can identify the change, you can often identify the word.

Combinations of consonants are often easy to recognise:

Old English	OE Example	Present-day English	PDE Example
cw	*cwic*	qu	quick (i.e. 'alive')
sc	*biscop*	sh	bishop
hl and hr	*hlaford, hrōf*	l and r	lord, roof
hw	*hwǣr*	wh	where
ht	*niht*	ght	night

There are no 'silent' letters in Old English: all vowels and consonants are pronounced. Silent letters in today's English, such as 'gh' in 'night' and 'k' in 'knee', often represent sounds that were pronounced in Old English and have now become fossilised in the spelling system. Can you guess what these words might mean?

cwæð	*scip*	*æsc*	*hlēapan*	*hring*
hrefn	*hwæt*	*riht*	*miht*[5]	

It is also useful to learn some of the common changes that occur to 'long vowels', those vowels that are usually marked with a ‾ over the letter (as in ī, ū and so on):

wīf (pronounced something like 'weef') becomes 'wife'.
hūs (pronounced something like Scots 'hoose') becomes 'house'.
bāt (pronounced something like 'baht') becomes 'boat'.
tōþ (pronounced something like 'toth') becomes 'tooth'.
fēt (pronounced something like 'fate') becomes 'feet'.
brȳd (pronounced something like 'brüd', with the same vowel as in German *Füße*) becomes 'bride'; however, sometimes the vowel is shortened, so that *lȳtel* becomes 'little'.

Bearing these changes in mind, what do you think the following words mean?

wīf	*līf*	*mīl*	*hwīt*	*wīs*
hūs	*mūs*	*hlūd*	*sūþ*	*mūþ*
bāt	*hām*	*stān*	*bān*	*hlāf*
tōþ	*hrōf*	*stōd*	*blōd*	*bōc*
fēt	*hēr*	*hē*	*swēte*	*gēs*[6]

And how do you think the following words would look in Old English?

mine   wine   why   good   foot   out   town   rope   teeth[7]

Two tricky consonants

Some sounds are a little more complicated. The consonants *c* and *g* are pronounced differently in different positions and in different combinations of letters:

> Old English *c* was usually pronounced *k* as in 'king'. However, before *e* and *i*, and at the end of a word, it can be pronounced *ch* as in 'chill'.

> Old English *g* was usually pronounced as in 'girl'. However, before *e* and *i*, and at the end of a word, it can be pronounced like the *y* in 'yet'.

> The combination *cg* was pronounced *j* as in 'judge'.

Knowing this, can you recognise the following expressions?

æl-mihtig	*benc*	*bysig*	*cræftig*	*dæg*
candel	*cirice*	*fæger*	*geong*	*manig*
ecg	*hālig*	*wērig*	*gēar*	*weg*[8]

Spelling variations

Some Old English words have a range of spellings, only one of which survives into today's English. For instance, some varieties of Old English have *a* where others have *o*, particularly before *m* or *n*, so that some texts have *ond* and *hond* rather than the more familiar *and* and *hand*. There is also variation between *a* and *ea*, particularly before *l*: for instance, the word for 'old' may be spelled *ald* or *eald*, and *fela* 'many' can also be spelled *feala*. Can you recognise the following words?

eall	*fram*	*mon*	*strang*	*lond*	*lang*	*weall*[9]

Changes in meaning

Sometimes, unfortunately, it is not enough simply to recognise a word. Sometimes its meaning has changed over the centuries. For example, two Old English words that could simply mean 'woman' were *cwēn* and *wīf*. Only their narrower meanings 'queen' and 'wife' (= 'married woman') survive in current standard English, although in some varieties, such as that of north-eastern Scotland, 'quine' still means a young woman more generally. Can you figure out the present-day meanings of the following Old English words? The first one is done for you.

Old English form	Present-day English form	Old English meaning
ǣrǣnde	errand	any kind of message
crǣftig		skilful
dōm		judgement
gāst		spirit
sōna		immediately
winter		year[10]

100 Old English words you already know

One message of this chapter is that there are many Old English words that quickly become recognisable, especially once you take into consideration the changes in spelling and pronunciation explained above. See how many of the following words you recognise. Some have already been given in the examples above. Verbs end in *-an*, for example *lufian* 'to love'.

People (*cynn*)

bearn, brōþor, brȳd, cild, dohtor, fæder, frēond, mōdor, sunu, sweoster, widewe, wīf, wīfmann[11]

Professions (*cræft*)

scēap-hierde, fiscere, bæcere, cōc, smiþ, gold-smiþ, þēof, wrītere[12]

Animals and birds (*dēor and fugol*)

fisc, gōs, hors, mūs, oxa, scēap, wulf, wyrm[13]

6   Eighth-century helmet ('helm'), found at Coppergate, York

Food and drink (*mete and drinc*)

bēor, ealu, etan, hlāf, hungrig, hunig, medu, þurst, wæter[14]

Religion (*ǣ-fæst-nes*)

abbod, æl-mihtig, ærce-biscop, āþ, cirice, dēofol, engel, hālga, god, hǣþen, heofon, munuc, mynster, prēost, sāwol, scrīn[15]

War (*beadu, gūþ* or *hild*)

helm, sceaft, scyld, spere, swurd, wǣpen[16]

Time (*tīma*)

ǣfen-tīd, æfter, dæg, gēar, hwīl, mōnaþ, morgen, niht, nū, winter[17]

Numbers (*getæl*)

ān, twā, þrēo, fēower, fīf, siex, seofon, eahta, nigon, tīen, endleofan, twelf, twentig, þrītig, fēowertig, hund, þūsend[18]

To move (*āstyrian*)

ārisan, cuman, feallan, flēogan, gangan, hlēapan, rīdan, swimman[19]

To say and to write (*secgan and āwritan*)

andswarian, āscian, bōc, spell, word[20]

Compounds

Like present-day English, Old English tended to use compounds as a way of forming new words from existing ones. For instance, three words for 'hall' were *heall, reced* and *sele*. In the heroic society portrayed in much Old English poetry, the hall was the focal point for eating, drinking, and the distribution of wealth by the lord to his retainers. Hence we find compounds such as *dryht-sele* 'lord-hall', *gold-sele* 'gold-hall', *heall-þegn* 'hall-retainer', *wīn-reced* and *wīn-sele* 'wine-hall'. Similarly, words for 'battle', such as *beadu, gūþ, hild* and *wīg*, can combine with words for 'man' or 'warrior', such as *rinc*, to give compounds such as *gūþ-rinc* and *hilde-rinc* – both meaning 'man of battle; warrior' – and with *plega* 'play' or *rǣs* 'rush' to give compounds such as *beadu-rǣs* 'rush of battle', *gūþ-plega* and *wīg-plega* 'play of battle; conflict'. The following compounds all use vocabulary that we have already encountered. Can you work out what they mean?

  dōm-dæg   medu-benc   niht-weorc   sǣ-man   sǣ-rinc[21]

Some useful words you should quickly learn

A small number of words occur many times in texts, and it is useful to learn and remember them, so that you do not have to look them up every time you come to read a new text. They are mainly grammatical words.

Questions		Pronouns	
hū	how	*ic*	I
hwā	who	*þū*	you (singular)
hwǣr	where	*hē*	he
hwæt	what	*hēo*	she
hwelc	which	*hit*	it
hwȳ	why	*wē*	we
		gē	you (plural)
		hīe	they, them

Question words and pronouns can be combined in a number of basic sentences, such as:

Hwā eart þū?   *Hwæt dēst þū?*   *Hwæt segst þū?*
Hwæt drincst þū?   *Ne drincst þū wīn?*   *Hwǣr slǣpst þū?*[22]

Two further small groups of grammatical words that occur frequently and are worth trying to memorise are conjunctions and common adverbs. Conjunctions link other words together, while adverbs often give information about time, frequency or manner (see further, Chapter 4). Some words, such as *þā* and *þonne*, can function as either conjunctions or adverbs, with slightly different meanings.

Conjunctions		Adverbs			
ac	but	*ǣr*	before	*oft*	often
for	before, because of	*ǣfre*	ever, always	*þā*	then
oþ-þæt	until	*ēac*	also	*þonne*	then
þā	when	*nū*	now		
þonne	when				

Learning unfamiliar vocabulary

The most effective way to learn vocabulary is to encounter it frequently, in different meaningful contexts. When learning a spoken language, like Arabic, Portuguese or Russian, there are opportunities to speak and hear the language in everyday conversations as well as to see it on the page. When learning languages that are no longer spoken, like Latin or Old English, we are normally restricted to reading texts, and so we meet particular words infrequently and in restricted contexts. If reading Old English is to become a pleasurable activity – which it should – then we have to make an effort to improve our reading fluency by enhancing our word-recognition skills. We have to make Old English vocabulary come alive.

The traditional way of engaging with an Old English text is to have a glossary (and perhaps an earlier translation) beside the original language, and to plough through each passage slowly, perhaps looking up most words in the glossary and comparing difficult passages with the translation. Generations of Old English scholars have been shaped by this process, and enthusiasts no doubt gain pleasure from the mental discipline required and the real sense of achievement when a particular work has been understood and appreciated. Readers with little earlier experience of learning another language perhaps need more support when approaching Old English for the first time, and the following advice is directed primarily at them.

Using dictionaries and glossaries

Dictionaries and glossaries are essential tools (and there is a good online dictionary of Old English at http://home.comcast.net/~modean52/oeme_dictionaries.htm). Many people plunder glossaries and dictionaries and make up their own list of useful vocabulary items, in a notebook or a computer file, and revise it periodically. This kind of activity is useful but it is best done systematically with frequent revision of the vocabulary, particularly in the early days. If you decide to make a vocabulary list, group the words according to their meanings, for example:

Parts of the body

bæc back	*earm* arm	*līc* body
bān bone	*eaxl* shoulder	*mūþ* mouth
blōd blood	*folme, hand,*	*nos-þyrel* nostril
cinn-bān chin bone	*hond* hand	*tōþ* tooth
ēage eye	*fōt* foot	*tunge* tongue
ēare ear	*hēafod* head	
	heorte heart	

As you build up your word-list, try to put aside a little time each day to review it. We can only internalise new words when we see them frequently, in different contexts and when they mean something to us. So use your imagination when you are memorising the words – visualise a huge, sharp *tōþ* in the *mūþ* of a creature whose *līc* is also large and misshapen. The more you make the words meaningful, the easier it should be to recall them when required.

The process of really getting to *know* what a word means is a slow one, and it cannot depend simply on looking the word up in a glossary or dictionary. To comprehend a word fully, we need to know various things, for example:

- What the word looks like; how it changes its form in different contexts, e.g. *þū* 'you' is sometimes found in the form *þē*. Why? (The answer will be revealed in Chapter 3.)
- What the word means – which involves not just knowing the dictionary sense of the word, but also knowing which words it is normally found alongside, what associations it might have (with family, or war), how it fits into a pattern of words with similar or opposite meaning, and so on.
- How the word behaves in combination with other words; that is, how it behaves grammatically.

We suggested above that the best way to learn individual items is to arrange them in meaningful groups (like 'parts of the body'), and to revise them frequently. When noting a word, it is useful to give more than just the bare dictionary meaning: give some useful grammatical information, and, ideally, show how it works in the text you have been reading. In this way you will build up a fuller knowledge of the word, how it behaves in sentences, and what other words it is associated with. For example, there are various words in Old English to express the concept of 'battle', including *hild* and *gūþ*. In your notebook, under a section such as 'War' you might note the words as follows:

> *hild*, f. war, battle   Hē tō þǣre **hilde** stōp.
> *gūþ*, f. war   Hē ongan þā forþ beran gār to **gūþe.**

The example sentences used here are adapted very slightly from the opening lines of *The Battle of Maldon* (Text C), a poem which naturally uses a lot of words to do with war. The first example means 'He advanced to the battle', and the second means 'He began then to bear forth his spear to battle'.

Both *hild* and *gūþ* are nouns, and the *f.* shows that they are feminine. This affects the words around the noun; for example, *hilde* is preceded by the feminine form *þǣre* 'the', rather than the equivalent form *þǣm* 'the', which would be used if the noun were masculine (see Chapter 3 for further information on this topic). The example sentences also show that after a preposition like *tō* these nouns add an -*e* to their stem, *hilde* and *gūþe* (see Chapter 4 for more on this topic). Finally, the example sentences help us to begin to build up a network of words associated with battle, like *stōp* ('advanced') and *gār* ('spear').

Efficient readers gradually build up a set of familiar vocabulary items that they can quickly and easily recognise in texts. The more work you are prepared to put into actively developing your vocabulary, the greater the reward you will gain in increased reading speed and enjoyment. There are various strategies you can use to make vocabulary enrichment a more enjoyable process. A few examples are given below.

Using diagrams

A familiar way of grouping words expressing personal relationships is by a 'family tree'. The group of words denoting relatives can easily be expanded and shown in such a fashion:

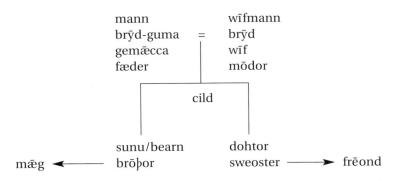

By constructing a simple 'family tree' that here extends to *mǣg* 'relative' and *frēond* 'friend', we are forced to think about the relationship between the words used to express kinship in Anglo-Saxon times – which may not, of course, correspond to the ways in which modern society conceives of and expresses family relations.

Similar diagrams can be used to express concepts like social hierarchy and physical location. To take two examples:

1.   How would you draw a map showing the following locations?

eorþe, folde	earth
middan-geard	middle-earth
heofon	heaven
hell	hell
rīce	kingdom
eard	homeland
sele	hall
hām	home
woruld	world
land	land
sǣ	sea

2.   Old English has an abundance of vocabulary expressing degrees of social rank. Group the following words according to their position in the royal family, the nobility and the people who followed them.

aldor-mon, ealdor-man	nobleman, king's representative
æþeling	prince
beorn	man, warrior
ceorl	freeman, peasant ('churl')
cyning	king
cwēn	queen
dryhten	lord
ealdor	lord
eorl	nobleman, warrior
frēa	lord
hlāford	lord
rinc	warrior
þegn	warrior, retainer
þēoden	lord

Representing rank as a hierarchy, with royal family at the summit and retainers at the base, gives a visual sense of the Anglo-Saxon social order and encourages us to process the vocabulary used by the speakers themselves, a thousand years ago, to articulate their place in the community.

Affective vocabulary (emotion and evaluation)

Language teachers have long observed that learners quickly acquire those words that are personally meaningful to them. Into this category often fall those words that convey emotion or evaluations, for example, terms of praise and endearment, or insults and abuse. These are, in Old English, to do with the *mōd*, that is, the spirit or heart (it obviously gives us today's word 'mood'). In your developing word-list you can ask yourself which words you would apply to (a) the person you love, (b) your lord and master, and (c) the monster from the moorland who is terrorising your community. Possible expressions include:

lēof	dear		*æþele*	noble
grim	fierce, cruel		*frōd*	old, wise
ǣttren	poisonous		*mōdig*	spirited, daring
unearh	not cowardly, brave		*ælf-scīne*	beautiful (lit. elf-bright)
heard	hard, harsh		*cynelic*	royal

Of course, different people might wish to categorise these terms differently, depending on how they feel about monsters and masters. The point is to make these words – and the others you come across in this book – as meaningful to *you* as possible, so that you have a better chance of recalling them when you see them in reading passages.

Names

Old English personal names were made up of vocabulary words, often in compounds that do not make literal sense. The main characters in one of the texts we shall read in Part II are called Cynewulf and Cyneheard, names that translate as 'royal-wolf' and 'royal-hard'. The hero of the epic poem *Beowulf* has a name that literally means 'bee-wolf', but figuratively perhaps means 'bear' (bee = honey, wolf = fierce animal; fierce animal that steals honey = bear). This is an aspect of Old English on which J. R. R. Tolkien drew extensively when naming characters in *The Lord of the Rings*. For instance, the name of the villain, Saruman (Illustration 7), is taken from OE *searu* 'trickery' plus

7   Saruman from *Lord of the Rings*

'man', to give a compound with the sense of 'man of trickery'. Can you work out the meanings of the place-name Mordor, and the name of Tolkien's hobbit hero, Frodo?[23]

Summary

This chapter has reviewed some of the issues involved in recognising Old English words and their meanings, and offered advice on building up an active reading vocabulary. As anyone who has learned another language will know, knowledge of words alone is insufficient to understand texts. Readers also need to know how words behave in sentences and longer texts. In other words, readers need to experience how words combine into sentences and ultimately into stories, riddles and poems. The following three chapters turn to those basic aspects of Old English grammar that need to be understood in order to make sense of texts.

Answers

1   and, east, gold, help, bliss, god, west, understand, word, wonder
2   death, thing, this, north, murder, other, brother, earth
3   devil, drink, dizzy, folk, over, work
4   bright, grass, three, third, thirty, through
5   quoth (= said), ship, ash (= something made of ash-wood), leap, ring, raven, what, right, might (= power)
6   life, mile, white, wise; mouse, loud, south, mouth; home, stone, bone, loaf; roof, stood, blood (northern English pronunciation), book; here, he, sweet, geese
7   mīn, wīn, hwī or hwȳ, gōd, fōt, ūt, nū, tūn, rāp, tēþ
8   almighty, bench, busy, crafty, day, candle, church, fair, young, many, edge, holy, weary, year, way
9   all, from, man, strong, land, long, wall
10 crafty (= devious), doom, ghost, soon, winter (Old English *winter* can in fact mean either 'winter' or 'year')
11 child (Scottish 'bairn'), brother, bride, child, daughter, father, friend, mother, son, sister, widow, wife, woman
12 shepherd, fisher(man), baker, cook, smith, goldsmith, thief, writer
13 fish, goose, horse, mouse, ox, sheep, wolf, worm (= serpent)
14 beer, ale, eat, loaf, hungry, honey, mead, thirst, water
15 abbot, almighty, archbishop, oath, church, devil, angel, holy one (=

saint), god, heathen, heaven, monk, minster (= monastery), priest, soul, shrine

16 helmet, shaft, shield, spear, sword, weapon

17 evening ('eventide'), after, day, year, while, month, morning, night, now, winter (= year)

18 one, two, three, four, five, six, seven, eight, nine, ten, eleven, twelve, twenty, thirty, forty, hundred, thousand

19 arise, come, fall, fly, go (Scottish 'gang', also gangplank, gangway), leap, ride, swim

20 answer, ask, book, spell (= story, message), word (= speech)

21 Judgement Day, mead bench, night's work, sailor, sailor

22 Who are you? What do you do? What do you say? What do you drink? Don't you drink wine? Where do you sleep?

23 Mordor, the Land of Shadows = 'murder'; Frodo = old, wise

3 People and Things

This chapter continues to build up your basic reading skills in Old English. We start by considering what happens when we combine words in Old English; that is, we begin to explore the grammar of Old English. Old English grammar differs in a number of interesting ways from that of English today. In this chapter, in particular, we shall concentrate on the vocabulary and grammar used to express *people* and *things*.

Pronouns

One of the most common groups of words in Old English is the set of pronouns, that is, words such as

- *he*, which takes the place of full **masculine** noun phrases such as *the angel Gabriel*;
- *she*, which takes the place of **feminine** noun phrases like *the holy mother Mary*;
- *it*, which replaces **neuter** noun phrases, like *the child*.

In other words, rather than repeating 'the angel Gabriel' or 'Beowulf' in sentences like 'Beowulf leapt up. Beowulf killed the dragon,' we can use a pronoun to substitute for the second noun phrase: 'Beowulf leapt up. *He* killed the dragon.'

Pronouns are one of the few types of word in today's English that still change their form according to how they are used in the sentence. Put simply, the form *he* is used as a substitute for masculine singular noun phrases, when the person referred to is performing the action of the verb; for example, '*He* killed the dragon.' In such sentences, linguists make a distinction between the role that the pronoun is playing in the sentence (namely, the Subject) and the form that it takes (that is, the Nominative form). So in this case, the form that the pronoun takes when it plays the role of the Subject is the Nominative, *he.*

When the pronoun is the Object of the sentence, it takes a different form, which we call the Accusative; that is, *him*, as in 'The dragon killed *him.*' Here the pronoun is not responsible for the action; it is affected by it. In today's English, then, we have two forms for most pronouns, *I/me, he/him, she/her, we/us, they/them, who/whom,* depending on whether they are Nominative (i.e. functioning as Subject in the sentence) or Accusative (functioning as Object). This is an important point to grasp, because, as we shall soon see, this grammatical characteristic – that the form of a word changes according to the role that it plays in a sentence – is much more general in Old English than it is in today's English. While today only pronouns change their form depending on their grammatical role in the sentence, in Old English entire noun phrases, like *the dragon* and *the holy mother, Mary,* also change their form to indicate which role in the sentence they are playing.

Three common Old English pronouns are *hē* ('he'), *hēo* ('she') and *hit* ('it').

Although in some respects these Old English pronouns look a little different from those of today's English, in other important ways they are similar. As we have seen in English today, pronouns change their form according to their *gender* (masculine, feminine and neuter) as well as the way they are used in a sentence. In the following examples, we can see further how pronouns replace singular nouns and noun phrases in a few simple sentences:

	Subject	**Verb**	**Object**
Masculine	God	sent	his angel, Gabriel
	He	sent	*him*
Feminine	Mary	sent	her mother
	She	sent	*her*
Neuter	The child	sent	his dog
	It	sent	*it*

In Old English, the table looks like this:

	Subject	**Verb**	**Object**
Masculine	God	āsende	his engel, Gabrihel
	Hē	āsende	*hine*
Feminine	Māria	āsende	hire mōdor
	Hēo	āsende	*hīe*
Neuter	Þæt cild	āsende	his hund
	Hit	āsende	*hit*

As well as changing their form for gender, pronouns change form to indicate plurals. The full range of pronouns, singular and plural, is given below:

Present-day English

	Singular					*Plural*		
Nominative	I	you	he	she	it	we	you	they
Accusative	me	you	him	her	it	us	you	them

Old English

	Singular					*Plural*		
Nominative	ic	þū	hē	hēo	hit	wē	gē	hīe
Accusative	mē	þē	hine	hīe	hit	ūs	ēow	hīe

As you might have noticed, the form *hīe* is used to mean different things in Old English – effectively when you see *hīe* in an Old English text, you have to decide from the context whether it means 'her', 'they' or 'them'. As in today's English, when the pronoun is plural (i.e. when *hīe* means 'they' or 'them'), it can substitute for nouns that are masculine ('three warriors' > 'they'), feminine ('three girls' > 'they') or neuter ('three ships'> 'they').

The meaning of 'case'

So far we have noted that, in both present-day and Old English, the form of the pronoun often changes, depending on whether it is expressing the Subject ('he/she') or the Object ('him/her') of the sentence. This grammatical signal, known as *case*, is used in many languages, ancient and modern, in order to tell us, for example, who is acting in any sentence (i.e. the Subject), and who is being acted upon (i.e. the Object). Different languages have different numbers of cases that express different kinds of meaning. As we shall see, Old English actually has four cases; that means that there are up to four different forms of the pronoun, depending on what meaning it is being used to express.

It is a good idea to familiarise yourself with the pronouns, particularly because they occur so frequently in Old English texts. Take note of the idiosyncrasies of the pronoun system – be aware, for example, that *hēo* means 'she'. The second person pronoun is easier to memorise if you recall that *þū* and *þē* correspond to the older forms 'thou' (Nominative) and 'thee' (Accusative).

So far we have focused mainly on the Nominative and Accusative cases, that is, the forms used when the pronoun is Subject or Object. The third case, the Genitive, is easy for today's English speakers to master because it is simply the form that signifies possession. When Old English pronouns are in the Genitive case, they identify other nouns, for example '*my* horse, *your* hound, *his* lady'. The Old English Genitive forms of the pronoun, with their present-day equivalents, are given below:

Present-day English

	Singular					*Plural*		
Genitive	my	your	his	her	its	our	your	their

Old English

	Singular					*Plural*		
Genitive	mīn	þīn	his	hire	his	ūre	ēower	hira

Summary

In Old English, words that refer to people and things can be found in different forms, according to their gender (masculine, feminine, or neuter), their number (singular or plural), and their grammatical function in the sentence (Nominative forms express the Subject, Accusative forms express the Object, and Genitive forms express possession). The pronouns of both current English and Old English show these different forms. As we shall shortly see, however, the case system in Old English is much more extensive than it is in English today. One difference is that in Old English there is another case, the Dative, which is often used after a preposition, e.g. *for* him, *by* him, *to* him, *with* him, and so on. We will consider the meaning, form and use of the Dative case in detail in Chapter 4.

Reading practice

Let us look at these pronouns as they appear in different short excerpts from Henry Sweet's version of a translation into Old English of Ælfric's Latin *Colloquy*, one of the earliest surviving language-teaching manuals produced in the British Isles. In these extracts, the speaker asks various workers who they are and what they do. In each of the three dialogues, identify the occupation being described. Remember it is not yet necessary to identify every word in the passage; at the moment we are looking simply for a general under-standing of the text. However, some useful words are listed in alpha-betical order and defined briefly before each excerpt. The answers to the questions and some discussion follow the excerpts.

Occupation (1)

bēag ring	*hwīlum* sometimes	*swā hwæt swā* whatever
fētt feeds	*oþþe* or	*ymb* concerning
for-þǣm because	*scrytt* clothes (verb)	
gefō capture	*selle, selþ* give(s)	

> *Canst þū ǣnig þing?*
> Ānne cræft ic cann.
> *Hwelcne cræft canst þū?*
> Ic eom hunta.
> *Hwæs hunta eart þū?*
> Ic eom þæs cyninges hunta.
> *Hwæt dēst þū ymb þīnne huntoþ?*
> Ic selle þǣm cyninge swā hwæt swā ic gefō, for-þǣm ic eom his hunta.
> *Hwæt selþ hē þē?*
> Hē scrȳtt mē wel and fētt, and hwīlum hē mē hors selþ oþþe bēag.

Occupation (2)

be about *magon* can

būtan without   *secge* say

beþurfon need   *tō āwihte* at all, 'a whit'

furþum even   *ūt-ādrifaþ* cast out, banish

gefērscipe community   *wyrta* vegetables

Hwæt secge wē be þæm cōce? Hwæþer wē his cræftes tō āwihte beþurfon?

Gif gē mē of ēowrum gefērscipe ūt-ādrifaþ, gē etaþ ēowre wyrta grēne and ēowre flǣsc-mettas hrēawe; ne magon gē furþum fǣtt broþ habban būtan mīnum cræfte.

Occupation (3)

ac but   *nīetenu* animals

andgiete understanding, intellect *nyllaþ* do not wish

ascige ask   *nyton* do not know

būton except   *sprǣc* talk, speech

dēoplīce deeply   *spricst* say

Ēalā Oh!   *stunt* stupid

geornlīce eagerly   *swā-swā* as, like

leornige learn   *þearle* very

līcaþ please   *þonne* then

mǣþ capacity   *wille, willaþ* wish, wishes

Ēalā gē cild, hū līcaþ ēow þēos sprǣc?

Wel hēo ūs līcaþ; ac þearle dēoplīce þū spricst and ofer ūre mǣþ. Ac sprec wiþ ūs æfter ūrum andgiete, þæt wē mægen understandan þā þing þe þū spricst.

Ic āscige ēow, 'For hwȳ leornige gē swā geornlīce?'

For-þǣm wē nyllaþ bēon swā-swā stunt nīetenu, þe nān þing nyton būton gærs and wæter.

Hwæt wille gē þonne bēon?

Wē willaþ wīse bēon.

Discussion

With a little effort you have probably realised that the first dialogue is with the king's hunter, the second with a cook, and the third with a group of young scholars, keen to learn, and so probably intending to be monks. At this point we are mainly concerned with exploring in detail how the pronouns work in these passages, because once we have grasped the principles of pronoun use, we can extend our understanding to nouns and noun phrases in general. Let us therefore look at one sentence from each of the above texts:

(1) Hē scrȳtt mē wel and fētt, and hwīlum hē mē hors selþ oþþe bēag.
(2) Gif gē mē of ēowrum gefērscipe ūt-ādrifaþ, gē etaþ ēowre wyrta grēne and ēowre flǣsc-mettas hrēawe . . .
(3) Wel hēo ūs līcaþ; ac þearle dēoplīce þū spricst and ofer ūre mǣþ.

Sentence (1) corresponds to present-day English 'He clothes and feeds me well, and sometimes he gives me a horse or ring'. Notice that the word order is different in present-day and Old English, where the actual order of words is 'He clothes me well and feeds, and sometimes he me horse gives or ring'. The order of words is more flexible in Old English than in English today, partly because in Old English the cases of the pronouns and, as we shall see, the noun phrases, often tell us who is doing what to whom. For example, in the sequence, *hē mē hors selþ*, we know that the king is doing the giving, because *hē* is in the Nominative case, which is the form that expresses the Subject (**'he** gives'), while *mē* can be read as the Accusative ('he gives **me**') or the Dative ('he gives **to me**').

One lesson to learn from this sentence is to expect flexibility in word order in Old English sentences, and to pay attention to the cases of pronouns and nouns. Indeed, Sentence (2) also has a word order that departs from the order expected in English today. Its actual word order is 'If **you me** of your community cast out, you eat your vegetables green and your meats raw'. To translate the cook's comment into current English, we have to rearrange the pronouns and the verb: 'If **you** cast **me** out of your community, you eat your vegetables green and your meats raw'. 'Green' has the sense of 'unripe' here. Again, the case of the pronouns tells us who is doing the casting out and who is being cast out.

Sentence (3) also has an unusual word order, seen from today's perspective: 'Well **it us** pleases, but very deeply you speak, and beyond ('over') our understanding'. Once more, to render this sentence in today's English we would change the word order: '**It** pleases **us** well, but you speak very deeply, and beyond our understanding'. Here Ælfric's young monks, like many language beginners, are keen to learn but feel that their teacher is moving too fast.

Nouns and noun phrases

At the risk of emulating Ælfric's stern teacher, let us now move on to consider nouns and noun phrases in full. So far we have looked only at pronouns, like 'he' 'she' and 'it', in present-day and Old English. The advantage of starting with pronouns is that some of them today still have the case forms that we find in Old English, for example 'I/he/she' (Nominative) and 'me/him/her' (Accusative). They also have separate singular and plural forms (e.g. 'I/we' and 'he/they') and they have masculine, feminine and neuter forms ('he/she/it'). The present-day English pronoun system is therefore not in principle different from the Old English system. But the noun system is.

Nouns are those words, like 'angel' or 'mother' or 'ship', that name people and things. They generally have singular and plural forms, and they can be expanded into phrases by adding descriptive *adjectives* ('**good/bad** angel') and a set of other types of word, generally called *determiners* because they specify *which* noun we are talking about ('**a/the/this/that/any** good angel').

With a single exception, nouns and noun phrases in today's English do not explicitly signal their case. That is, there is no way of knowing whether, out of context, a noun phrase like 'the good angel' is the Subject or the Object of a sentence. (The exception is that the apostrophe used in the present-day possessive form, as in 'the angel's head', is a relic of the old Genitive case *þæs engles hēafod*.) In Old English, the noun phrase contains a number of extra grammatical clues that signal this kind of subtle information.

Let us look first at the noun itself. The Old English word *engel* 'angel' does not change its form in the Nominative and Accusative. Therefore, out of context, we have no clue as to whether this word would function as the Subject or Object in a complete sentence. However, when we add a determiner and an adjective to make a full noun phrase, something interesting happens. There are different possible forms of the phrase 'the good angel', for example:

se gōda engel

þone gōdan engel

In the first instance, the *Nominative* form of both 'the' (*se*) and 'good' (*gōda*) tell us that, in the context of a sentence, this phrase will act as the Subject. In the second instance, the *Accusative* form of 'the' (*þone*) and 'good' (*gōdan*) tell us that in a sentence this phrase will act as the Object.

One of the main differences between today's English and Old English is that in the latter, the individual members of *all* full noun phrases change their form to signal number (singular or plural), gender (masculine, feminine or neuter), and case (Nominative, Accusative, Genitive or Dative). Moreover, masculine, feminine and neuter nouns have different case endings: the Accusative ending of a masculine noun will be different from the Accusative ending of a feminine or a neuter noun. The result is that Old English nouns have – to modern eyes – a bewildering variety of forms. Let us look at three examples (a masculine noun phrase, a feminine one and a neuter one) simply to illustrate this variety:

	Masculine	Feminine	Neuter
	'the good angel'	*'the good mother'*	*'the good ship'*
Nom.	se gōda engel	sēo gōde mōdor	þæt gōde scip
Acc.	þone gōdan engel	þā gōdan mōdor	þæt gōde scip
Gen.	þæs gōdan engles	þǣre gōdan mōdor	þæs gōdan scipes
Dat.	þǣm gōdan engle	þǣre gōdan mōdor	þǣm gōdan scipe
	the good angels'	*'the good mothers'*	*'the good ships'*
Nom.	þā gōdan englas	þā gōdan mōdor	þā gōdan scipu
Acc.	þā gōdan englas	þā gōdan mōdor	þā gōdan scipu
Gen.	þāra gōdra engla	þāra gōdra mōdra	þāra gōdra scipa
Dat.	þǣm gōdum englum	þǣm gōdum mōdrum	þǣm gōdum scipum

For learners of the language, the numerical complexity of the combination of forms can be understandably off-putting. Added to the complexity is the fact that in Old English the gender of many words is conventional rather than 'natural'. Thus *sumor* 'summer' and *winter* 'winter, year' are masculine, *spræc* 'speech' and *miht* 'power' are feminine, and *gold* 'gold' and *dēor* 'wild animal' are neuter. When we come to read an Old English text, we have to realise that *all* words change cases according to their gender, and that it is not immediately obvious what is masculine, what is feminine and what is neuter. Even more perplexingly, for each gender there are several possible patterns of variation, similar to the ones given above. Each possible pattern is traditionally called a 'declension', or sometimes a 'paradigm'. For example, here are some examples of masculine, feminine and neuter words in the Nominative and Accusative cases: *hlāf* 'loaf', *gefēra* 'comrade', *rōd* 'cross', *hlǣfdige* 'lady', *dēofol* 'devil' and *ēage* 'eye'. The first of each pair belongs to the type of declension sometimes referred to as 'strong'; the second belongs to the type sometimes referred to as 'weak'. Each noun is preceded by the appropriate form of the Old English word for 'the'.

Masculine	*Singular*		*Plural*	
Nominative	se hlāf	se gefēra	þā hlāfas	þā gefēran
Accusative	þone hlāf	þone gefēran	þā hlāfas	þā gefēran
Feminine				
Nominative	sēo rōd	sēo hlǣfdige	þā rōde/a	þā hlǣfdigan
Accusative	þā rōde	þā hlǣfdigan	þā rōde/a	þā hlǣfdigan
Neuter				
Nominative	þæt dēofol	þæt ēage	þā dēoflu	þā ēagan
Accusative	þæt dēofol	þæt ēagan	þā dēoflu	þā ēagan

Faced with a variety of word forms that at first glance seems overwhelming, the beginner might simply give up. However, there are ways to navigate the difficulties. There is a set of tips that can help beginners to deal with the complexity of Old English noun phrases while slowly familiarising themselves with the more finicky details.

- Pay particular attention to the different forms of 'the'. This is a limited number of words, and the different forms of 'the' in Old English have the virtue of letting the reader know the gender, case and number of the nouns they precede. Thus if you see *se gāst* 'the spirit', you know from the determiner *se* that the noun *gāst* 'spirit' is masculine, that it is singular and that it is in the Nominative case. In other words, the spirit is doing something in the sentence. If, on the other hand, you see *þone gāst* 'the spirit', you still know from the determiner *þone* that *gāst* is masculine and singular, but this time the noun is in the Accusative case, and something is being done to the spirit.
- As suggested earlier, pay attention to the *pronouns*. This is again a limited set of words and word-forms, and they are used frequently.
- Notice that the plurals of nouns and pronouns generally vary less than the singular forms. Try to familiarise yourself with the rela-

tively few plural forms, so as to be able to recognise them in a text. From the examples given above, you can see that some noun plurals end in -*s*, while many others end in -*n* and a few in -*u* or -*e* or -*a*. Most present-day English plurals end in -*s*, of course, but a few keep one of the ancient alternative endings, as in *children* and *oxen*.

• Notice that plural forms of the determiner 'the' are the same for all genders.

Some people like to memorise by rote *all* the possible variations in the forms of noun phrases; however, this is not necessarily the most effective way of coming to terms with these different forms in Old English. Another way is to read as much Old English as you can, referring only where necessary to tables of declensions to identify Nominatives, Accusatives, Genitives and so on. Often the sense of a passage will be clear without your having to refer to such tables. At the start you will find reading a little slow, but with frequent practice you will find that you can explore quite a lot of Old English with the help of a little grammatical information and a good glossary.

Let us look at a fairly simple passage of Old English – one so simple that, with a little patience and some thought, it should be almost comprehensible to a speaker of today's English. It is a version of 'The Incarnation' (see Illustration 8), that is, the Christian story of how God became embodied in the person of Jesus Christ, and of his childhood and adolescent years. It is typical of the kind of written text that survives from Anglo-Saxon culture, since, as has been mentioned already, most of the literate population had a religious occupation. The extract is adapted from a 'homily' or sermon, again by Ælfric. The sentences have been numbered for ease of reference.

Try reading the passage and picking out the words you understand, using the vocabulary-recognition strategies suggested in Chapter 2. Do not worry if you do not understand all the words in your first few readings of the text; we shall be looking at it in some detail shortly. However, it is important for you to get an early taste for – and to develop an enjoyment of – the struggle to make meaning of these challenging texts.

The Incarnation
(1) Þā se tīma cōm þe God fore-scēawode, þā āsende hē his engel Gabrihel tō ānum mǣden, sēo wæs Maria gehāten. (2) Þā cōm se engel tō hire, and hīe gegrette mid Godes wordum, and cȳdde hire

8   Annunciation Panel, Ruthwell Cross

þæt Godes Sunu sceolde bēon ācenned of hire, būton weres gemānan. (3) And hēo þā gelȳfde his wordum, and wearþ mid cilde. (4) Þā þā hire tīma cōm, hēo ācende, and þurh-wunode mǣden. (5) Sēo hālige mōdor Maria þā āfēdde þæt cild, and hit wēox swā-swā ōþre cild dōþ, būton synne ānum.

Recognising words

Using the suggestions given in Chapter 2, and a little imagination, you might have recognised quite a few of the words in these five sentences. For example, in sentence (1):

tīma	time	*hē*	he	*tō*	to
cōm	came	*his*	his	*mǣden*	maiden
God	God	*engel*	angel	*wæs*	was
āsende	sent	*Gabrihel*	Gabriel		

A fairly literal translation of these five sentences would be:

> (1) When the time came that God pre-ordained (or 'had pre-ordained'), then he sent his angel, Gabriel, to a maiden, who was called Mary. (2) Then the angel came to her, and greeted her with God's words, and made known to her that God's Son should be born by her, without intercourse with a man. (3) And she then believed in his words, and became pregnant ('with child'). (4) When her time came, she gave birth, and remained a maiden (i.e. 'a virgin'). (5) The holy mother Mary then fed the child, and it grew ('waxed', as in 'waxed and waned') just as other children do, without a single sin.

Let us look now in more detail at some of the key features of this text, the people and things, highlighted below.

> (1) Þā **se** tīma cōm þe **God** fore-scēawode, þā āsende **hē his engel Gabrihel** tō ānum mǣden, sēo wæs **Maria** gehāten. (2) Þā cōm **se engel** tō hire, and **hīe** gegrette mid Godes wordum, and cȳdde hire þæt **Godes Sunu** sceolde bēon ācenned of hire, būton weres gemānan. (3) And **hēo** þā gelȳfde his wordum, and wearþ mid cilde. (4) Þā þā **hire tīma** cōm, **hēo** ācende, and þurh-wunode mǣden. (5) **Sēo hālige mōdor Maria** þā āfēdde **þæt cild**, and **hit** wēox swā-swā ōþre cild dōþ, būton synne ānum.

If we focus for the moment only on the highlighted words in this text, we can see how many of the people and things mentioned relate to each other. Let us look at the nouns and pronouns in the Nominative and Accusative cases:

Nominative forms (i.e. those words usually expressing Subjects of their sentences)

se tīma	God	hē	sēo ... Maria	se engel
Godes Sunu	hēo	hire tīma	hēo	mǣden
Sēo hālige mōdor Maria	hit	ōþre cild		

Again, if we pay attention to the determiners of these Nominative forms, we can see that *se tīma* 'the time' and *se engel* 'the angel' are masculine, singular noun phrases, while *sēo hālige mōdor Maria* 'the holy mother Mary' is feminine singular. The pronoun *hit* 'it' shows that *cild* 'child' is considered to be neuter. Within the noun phrases, there are a number of Genitive forms, expressing possession: **Godes Sunu**, 'God's Son' and **hire tīma** 'her time'. A trickier example is the expression *sēo wæs Maria gehāten*, which literally means 'the/that was called Mary' but which we have translated as 'who was called Mary'.

Accusative forms (i.e. those words usually expressing Objects of their sentences)

his engel Gabrihel	hīe	þæt cild

As we expect of the Accusative case, things are happening to these people: God sent his angel Gabriel (*his engel Gabrihel*), Gabriel in turn greeted her (*hīe*, i.e. Mary), and Mary fed the child (*þæt cild*).

If we look at the text again, we can see, for example, different words for 'she/her': *hēo* 'she' when the pronoun is the Subject ('she believed in his words'), and *hīe* 'her' when the pronoun is the Object ('the angel greeted her'). In addition, the Genitive *hire* 'her' is used with another noun to express possession in *hire tīma* 'her time'. The same form, *hire* 'her', is also used in the Dative case, when some kind of prepositional meaning is made explicit or implied, as in *tō hire* 'to her', *of hire* 'from/by her', and *cȳdde hire* 'made known (to) her'. (A further example of the Dative, this time a neuter plural noun phrase, is found in *gelȳfde **his wordum*** 'believed **(in) his words**'. Again, a prepositional meaning is implied.)

Further reading practice

As Ælfric's story of the Incarnation continues, it becomes clear that
what the monk wishes to communicate is the divine nature of Jesus.
The excerpt we have just considered ends with him stating that Jesus
was exceptional as a child in that he was *būton synne ānum* 'without a
single sin' (literally, 'without sin one'). In the unfolding of Ælfric's
story, the monk is careful to emphasise the exceptional and supernat-
urally powerful qualities of Jesus as he grows older. Read the passage
and check how many of the questions you can answer.

- How old was Jesus when he began to perform miracles?
- Why, in Ælfric's view, did Jesus work miracles?
- Which four miracles does Ælfric mention?

Some useful vocabulary is given below. However, some relevant
vocabulary is contained in the first excerpt, translated above, and
some vocabulary (e.g. *āwende*) can be guessed from the context of the
passage. The answers to the questions are given in the discussion that
ends the chapter.

ǣr-þan þe before	*hǣse* command
bearn child (compare	*on þǣre mennisc-nysse* in
Scots 'bairn')	human form, 'in the
ēode went	incarnation'

(6) Hē wæs būton synnum ācenned, and his līf wæs eal būton
synnum. (7) Ne worhte hē þēah nāne wundra openlīce ǣr-þan þe hē
wæs þrītig-wintre on þǣre mennisc-nysse. (8) Þā worhte hē fela
wundra, þæt men mihton gelȳfan þæt hē wæs Godes bearn. (9) Hē
āwende wæter tō wīne, and ēode ofer sǣ mid drīum fōtum, and hē
gestilde windas mid his hǣse, and hē forgēaf blindum mannum
gesihþe.

As well as telling the story of the Gospel, monks like Ælfric needed to
impress upon their Anglo-Saxon listeners the relevance of the
Christian message to their own experience and history. Old English
literature is full of stories of saints' lives (and deaths) and the miracu-
lous deeds performed by holy men in England. Saint Cuthbert, the
seventh-century bishop of the island monastery of Lindisfarne, was

the subject of no fewer than three 'Lives', one of them by an anonymous monk and the other two by Bede (see Illustration 9).

In the following tale from another of Ælfric's homilies, Cuthbert is consulted by an Abbess, Ælfflæd, about the future of her brother, Ecgfrid. Try reading the story and answering the questions. To do this you do not need to understand every single word, though some keywords are explained and others have already appeared in earlier passages. It is a good idea when reading this passage to focus on the forms of the nouns and pronouns, paying attention to which are masculine and which are feminine, which are singular and which are plural, and which case each is in. By attending to these issues, it should be easier to make sense of the story.

- What was Ecgfrid's position in society?
- What did the Abbess wish to know about him?
- What was Cuthbert's response?
- After hearing his response, what was the Abbess's main concern?
- How did Cuthbert attempt to calm her fears?
- How was Cuthbert's prophecy fulfilled?
- At what point in Cuthbert's life did this event happen?

æþela	noble	*næfþ*	does not have (*ne* + *hæfþ*)
befrān	asked	*ofer Drihtnes willan*	against God's will
brūcan	possess	*Peoht*	Pict
fela	many	*rīces*	kingdom
fōn	succeed, take over	*rīxode*	reigned
gecorenne	chosen (one)	*Scyppend*	Creator
gehealden	held	*siþþan*	afterwards
hālga	holy, holy one	*þonne*	since
hālsigenne	entreat	*þyssere*	this
lēode	people	*ylcan*	same
lēof	beloved, dear		

Fela wundra wurdon geworhte þurh þone hālgan Cuþberht. Þā cōm him tō sum abbudysse, sēo wæs Ælflæd gehāten, þæs cyninges sweostor Ecgfrides. Þā begann hēo to hālsigenne þone hālgan wer þæt he sceolde hire secgan hū lange hire brōþor Ecgfridus mōste his rīces brūcan.

9   King Athelstan presents Bede's *Lives of St Cuthbert* to St Cuthbert: Cambridge, Corpus Christi College, MS 183, fol. 1ᵛ

Þā andwyrde hire se hālga, and cwæþ þæt se brōþor ne mōste his līfes brūcan ofer þǣm ānum gēare. Hēo befrān, 'Hwā sceal tō his rīce fōn, þonne hē bearn næfþ?' Þā cwæþ se hālga wer eft to þǣm mǣdene, 'Se æl-mihtiga Scyppend hæfþ gehealden sumne gecorenne þyssere lēode tō cyninge, and sē biþ þē swā lēof swā nū is se ōþer.'

On þǣm ylcan gēare wearþ ofslegen Ecgfridus, se æþela cyning, þā þā hē on Peohtum begann to feohtenne ofer Drihtnes willan; and his brōþor siþþan rīxode. Þā wæs gefylled sēo fore-sǣde sprǣc, swā swā se hālga wer sǣde þǣm mǣdene be hire gebrōþrum, ǣr he biscop wǣre.

Discussion of further reading

At this stage, the above passages for further reading will no doubt be deciphered only partially and with some labour. This is to be expected; however, with regular practice and revision your reading fluency will increase. To revise the vocabulary, as suggested in Chapter 2, begin devising your own glossary, grouping the unknown words according to their meaning (e.g. words for God: *God, Scyppend, Drihten*) and review them regularly.

Your understanding of the first of the two passages will probably be easier if you are familiar with the Christian story. Ælfric tells his listeners that Jesus did not perform miracles ('wonders') openly until he was thirty years old (or 'thirty winters in human form'). He also tells us that Jesus performed miracles so that the people would believe that he was God's child (*Godes bearn*). The four miracles mentioned are the turning of water into wine, going across the sea with dry feet ('walking on water'), calming ('making still') the winds with his command, and giving blind men sight.

The second passage is probably more difficult, in part because the story is less well known. A fairly literal translation is given below, in unidiomatic present-day English, and it contains the answers to the questions posed above.

Many wonders were wrought through the holy Cuthbert. Then a certain abbess came to him, who was called Ælfflæd, sister of the king Ecgfrid. Then she began to entreat the holy man that he would tell her how long her brother Ecgfrid might be allowed to possess his kingdom.

Then the holy (one) answered her, and said that the brother would not be allowed to possess his life beyond the one year. She asked, 'Who shall succeed to his kingdom, since he has no child?' Then the holy man said again to the maiden, 'The almighty Creator has preserved a certain chosen (one) as king of this people, and he will be as dear to you as now the other is.'

In the same year, Ecgfrid, the noble king, was slain when he began to fight the Picts against God's will; and his brother ruled afterwards. Then the aforesaid speech was fulfilled, just as the holy man told the maiden about her brothers, before he was bishop.

Summary

In this chapter, we focused on the means of expressing people and things, through pronouns and noun phrases, and we looked at the way in which Old English grammar signals the gender, number and case of the participants in narratives, fables and legends. In the following chapter, we continue our exploration by turning our attention to ways of expressing place, time, manner and reason.

4 Place, Time, Manner and Reason

Review

In Chapter 3 we introduced some basic concepts that need to be grasped if we are to make sense of Old English literature. We looked at the way in which those Old English words that express people and things (namely pronouns and noun phrases) change their form according to *number* (singular and plural), *gender* (masculine, feminine and neuter) and *case*.

It is the concept of case that is probably least familiar to today's speakers of English. English today has lost most of the signals of case that were present in Old English; only the present-day pronoun system preserves the distinction between, for example, the Nominative forms *he/she/we/they* that express the Subject of a sentence, and the Accusative forms *him/her/us/them* that express the Object of a sentence. A full noun phrase like *the brave warrior* can be either Subject or Object in today's English:

The brave warrior killed the dragon.

The dragon killed *the brave warrior.*

In Old English, however, speakers and writers had to choose the appropriate case form. Depending on how the phrase as a whole is used in the sentence, all the individual words in the noun phrase could potentially change their form: the determiner *the*, the adjective *brave* and the noun *warrior*. Today, there is little evidence of this sophisticated case system in English nouns. Only the Genitive case of the noun, indicating possession, is still signalled, by the apostrophe -*s* found in words like *warrior's* and *brother's*.

In this chapter we look more closely at ways of expressing concepts like place, time, manner and reason in Old English texts. The words and phrases that express these concepts give crucial or optional extra information in the sentences in which they appear. Grammatically, this kind of extra information is signalled in three main ways:

- Using a prepositional phrase, like *at midnight*
- Using an adverb, like *quickly*
- Using a subordinate clause, like *because he was angry*

In the sections that follow, we explain these grammatical features in more detail, and show how they work in further examples of Old English texts.

Place and time

The expressions used for place and time are similar; in fact some expressions can be used to communicate location either in time or in space. A good example is *hēr*, literally 'here', an adverb that begins many entries in the *Anglo-Saxon Chronicle*, a record of the history of early England. In context, we can take the word to mean something like 'at this point'. Illustration 10 shows a page from the earliest surviving *Chronicle* manuscript, with the annals dated 752–5 each beginning with *hēr*. We shall look at one of these annals in detail in Part II (Text A).

One of the earlier entries in the *Chronicle* looks back at the year AD 47, and it deals largely with the relationship between Rome and Britain at that time. Read the passage and see if you can pick out answers to the following questions:

- Which Roman emperor ('king') came with an army to Britain in AD 47?
- Which tribes did he subject to Roman rule?
- In which year of his reign did he carry out this campaign?
- In the same year, what kind of catastrophe affected Syria?
- Which book of the Bible foretold this catastrophe?
- Which Roman emperor's neglect resulted in the loss of Britain to the Romans?

æt nȳstan	finally	*fore-witgod*	foretold
fēng	succeeded	*forlēt*	lost

10   The *Anglo-Saxon Chronicle*: Cambridge, Corpus Christi College
MS 173, fol. 10ʳ (*detail*)

geēode conquered	*mycla* great
gefeoht military campaign	*under-þēodde* subjected
gefremede carried out	*uncāfscipe* neglect
gewāt went	*wītegan* prophet
gewearþ arose	*þe* which
here army	

47. Hēr Claudius, Rōmāna cyning, gewāt mid here on Brytene, and
þæt īg-land geēode, and ealle Pihtas and Walas under-þēodde
Rōmāna rīce. Þis gefeoht hē gefremede þǣm fēorþan gēare his rīces.
On þǣm gēare gewearþ se mycla hungor on Siria, þe wæs fore-witgod
on þǣre bēc Actus Apostolorum þurh Agabum þone wītegan. Þā fēng
Neron tō rīce æfter Claudie, sē æt nŷstan forlēt Brytene īg-land for his
uncāfscipe.

Look at the passage again and focus on those expressions that convey
time and place:

Time
hēr   at this point
þǣm fēorþan gēare his rīces   the fourth year of his reign
on þǣm gēare   in that year
þā   then
æt nӯstan   at last, finally

Place
on Brytene   in Britain
on Siria   in Syria
on þǣre bēc Actus Apostolorum   in the book, the Acts of the Apostles

Other prepositional expressions in the passage tell us that Claudius came to Britain with an army (*mid here*) and conquered the Picts and Welsh, that the famine in Syria was foretold in the Acts of the Apostles by the prophet, Agabus (*þurh Agabum þone wītegan*), and that Nero's loss of Britain was due to his neglect (*for his uncāfscipe*). From these examples, it is evident that prepositional phrases express concepts such as accompaniment, agency and reason, as well as time and place.

Further practice

The entry in the *Anglo-Saxon Chronicle* for the year AD 787 details events that were much closer in history to the era of the chroniclers. This entry contains the first mention of the Viking ships of the Danes that were to arrive in increasing numbers and terrorise the population for centuries to come. Although it is short, this is quite a tricky little passage to understand. Read the entry and check how much you can figure out with the help of the words given beforehand. In particular, can you answer the following questions?

* How many Danish ships were there?
* How did the sheriff (*gerēfa*) travel to meet the ships?
* Where did the Danes wish to go?

ǣrest, ǣrestan first	*man ofslōg* they killed (literally 'one slew')
drīfan drive	*nam* took (in marriage)
gerēfa sheriff	*nyste* did not know
gesōhton visited	*þӯ* because

787 Hēr nam Beorhtrīc cyning Offan dohtor Ēadburge. And **on his dagum** cōmon **ǣrest** þrēo scipu; and þā se gerēfa **þǣr-tō** rād, and hīe wolde drīfan **tō þæs cyninges tūne**, þȳ hē nyste hwæt hīe wǣron; and hine man ofslōg. Þæt wǣron þā ǣrestan scipu Deniscra manna þe Angel-cynnes land gesōhton.

The first sentence of this entry can be difficult to decipher, again partly because the word order of Old English differs from that of English today. This is one reason why it is so important to pay attention to case endings. A literal translation, paying no attention to case endings, would be something like 'Here took in marriage Berhtric king Offa daughter Eadburg'. As we saw in the previous chapter, we can make sense of the relationship between people and things only by considering the case forms. In this sentence, *Beorhtric cyning* is the Nominative form, the *-n* of *Offan* shows that the phrase *Offan dohtor* is in the possessive or Genitive form ('Offa's daughter'), and the *-e* of *Ēadburge* indicates the Accusative case. So the sentence can be translated more idiomatically into today's English as 'In this year, King Berhtric took Offa's daughter, Eadburg, in marriage.' The next few sentences continue the story:

And **in his days** three ships **first** came; and **then** the sheriff rode **to them**, and wished to drive them **to the king's village**, because he did not know what (i.e. what kind of men) they were; and they killed him. These were the first ships of the Danish men that visited the land of the English people.

Here location in time and place is given in two ways:

(i)   by adverbs *ǣrest, þā*

(ii)   by prepositional phrases *on his dagum, tō þæs cyninges tūne, þǣr-tō*

Adverbs of time and place

Adverbs of time and place in English today include words like 'first', 'then', 'before', 'here', 'afterwards' and so on. In Old English, common adverbs of time and place include:

| *ǣr* | before | *þā* | then |
| *hēr* | here | *æfter* | afterwards |

Of these words, *þā* is one of the most frequently used; it is, however, a deceptive word and one to observe carefully. It appears twice in the entry from the *Anglo-Saxon Chronicle* given above:

and þā se gerēfa þǣr-tō rād

þā ǣrestan scipu

The first occurrence of *þā* means 'then'. However, in the second example, *þā* is part of a noun phrase: it is the Nominative plural form of 'the'. The form *þā* can also be the Accusative plural and the feminine Accusative singular form of 'the'. We need to look hard at how individual words function in the context of sentences. Indeed, when *þā* is closely followed by another *þā* their meaning corresponds to 'when . . . then'.

Prepositional phrases

Prepositional phrases are made up of a preposition like *on* or *tō* plus a noun phrase like *his dagum* 'his days' and *þæs cyninges tūne* 'the king's town' or 'the king's village'. There is a small set of Old English prepositions, including:

| *on* | in, on | *ofer* | on, over | *mid* | with | | *wiþ* | against |
| *of* | from | *fram* | by | *ǣr* | 'ere', before | *tō* | to, at |

Some have a range of meanings in different contexts. Note also that some words, like *ǣr*, sometimes work in a sentence as an adverb, at other times as a preposition. The grammatical label depends on whether or not the word is linked to a noun phrase: compare 'he went out *before*' (adverb) and 'he went out *before the dawn*' (preposition). It will also be clear from this list that the meanings of many of the prepositions have changed over the centuries, although some older meanings survive in particular phrases, e.g. 'he fought with (i.e. 'against') his brother all the time'.

In today's English, noun phrases follow prepositions – that is in fact why this group of words is called *pre*positions. However, in Old English prepositions can either precede or follow the noun phrases to which they are attached:

on his dagum   'in his days'

his dagum on

The relationship between the preposition and the noun phrase is signalled by the case: nouns that are linked to prepositions are usually found in the Dative case. Here *dagum* has the distinctive *-um* ending that signals the Dative plural 'days'. In *to þæs cyninges tūne*, the *-e* ending of *tūne* signals that this is a Dative singular. Certainly if you see a noun ending in the common Dative plural *-um* then you should be looking for a preposition close by; and you should also remember that the meaning of the preposition will probably be slightly different from its present-day meaning.

Prepositions expressing movement

There are, as usual, exceptions to the grammatical rule that prepositions are associated with noun phrases in the Dative case. A number of prepositions are associated with noun phrases in the Accusative case, not the Dative. These tend to be prepositions expressing movement, like *þurh* 'through'. There are also some special cases, like *þǣr-tō* in the extract given above. Here a pronoun signifying some kind of thing or things (here ships) has been replaced by *þǣr* and the pronoun *tō* has been added, to give the meaning, in this context, of 'to them'. Over time, of course, this phrase solidified into the single, now rather old-fashioned, English adverb 'thereto'.

To summarise thus far, then, time and place in English today and in Old English are usually expressed by adverbs and prepositional phrases. Prepositional phrases are made up of words like *in*, *tō*, *mid*, *æfter*, followed or preceded by noun phrases. To show their status as members of prepositional phrases, in Old English the noun phrases are usually found in the Dative case, although sometimes, especially when the preposition has the sense of motion, the noun phrase is found in the Accusative case.

Reading practice

Let us look particularly at how place and time are expressed in a further short passage of Old English, another biblical story, this time from the Old Testament: the tale of the fall of the city of Jericho. Before we look at the passage in detail, try reading it and answering the following questions.

- What surrounded the city of Jericho?
- What three things did God promise to put into Joshua's power?
- For how long did God tell Joshua to go around the city?
- How many priests did God say should blow upon the trumpets?
- What event happened to allow Joshua's army to enter the city?

æt-foran	before	*hrȳmde*	shouted
bǣron	carried	*rǣdde*	advised
belocen	enclosed	*sācerdas*	priests
bȳmum	trumpets	*scrīn*	shrine
ēodon	went	*wuniaþ*	live
faraþ	go	*ymb*	around
gewealde	power	*ymb-trymed*	surrounded

Hierichō sēo burh wæs **mid weallum** ymb-trymed and fæste belocen. Drihten cwæþ **þā tō Iōsue**, 'Ic dō þās burh Hierichō **on þīnum gewealde** and þone cyning samod and þā strengstan weras þe wuniaþ **in Hierichō**. Faraþ **nū** siex dagas **ymb þā burh**, þā hwīle þe seofon sācerdas mid bȳmum **ēow æt-foran** blāwaþ.' Iōsue þā swā dyde and sācerdas bǣron þæt Godes scrīn **ymbe þā burh**. Þā þā sācerdas blēwon, and þæt folc eall hrȳmde, swā swā Iōsue rǣdde, þā burston þā weallas and hīe **þā in** ēodon.

In the above passage there are several prepositional phrases, highlighted. Their form and meaning can be summarised as follows:

Old English phrase	Preposition	Case of noun phrase	Meaning
mid weallum	*mid*	Dative plural	with walls
tō Iōsue	*tō*	Dative singular	to Joshua
on þīnum gewealde	*on*	Dative singular	in your power
in Hierichō	*in*	Dative singular	in Jericho
ymb(e) þā burh	*ymb, ymbe*	Accusative singular	round the city
ēow æt-foran	*æt-foran*	Dative plural	in front of you (pl.)

The passage also highlights some adverbs of time and place:

Old English adverb	Meaning
þā	then
nū	now
in	in

There are various points to note about these prepositional phrases and adverbs. First, note that the phrases which are made up of a prepositional phrase and an Accusative noun phrase indeed imply motion – Joshua's army goes *round the city* for six days. The case of the noun phrase is most easily seen from the determiner *þā*, the feminine Accusative singular form. The majority of phrases, however, consist of a preposition and a noun phrase in the Dative case. Dative plural nouns can be identified by the distinctive ending -*um* as in *weallum* 'walls'. Finally, there is an example of the preposition following a noun – or, in this case, a pronoun, *ēow æt-foran* literally 'you in front of', meaning 'in front of you'.

A fairly literal translation of the passage is:

> Jericho the city was surrounded by walls and firmly enclosed. The Lord then said to Joshua, 'I shall put this city Jericho in your power and also the king and the strongest men who live in Jericho. Go now six days round the city, while seven priests blow with trumpets in front of you.' Joshua then did so and priests carried the shrine of God round the city. When the priests blew, and all the people shouted, just as Joshua advised, the walls then burst and they then went in.

Manner

Prepositional phrases and adverbs are also used to express *manner*, or how things were done. Some good examples of prepositional phrases expressing manner can be seen in Ælfric's story of the Incarnation, which we looked at in Chapter 3:

> Hē āwende wæter tō wīne, and ēode ofer sǣ **mid drīum fōtum**, and hē gestilde windas **mid his hǣse**, and hē forgēaf blindum mannum gesihþe.

Here we are told that Jesus went over the sea *mid drīum fōtum* 'with dry feet' and that he stilled the winds *mid his hǣse* 'with his command'. The noun phrases are Datives; the first is a plural, as can again be seen by the distinctive *-um* ending of the Old English words for both 'dry' and 'feet'. (Remember that this ending is also found in *blindum mannum* 'to blind men', although the preposition 'to' is absent in Old English.) The *-e* ending of the singular noun *hǣse* 'command' indicates that it is a Dative singular.

Adverbs of manner also tell us how things were done. A common way of forming this group of adverbs is to add *-līce* to the adjective. In today's English this ending has been reduced to *-ly*. Examples include:

blīþelīce	gladly, 'blithely'
fæstlīce	firmly, strictly, resolutely
geornlīce	eagerly, zealously

What do you deduce the Old English adjectives *blīþe*, *fæst* and *georn* mean?

Further reading practice

To see how some prepositional phrases and adverbs of manner work in context, let us look at two slightly longer passages based on the Anglo-Saxon epic poem *Beowulf*. We shall return to this poem in more detail when we compare translations in Chapter 7, and again when we read an excerpt from the original text in Part II of this book. In the meantime, the following passages are taken from a simplified prose version written by Henry Sweet expressly to teach Old English to beginners. At this point in the story, the hero Beowulf encounters and fights a monster, Grendel, who is terrorising the land of the Geats, or Goths, by attacking King Hrothgar's men in their great hall, Heorot.

In this episode, Grendel comes to Heorot by night. Some useful vocabulary is given beforehand, and the comprehension questions are intended to guide you through this passage.

āhlōg laughed	*ielde* delayed
ǣdrum veins	*līc-haman* body
ealne all	*māran* greater
faran go, act	*mōd* heart, mind
forswelgan devour, swallow	*ongeat* understood
forswolgen devoured, swallowed	*oþ-þæt* until
gefēng, fēng seized	*siþþan* then
gelǣhte seized	*sōna* immediately
gemētte met with	*stycce-mǣlum* little pieces
gesæt sat up	*tōbræc* broke in pieces
geseah saw	*tōbrǣgd* tore
hraþe quickly	*tōgēanes* towards

Text 1
- Where did Grendel see the Geats sleeping?
- What did Grendel intend to do to the Geats before daybreak?
- Was Beowulf awake or asleep at this point?
- How did Grendel break the bones of the first man he seized?
- What did Grendel drink?
- Where was Beowulf lying as Grendel went further into the hall?
- What did Beowulf seize hold of?
- What did Grendel immediately understand?

Þā geseah hē þā Geatas on þǣre healle slǣpan. Þā āhlōg his mōd: þōhte þæt hē hīe forswelgan wolde ānne æfter ōþrum ǣr dæg cōme. Ac Bēowulf wacode: behēold hū se fēond faran wolde.

Ne ielde Grendel nā lange, ac hē hraþe gefēng slǣpendne mann, and hine siþþan stycce-mǣlum tōbrǣgd: tōbræc þā bān mid his tuscum, and þæt blōd of þǣm ǣdrum dranc, oþ-þæt hē ealne þone līc-haman forswolgen hæfde mid handum mid fōtum mid ealle.

Hē ēode þā furþor, and Bēowulf gelǣhte, on his bedde licgende. Þā gesæt Bēowulf wiþ earm, and him tōgēanes fēng. Þā ongeat Grendel sōna þæt hē ne gemētte ǣr on ǣnigum menn māran hand-gripe!

You will probably need to read through the passage several times, referring where necessary to the unfamiliar vocabulary, before you make sense of it. Again, do not worry if you do not understand every single word. If you can answer most of the comprehension questions, you are doing well. Once you have completed this passage, try reading further to find out how the hand-to-hand combat between man and monster continues. Vocabulary and comprehension questions are once more given to support you, although some of the relevant vocabulary is explained before Text 1 above. Both passages are discussed briefly following Text 2.

ābugon were pulled	*īsen-bendum* iron bands
āhrure fell	*nīþe* violence, hostility
benca benches	*scuccum* demons
besmiþod fitted (with metal)	*swelce* as
drohtoþ condition	*swīþe* very
dynede resounded	*syllum* foundations, settings
fēoll fell	*þēah* though
for-þǣm þe because	*þȳ* the
forht afraid	*ungemetlice* excessive
ful-nēah very nearly	*ūtweard* outwards
gemunde remembered	*wearþ* became
gielp-worda boasting words	*winnende* fighting
grundlunga completely	*wiste* knew
innan and ūtan inside and out	*wununge* dwelling

- After meeting Beowulf, how did Grendel's mood change?
- Where did Grendel wish to flee?
- Who lived there?
- Why could Grendel not escape?
- How did Beowulf's fingers feel?
- What helped the great hall, Heorot, to survive the ferocity of the battle?

Text 2

Þā wearþ hē forht on mōde: wolde flēon tō þǣm mōrum, þǣr hē his wununge wiste mid þǣm ōþrum scuccum. Næs his drohtoþ on Heorote swelce hē ǣr gemētte!

Þā gemunde Bēowulf þāra gielp-worda þe hē ǣr gespræc: stōd þā ūp-

lang and him fæstlīce wiþ-fēng. Þā wæs Grendel ūt-weard. Ac
Bēowulf him fram nolde: gefēng hine þȳ fæstor, þēah him þā fingras
fulnēah bursten. Swā hīe mid ungemetlice nīþe winnende wǣron, oþ-
þæt sēo heall dynede, and manige þāra benca fram þǣm syllum
ābugon. Þæt wæs micel wundor þæt sēo heall ne āhrure grundlunga.
Ac hēo ne fēoll nā, for þǣm þe hēo wæs swīþe fæste mid īsen-
bendum besmiþod innan and ūtan.

Discussion

In this chapter so far, we have been looking mainly at the way prepositional phrases and adverbs are used to express time, place and location. Let us now focus on how some of these concepts are expressed
in Text 1:

> Þā geseah hē þā Geatas **on þǣre healle** slǣpan. Þā āhlōg his mōd:
> þōhte þæt hē hīe forswelgan wolde ānne **æfter ōþrum** ǣr dæg cōme.
> Ac Bēowulf wacode: behēold hū se fēond faran wolde.

> Ne ielde Grendel nā lange, ac hē **hraþe** gefēng slǣpendne mann, and
> hine **siþþan stycce-mǣlum** tōbrǣgd: tōbrǣc þā bān **mid his tuscum**,
> and þæt blōd **of þǣm ǣdrum** dranc, oþ-þæt hē ealne þone līc-haman
> forswolgen hæfde **mid handum mid fōtum mid ealle.**

> Hē ēode þā furþor, and Bēowulf gelǣhte, **on his bedde** licgende. Þā
> gesæt Bēowulf **wiþ earm**, and him tōgēanes fēng. Þā ongeat Grendel
> **sōna** þæt hē ne gemētte **ǣr on ǣnigum menn** māran hand-gripe!

Notice that many of the sentences begin with the adverb *þā* 'then'.
Other adverbs in this passage give a sense of time or urgency:

hraþe   quickly
siþþan   afterwards, then
sōna   immediately
ǣr   before, previously

The adverb *sōna* is an interesting word; it corresponds to present-
day 'soon' but its meaning has clearly weakened – 'soon' does not
mean 'immediately'. This process of weakening happens systematically through time to many adverbs expressing urgency.
    Some of the prepositional phrases give additional but crucial infor-
mation about location in space (*on þǣre healle* 'in the hall', *of þǣm
ǣdrum* 'from the veins', *on his bedde* 'in his bed', *on ǣnigum menn* 'on

any man'). Other prepositional phrases tell us about manner *(mid his tuscum* 'with his tusks', *mid handum mid fōtum mid ealle* 'with (his) hands, with (his) feet, with everything', *wiþ earm* 'against (his) arm').

Text 2 also has its share of prepositional phrases and adverbs:

> Þā wearþ hē forht **on mōde**: wolde flēon **tō þǣm mōrum**, þǣr hē his wununge wiste **mid þǣm ōþrum scuccum**. Næs his drohtoþ **on Heorote** swelce hē **ǣr** gemētte!

> Þā gemunde Bēowulf þāra gielp-worda þe hē **ǣr** gespræc: stōd þā **ūp-lang** and him **fæstlīce** wiþ-fēng. Þā wæs Grendel **ūt-weard**. Ac Bēowulf **him fram** nolde: gefēng hine þȳ fæstor, þēah him þā fingras ful-nēah bursten. Swā hīe **mid ungemetlice nīþe** winnende wǣron, oþ-þæt sēo heall dynede, and manige þāra benca **fram þǣm syllum** ābugon. Þæt wæs micel wundor þæt sēo heall ne āhrure grundlunga. Ac hēo ne fēoll nā, for þǣm þe hēo wæs swīþe fæste **mid īsen-bendum** besmiþod **innan and ūtan**.

Again some of these prepositional phrases and adverbs express location in time and physical or metaphorical space: *on mōde* 'in spirit', *tō þǣm mōrum* 'to the moors', *on Heorote* 'in Heorot', *him fram* 'from him', and *fram þǣm syllum* 'from the foundations'. Others again express manner: *mid ungemetlice nīþe* 'with extreme violence'. Still others express other types of prepositional meaning, including accompaniment, e.g. *mid þǣm ōþrum scuccum* 'with the other demons', and *mid īsen-bendum* 'with iron bands'.

The adverbs cover meanings of time, manner and place in a similar way to those we have encountered before:

ǣr	before, previously
fæstlīce	firmly
innan and ūtan	inside and out
þā	then
ūp-lang	upright
ūt-weard	literally 'outward'; here 'at the door/exit'

Summary of the texts

The first text, then, tells us that Grendel saw the Geats sleeping in the hall; he laughed inwardly as he planned to kill them, one after the other, before daybreak. But Beowulf was awake and he watched to see how Grendel would act. Without delay, Grendel seized one sleeping man, tore him to bits, broke his bones with his tusks and drank his blood from his veins. Then he went further into the hall and seized Beowulf, lying in his bed. Then Beowulf sat up against his arm and seized him. Grendel immediately understood that he had never before encountered a greater handgrip in any man.

The second text continues the story. Grendel was afraid, and wished to flee to the moors where he had his dwelling with the other demons. His experience in Heorot was not as he had encountered before. Then Beowulf remembered the words that he had previously spoken, he stood upright and held him firmly. Then Grendel made for the door. But Beowulf would not let him go: he held him more securely although his fingers were very nearly bursting. They were fighting with such extreme violence that the hall resounded and many benches came apart from the foundations. It was a great wonder that the hall did not completely collapse. But it did not fall, because it was fitted very securely with iron bands, inside and out.

Expressing reason

So far we have focused mainly on the way that noun phrases express people and things, and adverbs and prepositional phrases express time, place and manner. You have started to build up your Old English vocabulary, and by now you should be getting a 'feel' for reading short, simple texts in Old English. Even short, simple texts present their challenges, as we have seen. For example:

- We must expect the order of words to be different in Old English.
- We have to pay attention to the endings of words in Old English in order to spot clues that tell us about the number, gender and case of words.

As we move towards the conclusion of this chapter, let us look at some common ways in which sentences are extended, specifically by giving *reasons* or *causes* for events. Some of the words and phrases commonly used to signal reasons have been used in the reading passages already; some are new:

for-þǣm, for-þǣm þe	because
þȳ	therefore, because
(tō þǣm) þæt, (tō þon) þæt	in order that, so that

Here are some sentences – some of which you have already encountered – in which these expressions of reason are used. Take this opportunity to refresh your memory of the vocabulary you have already met. Since we are unfolding the means of expression in Old English gradually, whilst developing our reading skills, it is a good idea frequently to revisit the texts in the earlier chapters of this book as you read through it, and to consider in turn how different aspects of the language – for example, its ways of articulating people and things, places, time, manner and reason – are realised in the different texts.

Hwæt dēst þū ymb þīnne huntoþ?
Ic selle þǣm cyninge swā hwæt swā ic gefō, **for-þǣm** ic eom his hunta.

Ēalā gē cild, hū līcaþ ēow þēos sprǣc?
Wel hēo ūs līcaþ; ac þearle dēoplīce þū spricst and ofer ūre mæþ. Ac sprec wiþ ūs æfter ūrum andgiete, **þæt** wē mægen understandan þā þing þe þū spricst.

Ic ascige ēow, 'For hwȳ leornige gē swā geornlīce?'
For-þæm wē nyllaþ bēon swā-swā stunt nīetenu, þe nān þing nyton būton gærs and wæter.

Fela wundra wurdon geworhte þurh þone hālgan Cūþberht. Þā cōm him tō sum abbudysse, sēo wæs Ælflǣd gehāten, þæs cyninges sweostor Ecgfrides. Þā begann hēo tō halsigenne þone hālgan wer **þæt** he sceolde hire secgan hū lange hire brōþor Ecgfridus mōste his rīces brūcan.

Hēr nam Beorhtrīc cyning Offan dohtor Ēadburge. And on his dagum cōmon ǣrest þrēo scipu; and þā se gerēfa þǣr tō rād, and hīe wolde drīfan to þæs cyninges tūne, þȳ hē nyste hwæt hīe wǣron; and hine man ofslōg.

Þæt wæs micel wundor þæt sēo heall ne āhrure grundlunga. Ac hēo ne fēoll nā, **for-þǣm þe** hēo wæs swīþe fæste mid īsen-bendum besmiþod innan and ūtan.

Further reading

Let us look now at how Beowulf's battle with Grendel concludes, in Henry Sweet's prose adaptation. Some of the vocabulary is given below; other items have already been encountered and some items you should be able to guess, with a little thought. Again, some comprehension questions are interspersed among the extracts and should help to guide you through the climax of this episode.

ǣlce each	*gewundod* wounded
āsette set up	*gielp* vow
æt-berstan burst away	*grētan* literally 'greet'; here 'harm'
bēgen both	*hēowon* hewed, cut
burge save, protect	*hrīemde* shouted, roared
cempan warriors, champions	*nyston* did not know
drugon endured	*onsprungon* cracked
dura door	*sēcende* seeking
drȳ-cræfte sorcery, witchcraft	*sina* sinews
eaxle shoulder	*stapole* flight of steps
egeslīce terribly	*sweotol* clear
fǣlsode cleansed	*tācen* token, i.e. sign, proof
fæstenne stronghold	*tōburston* burst
feorh life	*tugon* tugged, pulled, drew
furþum even	*þanon* from there, thence
ge and	*þēah* however
gebētte amended	*urnon* ran
gefēran comrades	*wǣfer-sīene* spectacle
gefrēdde felt	*weardas* guards
gehīerdon heard	*wereden* protect
gelǣste kept	*wund* wound
gesīenu visible	*ymb-þrungon* crowded round, surrounded

- Why did Beowulf's comrades draw their swords?
- What did they do to Grendel?
- What protected Grendel?

Þā tugon Bēowulfes gefēran hire sweord þæt hīe hira hlāford wereden. Hīe þā þider urnon ealle, and þā cempan bēgen ymb-þrungon, and on ǣlce healfe hēowon, Grendles feorh sēcende. Hīe nyston þæt nān sweord ne mihte þone fēond grētan, for þǣm hē hæfde eallum wǣpnum forsworen mid his drȳ-cræfte.

- What did Grendel realise?
- What then did he do?
- How did the guards on the walls feel when this happened?

Hē þā Grendel, siþþan hē ongeat þæt hē þanon æt-berstan ne mihte, þā hrīemde hē egeslīce, swā þæt ealle Dene hit gehīerdon, ge furþum þā weardas on þǣm wealle āfyrhte wǣron.

- Where exactly was Grendel wounded?
- How serious was the wound?
- Where did he flee – and why?
- What was he aware of?

Þā wearþ wund gesīenu on Grendles eaxle, oþ-þæt þā sina onsprun-gon and þā bān tōburston. Hē þā ætbærst þanon, tō dēaþe gewun-dod: flēah tō þǣm mōrum, þæt hē him on his fæstenne burge. Hē gefrēdde þēah þæt his līf wæs æt ende.

- How had Beowulf kept his word?
- What did he take as a sign of his victory?
- Where did he put them?
- Who would see them there?

Swā Bēowulf gelǣste his gielp: fǣlsode þæs cyninges healle, and Denum þā yfel gebētte þe hīe lange drugon. Þæt wæs sweotol tācen þā Bēowulf genam Grendles earm and eaxle, and hīe on þǣm stapole āsette æt þǣre healle dura, eallum mannum tō wǣfer-sīene.

We shall return to *Beowulf*, both in the original text and in transla-tions, in greater detail in later chapters of this book. However, Henry Sweet's simplified adaptation of the most famous episode in the story gives an early taste of what many regard as the foundational work in English literature. By the end of this book, you will be able to read some of this masterpiece in its original poetic form, and you should be able to compare and comment on the many translations that have been made of it.

Still, we have come this far in our exploration of Old English without focusing on one of the most important aspects of the language: its means of expressing actions and events. That is the subject of the next chapter.

5 Actions and Events

Understanding the basic grammatical principles of a language is rather like putting a jigsaw puzzle together. Individually, the pieces do not make much sense; we can only apprehend the picture when the pieces are seen in combination. For that reason, it is sometimes frustrating to begin looking at the grammar of a language bit by bit – the bits make sense only when we see them in relation to each other. Our basic jigsaw of the grammar of Old English is very nearly complete. We have looked at some Old English texts and explored the vocabulary and grammar of the language without paying much attention to one of the most important types of word – the verb.

Verbs are those words that express actions and events. Today, the verb phrase can be made up of a single word, like 'give', or a group of words like 'might have given'. Other types of phrase orbit around the verb phrase, performing different functions with respect to it. For example, noun phrases usually act as Subjects and Objects of the verb phrase, while prepositional phrases, as we have seen, tend to give extra information about time, place, manner and so on. As we have also seen, the normal sequence of these phrases can differ in Old English and English today:

Verb	Subject	Object	Extra information
āsende	hē	his engel Gabrihel	tō ānum mǣden
sent	he	his angel Gabriel	to a maiden

Sequences of phrases such as the example above are known as *clauses*, and at the heart of each full clause, sitting like a pearl in an oyster, is the verb. The following sentence is made up of two clauses, and again the order of the phrases in Old English differs from that of English today:

Þā **tugon** Bēowulfes gefēran hire sweord // þæt hīe hira hlāford **wereden.**

Then Beowulf's comrades **drew** their swords // so that they **might protect** their lord.

While current English tends to follow a pattern in which Subject is followed by a verb that in turn is followed by Object –

Subject	Verb	Object
Beowulf's comrades	drew	their swords

– in Old English the verb can be followed or preceded by Subject and Object together:

drew	Beowulf's comrades	their swords
Beowulf's comrades	their swords	drew

Of course, in Old English we can often recognise the Subject and Object by looking at their case (that is, whether the words are in the Nominative or Accusative form), rather than by looking at their position with respect to the verb.

What the form of the Old English verb tells us

The *form* of the verb in Old English is packed with information about:

- Who is performing the action (1st, 2nd or 3rd *person*, i.e. I/we, you, he/she/it/they)
- How many are performing the action (*number*: singular v. plural)
- When it is being performed (*tense*: past v. present and future)
- Whether the sentence expresses a fact or not (*mood*: indicative v. subjunctive)
- Whether the Subject of the verb is the agent or is affected by the action (*voice*: active v. passive)

Changing the form of a verb, then, changes the information it gives about person, number, tense, mood and voice. It is unsurprising that in both English today and Old English the verb has many forms.

However, whereas today's writers of English frequently use a wide range of the forms available, Old English writers tended to restrict their palette to simple present and past forms. We therefore have to do some more interpretative work when we encounter these verb forms. For example, in a passage we shall shortly encounter, about the life of St Columba, we find the sentence:

Sūþ-Peohtas wǣron mycle ǣr gefullode.

A literal translation of this sentence would be 'The South Picts **were** baptised much earlier.' However, given the context of the sentence, and its use of the adverbial phrase *mycle ǣr* 'much earlier', we might venture the translation 'The South Picts **had been** baptised much earlier.' Our interpretation of the meaning of verb phrases therefore has to pay attention to the nuances of context and of any clues given by adverbs and prepositional phrases.

Let us consider some of the main forms that we will encounter in the reading passages.

Past v. present (and future)

In English today, we change the tense of some verbs by altering the vowel in the middle or end of the word (e.g. 'sing/sang'), while in most verbs we simply add -*ed* to the stem of the verb ('walk/walked'). The former are traditionally called *strong* verbs and the latter *weak* verbs. Over the history of English some verbs that were originally strong changed their form and became weak. A small group of verbs, in particular the verb *be*, are irregular and relatively unpredictable in form. The basic patterns in today's English are:

	Singular		**Plural**	
	Present	*Past*	*Present*	*Past*
1st	I draw	I dr**ew**	We draw	We dr**ew**
2nd	You draw	You dr**ew**	You draw	You dr**ew**
3rd	He draws	He dr**ew**	They draw	They dr**ew**
	She draws	She dr**ew**		
	It draws	It dr**ew**		

	Singular		Plural	
	Present	*Past*	*Present*	*Past*
1st	I protect	I protected	We protect	We protected
2nd	You protect	You protected	You protect	You protected
	He protects	He protected	They protect	They protected
3rd	She protects	She protected		
	It protects	It protected		

The present-day system has evolved from an older English system that is still recognisable, as we can see in the following strong verb *drīfan* 'to drive' and the common weak verb *habban* 'to have':

Strong verb: *drīfan* 'to drive'

	Singular		Plural	
	Present	*Past*	*Present*	*Past*
1st	ic drīfe	ic drāf	wē drīfaþ	wē drifon
2nd	þū drīfst	þū drife	gē drīfaþ	gē drifon
	hē drīfþ	hē drāf	hīe drīfaþ	hīe drifon
3rd	hēo drīfþ	hēo drāf		
	hit drīfþ	hit drāf		

Weak verb: *habban* 'to have'

	Singular		Plural	
	Present	*Past*	*Present*	*Past*
1st	ic hæbbe	ic hæfde	wē habbaþ	wē hæfdon
2nd	þū hæfst	þū hæfdest	gē habbaþ	gē hæfdon
	hē hæfþ	hē hæfde	hīe habbaþ	hīe hæfdon
3rd	hēo hæfþ	hēo hæfde		
	hit hæfþ	hit hæfde		

There are a few things to note about this table. The first is that the principle behind strong and weak verbs remains constant in English: strong verbs in Old English generally indicate past tense through a change in vowel, from *ic drīfe* 'I drive' to *ic drāf* 'I drove'. In contrast, weak verbs in Old English generally indicate past tense through a *d*, whether in the singular *hē hæfde* 'he had' or in the plural *hīe hæfdon* 'they had'. *Habben* is unusual in the interchange of *bb* and *f*; however, we include it here because it is one of the most common verbs that you will see.

Some grammatical signals remain fairly constant in both weak and strong verbs in Old English. Points to note in particular include:

- Third-person present singular forms with *hē*, *hēo* or *hit* often end in -*þ*.
- Second-person present singular forms with *þū* often end in -*st*.
- Present plural forms often end in -*aþ*.
- Past plural forms often end in -*on*.
- The infinitive form often ends in -*an*, e.g. *drīfan* 'to drive' and *habban* 'to have'.

We shall shortly look at other forms of the verb, but these should be sufficient for the time being to distinguish between past and present actions. Bear in mind that most narratives you read will usually have Subjects in the third person ('he/they'), and sometimes in the first-person singular ('I'). Second-person subjects will be restricted mainly to direct speech in the narrative. Usually, too, the narratives will be in the past tense. Therefore, at first you should focus on familiarising yourself with third-person forms (singular and plural) and the first-person singular.

Reading practice

Let us look now at several passages that illustrate how texts in Old English convey past and present actions and events. We will focus this time mainly on the verb forms. The first passage is again adapted from the *Anglo-Saxon Chronicle*. The entry for 565 focuses on momentous religious events. For Scottish readers this date holds particular interest as it tells of the arrival of Saint Columba, during the reign of Æthelbert of Kent, to convert the dominant Scottish tribe, the Picts, to Christianity. The abbey that stands on the beautiful island of Iona (Illustration 11), where Columba established his base, has been rebuilt and is still in use today.

Look at the questions below and see if you can figure out the answers from the text before we look at it in greater detail.

- How long did Æthelbert reign in Kent?
- Who brought the ritual of baptism to England?
- Where are the Picts described as living?
- Who gave Columba the island of Iona?

11   St Columba's Bay, Iona

fēng succeeded to	*Ii* Iona
fulluht baptism	*mæsse-prēost* priest
gecierde converted	*rīce* kingdom
gelēafan faith, belief	*wuniaþ* dwell
gesealde gave	

565   Hēr **fēng** Æþelbryht tō Cantwara rīce, and **hēold** þrēo and fīftig wintra. On his dagum **sende** Gregorius ūs fulluht, and Columba mæsse-prēost **cōm** to Peohtum and hīe **gecierde** to Crīstes gelēafan. Hīe **wuniaþ** be norþum mōrum. And hira cyning him **gesealde** þæt īg-land þe man **nemneþ** Ii.

Much of the *Anglo-Saxon Chronicle*, naturally, is concerned with the succession of kings, and here we are told that in 565 Æthelbert *fēng tō rīce* 'took the kingdom' or 'succeeded to the kingdom', which he held for 53 'winters' or years. Gregory, who was then pope, as the chronicler assumes his readers will know, sent baptism to England (via missionaries), and in the same year Columba came to the Picts and converted (*gecierde*) them. The chronicler tells us that the Picts live (*wuniaþ*) in the north moors, and that their king gave (*gesealde*) Columba the island called Iona (literally, 'that one calls Iona', *þe man nemneþ Ii*).

This brief extract has a good variety of verb forms in both past and present tenses. The present tenses can easily be identified by the plural -*aþ* and singular -*eþ* endings (*Hīe wuniaþ* 'they live'; *man nemneþ* 'one calls'). Most of the other verbs are past tenses, and can be identified as such by the *d*: *hēold* 'held', *sende* 'sent', *gecierde* 'converted', *gesealde* 'gave'. Only two verbs are left that do not fit the pattern, the strong verbs *fōn* 'seize', which has the past tense *fēng*, which here means 'succeeded', and *cuman* 'come', which has the past tense *cōm* 'came'.

Further reading

Now follow the *Chronicle* entry further, and find out how Columba fared.

- What did Columba build on Iona?
- What role did he perform there for 32 years?
- How old was he when he passed away?
- Which Pictish tribes had been baptised long before Columba's arrival?
- Who baptised them and where was he educated?
- In whose name is the abbey of Whithorn dedicated?
- Who rests at the abbey of Whithorn?

bodade	preached	*gelǣred*	educated
forþ-fērde	died (literally, 'travelled forth)	*getimbrode*	built
fulwiht	baptism	*mynster*	abbey
gefullode	baptised	*ierfe-weardas*	heirs
gehālgod	dedicated (i.e. 'hallowed')		

Þǣr se Columba **getimbrode** mynster, and þǣr hē **wæs** abbod twā and þrītig wintra, and þǣr **forþ-fērde** þā þā hē **wæs** seofon and hund-seofontig wintra. Þā stōwe **habbaþ** nū gīet his ierfe-weardas. Sūþ-Peohtas **wǣron** mycle ǣr **gefullode**. Him **bodade** fulwiht Ninia biscop, sē **wæs** on Rōme **gelǣred**. His mynster **is** æt Hwīterne, on

Martines naman **gehālgod**. Þǣr hē **resteþ** mid manegum hālgum werum.

The chronicler here punctuates what is essentially a past-tense narrative with occasional references to the present that bring home to his readers the contemporary relevance of the historical events he describes. And so we learn that Columba built an abbey and that he was abbot there for 32 years, until he died at the age of 77 (*seofon and hund-seofontig*). The chronicler then switches to the present tense to say that even now his heirs have that place (*pā stōwe habbaþ*). The chronicler again shifts his focus to pre-Columban Scotland and tells us that the southern Picts were baptised long before (*wǣron mycle ǣr gefullode*), by Ninian, who was educated (*wæs . . . gelǣred*) in Rome. The chronicler returns to the present, as he tells us that Ninian's abbey, dedicated to St Martin, is in Whithorn – which is on the southwest coast of Scotland – and that the abbot rests there with many holy men.

These extracts together, then, illustrate a very common type of narrative in Old English: events in the past are recounted, with only occasional present-tense references if any. Here the narratives relate largely to the exploits of individuals – Æthelbert, Gregory, Columba and Ninian – so most of the verbs are in the singular past tense form, often identified by the *-de* ending.

Expressing the future

Old English – like English today – has only two tenses with which to express different points of time, usually present and past. Old English speakers and writers, like their present-day counterparts, therefore used the present tense to express future time as well as present time. It is important here to distinguish between *present tense*, which is the conventional name given by grammarians to a form of any verb, and *present time*, which is a non-linguistic, temporal phenomenon. Thus *present tense* can be used to refer to any number of points in time, both present and future. An example of present tense used to express future time can be found at the beginning of the story of Joshua and the siege of Jericho, which we looked at in Chapter 4.

Hierichō sēo burh **wæs** mid weallum **ymb-trymed** and fæste **belocen**. Drihten **cwæþ** þā tō Iōsue, 'Ic **dō** þās burh Hierichō on þīnum gewealde and þone cyning samod and þā strengstan weras þe **wuniaþ** in Hierichō.'

In Chapter 4, we translated these sentences like this:

Jericho the city **was surrounded** by walls and firmly **enclosed**. The Lord then **said** to Joshua, 'I **shall put** this city Jericho in your power and also the king and the strongest men who **live** in Jericho.'

Most of these verbs should not give many difficulties. The forms of *ymb-trymed* 'surrounded' and *belocen* 'enclosed' have different endings – but then so do modern forms like 'ask**ed**' and 'giv**en**'. The past tense of *cweþan* 'to say' does not contain -*d* but it does change the middle vowel, like other irregular verbs such as 'sing' and 'sang', and, as noted in Chapter 2, it reminds us of the old-fashioned term, 'quoth'. The plural present-tense form *wuniaþ* 'live' is exactly what we now expect.

Any difficulty lies in understanding the simple word *dō*, the first-person singular, present-tense form of the verb *dōn*, which in Old English could mean 'do', 'act', 'make' or (as here) 'put'. Only the context of the verb in this passage suggests that the best translation into today's English is 'shall put'.

The word 'shall' in English today has an Old English ancestor in the verb *sculan* 'ought to, have to, must', just as present-day 'will' has an ancestor in *willan* 'wish to'. However, it was not until towards the end of the Old English period that *sculan* and *willan* began to mark future events or predictions as they do in English today. The present-tense form was much more widely used to indicate future in the earlier periods. The lesson to be learned from this example is that we often have to make intelligent guesses about the detailed meaning of individual verbs, based on what we understand of the overall meaning of any passage. Intelligent guesswork, as we shall later see, is also essential when the verb is missed out completely.

Duration

In most languages, verbs not only identify the point in time of an action (past, present or future), they can also indicate other meanings; for example, using the verb 'to be' with another verb in a particular form can indicate *duration*, that is, there is the sense that the action is or was lasting a relatively long time. The form of the verb that expresses this concept is called the 'present participle' – in today's English it ends in -*ing*, and in Old English it usually ends in -*ende*. Its use can be seen in the following sentence:

> *Ond hīe alle on þone cyning **wǣrun feohtende** oþ-þæt hīe hine ofslǣgenne hæfdon.*

And they all **were fighting** against the king until they had killed ('slain') him.

Two verbs 'to be'

The verb 'to be' is a highly irregular verb in English today. It is actually derived from *two* Old English verbs, *wesan* and *bēon*, although in standard English the only remnant of the second form is the infinitive 'to be' itself, all the other forms descending from *wesan*. Even in Old English, *bēon* was only used in the present tense. It is worth stating here for reference what the different Old English forms of 'to be' are:

to be	*wesan*	*bēon*
I am	ic eom	ic bēo
you are	þū eart	þū bist
he is	hē is	hē biþ
she is	hēo is	hēo biþ
it is	hit is	hit biþ
we are	wē sindon	wē bēoþ
you are	gē sindon	gē bēoþ
they are	hīe sindon	hīe bēoþ
I was	ic wæs	
you were	þū wǣre	
he was	hē wæs	
she was	hēo wæs	
it was	hit wæs	
we were	wē wǣron	
you were	gē wǣron	
they were	hīe wǣron	

It might seem odd that Old English had two verbs meaning much the same thing; however, even in varieties of regional English today, 'I be fighting' is not an impossible construction. Such expressions have an ancient pedigree. It is likely that in Old English *wesan* and *bēon* had slightly different meanings, the former referring to the present state while the latter was used to express 'timeless' facts, e.g.

> *I am in the garden*   present state
> *I be the king's huntsman*   fact

However, the two meanings, and the verbs used to express them, merged over time.

The use of *wesan* and *bēon* with present participles to indicate duration was less common in Old English than it is today, although it does occur, as in:

> *Ond hīe þā ymb þā gatu **feohtende wǣron**, oþ-þæt hīe þǣr-inne fulgon.*

And they then around the gates **were fighting**, until they therein burst.

Since this is quite an unusual form in Old English, a more subtle translation into today's English might choose to stress the sense of duration that the Old English verb phrase probably conveyed, as in:

> And then they **continued fighting** around the gates, until they burst in.

Specific reference to time

Other combinations of verbs can specify nuances of time more subtly than we can with a blunt, two-fold distinction between past and present. In the previous section we looked at the following sentence:

> *Ond hīe alle on þone cyning wǣrun feohtende oþ-þæt hīe hine **ofslæ-genne hæfdon**.*

And they all were fighting against the king until they **had killed** him.

In English today, we find combinations made up of the verb 'to have' with what is called the 'past participle' of the verb, that is, words like 'walked', 'given' or 'slain'. In these combinations, the meanings change depending on whether 'have' is in the present or past tense:

He **has fought.**   *Present tense: 'has'*
He **had fought.**   *Past tense: 'had'*

Depending on the verb used and the context of its use, the present-tense form can have up to three meanings:

- Unspecified past time (e.g. 'He has fought, and I'm not specifying when')
- Recent past (e.g. 'He has just fought, moments ago')
- Past action extending into the present (e.g. 'He has fought in these competitions for years, and still does')

In its past tense form, the combination of words generally suggests an action that took place before another specified action, e.g.

He had fought Grendel before Grendel's mother turned up.

The present-day English system, with its nuances, has developed from a similar but not identical Old English set of combinations with both *habban* and *bēon*:

Hē hæfþ gefeohten   'He has fought'
Hē biþ gecumen   'He has come' (literally, 'He is come')

When did Old English writers use *habban* and when did they use *bēon* in combination with past participles? There was a pattern: *habban* was used when the verb was naturally associated with an Object, whilst *bēon* was used when the verb was *not* naturally associated with an Object.

Hē hæfþ **þone fēond** gefeohten   'He has fought **the enemy**'
Hē biþ gecumen   'He has come'

For the purposes of reading, it is sufficient to be aware that both *habban* and *bēon* can be used with the past participle to express these subtle nuances of time. We also need to be aware that Old English writers do not always use these verbal combinations in exactly the way that we would today. That is, sometimes Old English writers use simple present-tense forms when we would expect a combination of words that expresses duration, or they might use a phrase with *habban + past participle* when today we would use a simple past form. So long as we are familiar with the basic forms and are sensitive to the possibility of variation, we should become confident in our interpretations of older texts.

First-person narratives

The *Anglo-Saxon Chronicle*, not surprisingly, is largely a third-person narrative, so we should expect to encounter mainly third-person forms in it. To illustrate a first-person narrative, where the speaker is an actor in his own story, let us look at a short extract from one of the poems we shall return to in full in Part II, *The Dream of the Rood*. This extraordinary, visionary work tells us about a dream in which the narrator encounters the cross ('the rood') on which Christ was crucified, and listens to its story. It allows us a tantalising glimpse of Anglo-Saxon attitudes to religion, also reflected in the number of carved or decorated crosses surviving from the medieval period (see Illustration 12).

In the following section, the narrative of the crucifixion is told from the perspective of the cross itself. The verbs are shown in bold; the forms shift from third to first person as the cross switches between telling of other people's actions and then expressing its own responses. Like other Anglo-Saxon poems, this is written in half-lines (each is usually referred to as line *a* and *b*), and in the following extract we have numbered them 1–11 for convenience, although they are actually lines 28–39 in the original text. The original ð has here also been replaced by the more familiar character þ. Read through the extract, and identify the lines in which:

- the cross is made;
- the cross describes the approach of Christ;
- the cross explains its feelings about being used as the vehicle for Christ's execution.

12   MacLean's Cross, Iona

āhēawen   cut down
āsetton   set down
āstyred   removed
beorg   hill
bifian   tremble
būgan   bow down
eftstan   hasten
elne mycle   with great zeal
gēara iū   very long ago
gefyllan   fell, strike down
geman   remember
genāman   seized

genōge   enough (i.e. many)
gestīgan   climb
geworhton   made ('wrought')
gȳta   still, yet
hebban   lift up
holtes   of the forest
scēatas   surfaces
sēlesta   best
stefne   root
wǣfer-sȳne   spectacle
wergas   criminals

Þæt wæs gēara iū
þæt ic wæs āhēawen
āstyred of stefne mīnum.
geworhton him þǣr tō wǣfer-
        sȳne,
Bǣron mē þǣr beornas on
        eaxlum,
Gefæstnodon mē þǣr fēondas
        genōge.
efstan elne mycle,
Þǣr ic þā ne dorste
būgan oþþe berstan,
eorþan scēatas.
fēondas gefyllan,

(ic þæt gȳta geman)
holtes on ende,
Genāman mē þǣr strange fēondas,
hēton mē heora wergas hebban.

oþ-þæt hīe mē on beorg āsetton.   5

Geseah ic þā Frean man-cynnes

þæt hē mē wolde on gestīgan.
ofer Dryhtnes word
þā ic bifian geseah
Ealle ic mihte   10
hwæþre ic fæste stōd.

First-person forms include the present tense *ic geman* 'I remember' and the past-tense forms *Geseah ic* 'I saw', and *ic stōd* 'I stood'. Two verbs are followed by other verbs in their basic infinitive form, *ic ne dorste būgan oþþe berstan* 'I did not dare to bow or break', and *ic mihte gefyllan* 'I could have felled/struck down'. Third-person forms include *Genāman mē strange fēondas* 'strong foes took me' and *hīe mē on beorg āsetton* 'they set me up on a hill'. Another verb followed by an infinitive is *hēton mē heora wergas hebban* 'commanded me to raise up their criminals'. Note again that Old English word order is often different from that of English today – although an unexpected word order is still a characteristic of poetic language.
    The structure of this extract should now be clear: lines 1–6a tell that

the cross was hewed from the edge of a wood, and, intended as a spectacle, it was taken by strong enemies who commanded it to raise up their criminals. Men bore it on their shoulders, and set it up on a hill. Lines 6b and 7 tell of Christ approaching with great zeal to climb the cross. Lines 8–11 tell of the cross's inability to influence events: it did not dare to bow or break against the Lord's will, and when it saw the earth shake it could have felled many enemies, but it stood firm.

The unusual perspective taken by *The, Dream of the Rood* is a powerful means of defamiliarising a tale that would be an integral part of the life of the poet and his listeners and readers. The image of the hero hastening to meet his death at the hands of his foes is at odds with that of a hero such as Beowulf, who defeats his foes in battle; in the cross's frustration at not being able to scatter Christ's enemies we can see the heroic values of military conquest set against the Christian ethos of self-sacrifice at God's command.

The next few sections of this chapter focus on some of the peculiarities of verb uses in Old English that you will notice in the reading passages in Part II of this book.

Verbs and plural Subjects

One characteristic feature of Old English that has not survived into the modern idiom is the tendency to split up plural Subjects that have the form 'X and Y', for example 'Beowulf and his comrades' or 'Cynewulf and the counsellors of the West Saxons'. In today's English such plurals are treated as compound Subjects, and they are followed by a plural verb; however, in Old English the Subject is often divided and a singular verb is used. The following two sentences illustrate this usage, and are translated literally:

Bēowulf onhielde his hēafod tō þǣm bolstre, and his gefēran swā same.

Beowulf laid his head on the pillow, and his comrades likewise.

Cynewulf benam Sigebryht his rīces ond West-Seaxna wiotan.

Cynewulf deprived Sigebryht of his kingdom and the counsellors of the West Saxons.

When reading Old English texts, then, we have to be aware that noun phrases beginning *ond/and* that appear after the verb might actually be part of a plural Subject, and should be understood as 'Beowulf and his comrades' or 'Cynewulf and the counsellors of the West Saxons'.

Asking questions

English today has different ways of forming questions. The word order depends on the kind of question asked and the verb chosen.

Questions that have the answer 'yes' or 'no'
When the verb phrase includes *to be* or a modal auxiliary verb like *can, could, must, might, should* and so on, we reverse the order of the Subject and the first verb:

He is sick	>	**Is he** sick?
He is going	>	**Is he** going?
We can go	>	**Can we** go?
We should leave	>	**Should we** leave?

When we form yes/no questions with other verbs, we have to introduce the auxiliary verb 'do'. This precedes the Subject, which in turn precedes the main verb:

I recognise you	>	**Do you recognise** me?

Questions using 'wh' words: who(m), what, why and how
Questions that require a more informative answer than 'yes' or 'no' make use of a question word like 'who' or 'what'. Then we more or less add the 'wh' word to the kind of question form used in yes/no questions:

Why is he sick?
Where is he going?
When can we go?
How should we leave?
Whom do you recognise?

In Old English, the question form is similar but easier. In yes/no questions the order of Subject and verb is simply reversed; in wh- questions, the question word precedes the first or main verb, which then precedes the Subject:

Ic cann būtan nettum huntian	> **Canst þū** būtan nettum huntian?
	> Hū **canst þū** būtan nettum huntian?
I can hunt without nets.	> **Can you** hunt without nets?
	> How **can you** hunt without nets?
Ic gefō heorotas and haran.	> **Gefehst þū** heorotas and haran?
	> Hwelc wild-dēor **gefehst þū**?
I catch stags and hares.	> **Do you catch** stags and hares?
	> Which wild animals **do you catch?**

Reading practice

Look at the questions below and see if you can match them up to the appropriate answers.

begietst   obtain
bīleofan   sustenance
cīepst   trade
ceastre   city
ceaster-ware   citizens
feoh   money
rēwett   rowing
swā fela gefōn swā ic sellan mæge   catch as many as I might sell
scrūd   clothes

Questions
1.   Hwelcne cræft canst þū?
2.   Hwæt begietst þū of þīnum cræfte?
3.   Hwǣr cīepst þū þīne fiscas?
4.   Hwā bygþ hīe?
5.   For-hwȳ ne fiscast þū on sǣ?

Answers

(a)   On þǣre ceastre.

(b)   Ic eom fiscere.

(c)   Þā ceasterware. Ne mæg ic hira swā fela gefōn swā ic sellan mæge.

(d)   Hwīlum ic dō swā, ac seldon; for-þǣm hit is mē micel rēwett tō þǣre sǣ.

(e)   Bīleofan ic me begiete and scrūd, and feoh.

The answers are revealed at the end of the chapter.

Negatives

We have already come across a number of negatives in the Old English texts we have read, for example in the previous activity:

> **Ne** *mæg ic hira swā fela gefōn swā ic sellan mæge.*

> I can**not** catch as many as I might sell.

The negative is often formed as above by putting *ne* before the verb. There is also another word, *nā*, which can be translated as 'not'. Both *ne* and *nā* can be used in the same sentence to stress the negative meaning:

> **Ne** ielde Grendel **nā** lange.

> Grendel did **not** delay long. (Literally, 'Grendel didn't delay not long'.)

The grammatical rule that forbids present-day speakers and writers of standard English from using double negatives (as in 'I can't get **no** satisfaction') was popularised by eighteenth-century grammarians who were more concerned with mathematical logic than with how people actually used the language. Double – and even triple – negatives were common in speech and writing in earlier English, as they still are in other modern languages today.

Some common verbs, as you will have noticed, combine with *ne* to form a single negative word: *nis* (*ne* + *is* 'isn't'), *nylle* (*ne* + *wille* 'don't wish'), and *nyste* (*ne* + *wiste* 'don't know'). This kind of combination also occurs with the pronoun *nān* (*ne* + *ān* 'none').

Hīe **nyston** þæt **nān** sweord **ne** mihte þone fēond grētan.

They did not know that no sword could harm the enemy.

Commands

Commands in Old English are expressed using two verb forms, one for commanding an individual, the other for commanding a group. And so you might say:

Commanding one person	Commanding more than one	
gā	*gāþ*	go
ne hrīn	*ne hrīnaþ*	don't touch

The plural command usually ends in -*þ*, like plural present-tense verbs. We saw an example in the reading passage in Chapter 4, when God commands Joshua and his men:

Faraþ nū siex dagas ymb þā burh . . .

Go now round the city for six days . . .

Impersonal events

A curious characteristic that English shares with some other languages is that certain kinds of action and even experience are expressed as if there is no animate Subject. In English today we can say things like:

It is raining
It seems that . . .
It appears that . . .

We often use these expressions to distance ourselves from the experience described; for example, we might say 'It appears (to me) that you are wrong' rather than 'I believe you are wrong'.

In Old English there is a broader range of verbs that have impersonal uses. This category includes other verbs of experience, such as 'dream', as we can see in the opening lines of the poem *The Dream of the Rood*:

> Hwæt! Ic swefna cyst   secgan wylle
> hwæt **mē gemǣtte**   tō midre nihte

> Lo! I wish to tell the best of dreams
> that **I dreamed** (lit. 'it **dreamed to me**') in the middle of the night . . .

The point to remember from this example is that when you come across some verbs in Old English, particularly those expressing mental events or perceptions, the noun phrase is often in the Dative case.

Active and passive voice

English today has two ways of expressing very nearly the same thing, for example:

> Ninian **baptised** the Picts.   *Active voice*
> The Picts **were baptised** by Ninian.   *Passive voice*

The availability of these two options allows English speakers today to manage the 'flow' of information in the sentence – we can decide, for example, whether to put the agent of any action at the start of the sentence or at its climax. In the case of the passive, we can even delete the agent altogether: 'The Picts were baptised.'

Old English writers used passive forms of the verb frequently. The passive in Old English is formed in an identical way to that in today's English:

> *Peohtas **wǣron gefullode.***   The Picts **were baptised**.

Another kind of Old English grammatical construction is also usually translated as a passive form in today's English, that is the verb with the impersonal use of 'man', meaning 'one':

> *. . . þe man nemneþ Ii.*

While this kind of phrase might literally be translated as 'that man/one calls Iona', translators conventionally render it as a passive, 'which is called Iona'.

Expressing factual and non-factual events

The Old English verb had a grammatical form that has barely survived into English today. Compare the following forms:

1. hē giefþ   hīe gēafaþ
2. hē geaf   hīe gēafon
3. hē giefe   hīe giefen

In the first line, the verbs express facts in the present tense: 'he gives' and 'they give'. In the second line, the verbs express facts in the past tense: 'he gave' and 'they gave'. In the third line, however, the form of the verb shows that we are no longer in the world of facts – these forms express 'non-factual' events or states, such as hypotheses, desires or possibilities that in present-day English would normally be expressed using other verbs, for example 'he/they *would* give, *wish* to give, *could* give' and so on. The precise meaning of this verb form depends on the context in which the verb is found, but it always has a generally 'non-factual' sense.

The form of the verb shown in line three is known as the *subjunctive*, and it only survives in today's English in expressions like 'If I **were** to help you' or 'Lord **help** us!' where again the meaning suggests a hypothesis, a desire or even a prayer. The subjunctive form of the verb in Old English is also used in indirect speech, where in English today we would again use a verb like 'would'; for example, 'She said that she would return.'

Though the subjunctive form of the verb has largely been replaced by alternative grammatical resources in English today, other languages such as French and German still make use of it. In Old English, the subjunctive is used to express various hypothetical meanings, including doubt, desire, condition and intended result, as well as to signal indirect speech. The main thing to look for is an -*e* ending showing the singular, and an -*en* ending showing the plural (although this is sometimes abbreviated to -*n* in verbs ending in vowels, like *dō* which has the subjunctive *dōn*). When you spot these endings, then you need to ask yourself if a hypothetical meaning is required.

Some of the examples seen earlier in this chapter include subjunctive uses of the verb:

*Ne mæg ic hira swā fela **gefōn** swā ic **sellan mæge.***

I **cannot catch** as many as I **might sell**.

Here the difference between *mæg* and *mæge* signals a shift in meaning from the fact that the hunter *cannot* catch the quantity that he (hypothetically) *might* sell. Whereas in English today we capture this shift in meaning by using different auxiliary verbs, Old English writers simply changed the form of the verb *mæg(e)*. Another example of a shift from fact to hypothesis occurs in the sentence:

þā **tugon** Bēowulfes gefēran hire sweord þæt hīe hira hlāford **wereden.**

Then Beowulf's comrades **drew** their swords so that they **might protect** their lord.

The first verb in this sentence (*tugon*) is a simple past plural form ('drew') which indicates a fact, something that has happened in the past, while the second verb (*wereden*) is a plural subjunctive, indicating that the act of protecting their lord is something that still exists only in the realm of possibility. As in the previous example, in English today we tend to express this notion through the use of an auxiliary verb like 'might'.

Pause for thought

This chapter concludes our introduction to the basic grammar of Old English. We have covered the essentials, from noun phrases that express people and things, through prepositional phrases expressing place, time, manner and reason, to verbs expressing actions and events – past, present and future, factual and hypothetical.

You now have the essential tools to begin to read more extended Old English texts. Before we launch into these, however, we shall pause to consider how Old English verse works (Chapter 6) and how different people in different periods have tackled Old English translation (Chapter 7).

Answers

Answers to matching exercise: 1b, 2e, 3a, 4c, 5d.

6   Introducing Old English Poetry

About 30,000 lines of Old English poetry survive, mostly in four manuscripts copied during the late tenth or early eleventh centuries. These are:

- the Exeter Book, a collection of religious and secular poetry donated to Exeter Cathedral by Bishop Leofric in 1072;
- the Vercelli Book, a collection of religious poetry and prose probably taken to Vercelli in Italy during the eleventh century by pilgrims on their way to Rome;
- the Junius Manuscript, an illustrated collection of four long religious poems bequeathed to the Bodleian Library in Oxford by an early owner, Francis Junius;
- the *Beowulf* Manuscript, a collection of poetry and prose concerning marvels, once owned by Sir Robert Cotton and now in the British Library in London.

A smaller amount of poetry survives in other sources, such as the *Anglo-Saxon Chronicle*, whose annals are mainly in prose but occasionally in poetry. Since all Old English poetry is written in continuous long lines like prose, and may be copied alongside prose as in the *Chronicle*, the Vercelli Book, and the *Beowulf* Manuscript, it is only the form and style that identifies it as verse. The aim of this chapter is to provide an introduction to the main characteristics of Old English poetry, with examples from different genres. The following chapter will focus on the epic poem *Beowulf*, and an extract from *Beowulf*, together with two other complete poems, will be found in Part II.

From this point onwards, we shall no longer be simplifying the language and spelling of the texts, as in Chapters 2–5. You should therefore be aware that spellings may be inconsistent between (and even within) individual texts, and that some texts use letter ð ('eth') interchangeably with þ ('thorn').

Religious poetry: *Caedmon's Hymn*

The earliest Old English poetry was pre-Christian, but the conversion of the Anglo-Saxons during the seventh and eighth centuries resulted in a strong tradition of religious verse. Among the genres represented are biblical paraphrase, as in *Genesis, Exodus* and *Daniel* in the Junius Manuscript, saints' lives, as in *Guthlac A* and *Guthlac B* in the Exeter Book, and dream vision, as in *The Dream of the Rood* in the Vercelli Book. The earliest religious poem in English is recorded by the monk and historian Bede (*c.*673–735) within a miracle story which forms part of his most famous work, *Ecclesiastical History of the English People*. The main character is Caedmon, a herdsman on a monastic estate (probably Whitby in northern England), who was so bad at singing that whenever his fellow workers were entertaining each other by improvising secular songs at drinking parties, he would leave before his turn came. One evening when he had done so and gone to bed, a man appeared to him in a dream and ordered him to sing. Despite his protests that he was unable to do so, the man insisted, and Caedmon was divinely inspired to compose a poem about the creation of the world. On repeating it to the abbess of the monastery the following day, he was admitted as a lay brother and spent the rest of his life turning biblical stories into verse, thus founding the English tradition of vernacular religious poetry.

Bede's *Ecclesiastical History* survives in a number of manuscripts, both Latin and Old English, with different versions of Caedmon's original poem. Here is one of them, with a literal translation or 'gloss' under each word and a prose translation at the end.

Nū wē sculon herian	heofon-rīces Weard,
Now we must praise	*of the heavenly kingdom Guardian*
Metodes mihte	and his mōd-geþanc,
of the Creator might	*and his conception*
weorc Wuldor-fæder,	swā hē wundra gehwæs,
work of the Father of glory.	*as he of wonders each*
ēce Dryhten,	ōr onstealde.
eternal Lord	*beginning established*

Hē ǣrest scōp	eorþan bearnum 5
He first created	*of earth for the children*
heofon tō hrōfe,	hālig Scieppend.
heaven as roof	*holy Creator*
Þā middan-geard	man-cynnes Weard,
Then earth	*of mankind Guardian*
ēce Dryhten,	æfter tēode,
eternal Lord	*afterwards adorned*
fīrum foldan	Frēa æl-mihtig.
for men earth	*Lord almighty*

[Now we must praise the Guardian of the heavenly kingdom, the might and conception of the Creator, the work of the Father of glory, as he, eternal Lord, established the beginning of each wonder. He, the holy Creator, first created heaven as a roof for the children of earth. Then the Guardian of mankind, eternal Lord, Lord almighty, afterwards adorned the earth for men.]

As you can see, the poetry does not rhyme, and neither is there a fixed number of syllables per line. Instead, Old English verse is based on rhythm and alliteration (the use of the same initial sound to link words). Each line of poetry has four main stresses, with a variable number of unstressed syllables. In modern editions, the lines are usually printed with a break in the middle, so that there are two stresses in each half-line. The two half-lines – sometimes known as the '*a*-verse' and the '*b*-verse' – are linked by alliteration. The first stressed syllable in the *b*-verse is known as the 'headstave', and it alliterates with one or both stressed syllables in the *a*-verse. In line 1, the headstave is *heofon*, alliterating with *herian*. In line 2, the headstave is *mōd*, alliterating with *Metod* and *mihte*. The second stressed syllable in the *b*-verse must not alliterate with these, but may occasionally alliterate with a different stressed syllable in the *a*-verse, or with the following line.

The main stresses are usually long syllables (syllables with a long vowel, or a short vowel followed by more than one consonant), and tend to be important words like nouns and adjectives. There are in any case fewer grammatical words than in prose. Old English poetry is a very concentrated style of writing, and the omission of many of the grammatical words, which carry less meaning, packs each line full of significant terms. Line 2b has a conjunction *and*, and line 6a has a preposition *tō*, but otherwise this poem is composed entirely of adjectives, adverbs, nouns, pronouns and verbs.

Both stress and alliteration fall on word stems rather than on prefixes or inflexions, so they do not always come at the beginning of words. Many Old English words begin with an unstressed *ge-* prefix, so in line 3b, the fourth stress falls on the second syllable of *gehwæs*. In 4b, it falls on the second syllable of *onstealde*, and in 9b, it falls on the middle syllable of *æl-mihtig*. Some compound words may have two stresses, as on the first and third syllables of 2b *mōd-geþanc* and 7a *middan-geard*. Since line 3 alliterates on *w*, *gehwæs* might appear to break the rule whereby the second stressed syllable in the *b*-verse does not alliterate with the headstave. However, some consonant clusters such as *sc*, *sp*, *st* and *hw* alliterate only with themselves, not with single consonants. Conversely, all vowels alliterate with all other vowels, so in line 4 *ēce* alliterates with *ōr*, in line 5 *ǣrest* alliterates with *eorþan*, and in line 8 *ēce* alliterates with *æfter*.

Here is the poem again, with alliteration underlined (double for headstaves), and stressed syllables printed in bold:

Nū wē sculon **h**erian	**h**eofon-rīces **Weard**,	
Metodes **m**ihte	and his **m**ōd-geþanc,	
weorc Wuldor-fæder,	swā hē **w**undra gehwæs,	
ēce **Dryhten**,	**ō**r onstealde.	
Hē **ǣ**rest **scōp**	**eor**þan **bearnum**	5
heofon tō **h**rōfe,	**h**ā lig **Scieppend**.	
Þā **m**id**dan-geard**	**m**an-cynnes **Weard**,	
ēce **Dryhten**,	**æ**fter **tēode**,	
fīrum **f**oldan	**Fr**ēa **æl-mihtig**.	

But there is more to Old English poetry than a four-stress line linked by alliteration. Other features of the verse technique represented here are:

- circumlocution
- compounds
- formulas
- poetic diction
- synonyms
- variation

Anglo-Saxon poets often use roundabout expressions, known as 'circumlocution' or 'euphemism', in preference to more straightforward terminology. For instance, God is referred to here as *heofon-rīces Weard* 'Guardian of the heavenly kingdom' (1b) and *man-cynnes Weard* 'guardian of mankind' (7b), while people are described as *eorþan bearnum* 'the children of earth' (5b).

Compounding is particularly common in Old English poetry. It tends to increase the weight of meaning, since a compound can express an idea more concisely than a descriptive phrase. There are six examples in this short poem:

- 1b *heofon-rīce* 'heavenly kingdom' (*heofon* 'heaven' + *rīce* 'kingdom')
- 2b *mōd-geþanc* 'conception' (*mōd* 'mind' + *geþanc* 'thought')
- 3a *Wuldor-fæder* 'father of glory' (*wuldor* 'glory' + *fæder* 'father')
- 7a *middan-geard* 'earth' (*middan* 'middle' + *geard* 'dwelling')
- 7b *man-cynn* 'mankind' (*mann* 'human' + *cynn* 'kind, race')
- 9b *æl-mihtig* 'almighty' (*æl* 'all' + *mihtig* 'mighty')

Some compounds are metaphorical rather than literal, and are known as 'kennings'. The meaning of *middan-geard* ('middle-dwelling'; the source of Tolkien's 'Middle Earth', as noted in Chapter 1) derives from the medieval belief that earth was mid-way between Heaven and Hell.

Formulas are stock phrases – sometimes complete half-lines – which can be repeated either exactly or with minor variations in different contexts. They originated in oral tradition for the convenience of poets improvising as they went along, but formulas continued to be used in written composition. Here line 4a is identical to 8a: *ēce Dryhten* 'eternal Lord' was a useful formula to use in lines of religious poetry where the headstave alliterated either on a vowel or on *d*. Another formula is 1b, *heofon-rīces Weard* 'Guardian of the heavenly kingdom', an adaptation of the formula *rīces weard* 'guardian of the kingdom' used of kings in secular poetry. A similar phrase appears in 7b, *man-cynnes Weard* 'guardian of mankind': not a precise repetition of the formula, but a variant of it.

Partly because of the demands of alliteration, Old English poetry needed a wide vocabulary, with a range of synonyms for recurring themes such as man, warfare, and God. For instance, *Metod* (2a) and *Scieppend* (6b) both mean 'Creator', and *Dryhten* (4a, 8a) and *Frēa* (9b) both mean 'Lord'. The vocabulary of Old English poetry is to some extent different from the vocabulary of prose, and here the words *Metod* 'God' (2a), *firas* 'men' (9a, in the dative plural *firum* 'for men') and *Frēa* 'Lord' (9b) are recorded only in poetry. Later stages of the language also have a poetic register – a sense that certain words are primarily suitable for use in poetry – but this is particularly pronounced in Old English, where a sizeable proportion of the known vocabulary is restricted to the poetic corpus, and referred to as 'poetic diction'.

Finally, we come to variation. In lines 1–3a, the Subject is *wē* 'we' (1a), the verb phrase is *sculon herian* 'must praise' (1a), and there are four Direct Objects: *heofon-rīces Weard* 'Guardian of the heavenly kingdom' (1b), *Metodes mihte* 'the might of the Creator' (2a), *his mōd-geþanc* 'his conception' (2b), and *weorc Wuldor-fæder* 'the work of the Father of glory' (3a). This again is characteristic of Old English poetry. Poetry more than prose tends to have strings of parallel phrases in consecutive lines or half-lines. Sometimes these parallel phrases actually mean the same thing. In the next clause, *swā hē wundra gehwæs, ēce Dryhten, ōr onstealde* 'as he, eternal Lord, established the beginning of each wonder', the Subject is expressed twice, first as the pronoun *hē* 'he' (3b), and then as a noun phrase *ēce Dryhten* 'eternal Lord' (4a). Both refer to God, and both have the same function in the sentence. This repetition of an idea, using different words with the same meaning, is a common device in Old English poetry known as 'variation'. It appears twice more even in this short poem. The Subject of the verb *scōp* 'created' in 5a is the pronoun *hē* 'he' in the same half-line, but *hālig Scieppend* 'holy Creator' (6b) expresses the same Subject again in a different way: 'He, the holy Creator . . .' The final section, lines 7–9, has three parallel Subjects for the verb *tēode* 'adorned', all referring to God. The first is *man-cynnes Weard* 'Guardian of mankind' (7b), the second *ēce Dryhten* 'eternal Lord' (8a), and the third *Frēa æl-mihtig* 'Lord almighty' (9b). Here the purpose of the variation is to repeat and reinforce the idea of God as creator and protector, which is central to the poem. In other poems, variation may serve to create suspense, to heighten tension, or to strengthen characterisation. So too with other poetic devices: for instance, alliteration may emphasise major themes, while formulas bring in associations from other contexts where the same phrases are used. As with all poetry, the first step is to appreciate the rules governing the verse form; but what really matters is the skill with which the poets exploit the conventions they are working within.

Having considered a religious poem, let us now look at some of the other main types of Old English verse: riddles, elegies and heroic poetry.

Riddles

Anglo-Saxon poets delighted in word-play, and in the deliberate exploitation of ambiguities. The Exeter Book contains about 95 riddles, which characteristically describe one thing in terms of another – for instance, an inanimate object as though it were alive, or an animal as though it were human. Some of the riddles are self-explanatory, while others are more difficult to guess, and some have not yet been solved. In the former category is the 'Book-Moth' riddle, a poem of just six lines comprising what have been described as 'successions of interconnected puns organized around a central subject'.[1] It reads as follows:

Moððe word fræt.	Mē þæt þūhte
Moth words ate	*To me that seemed*
wrǣtlicu wyrd,	þā ic þæt wundor gefrægn,
marvellous event	*when I the wonder heard*
þæt se wyrm forswealg	wera gied sumes,
that the worm swallowed	*of men song of a certain one*
þēof in þȳstro,	þrym-fæstne cwide
thief in darkness	*glorious utterance*
ond þæs strangan staþol.	Stæl-giest ne wæs 5
and the strong foundation	*Thief not was*
wihte þȳ gleawra,	þe hē þām wordum swealg.
whit the wiser	*because he the words swallowed*

[A moth ate words. That seemed to me a marvellous event, when I heard of the wonder, that the worm, a thief in darkness, swallowed the song of a certain man (lit. of a certain one of men), a glorious utterance, and the strong foundation. The thief was no whit the wiser because he swallowed the words.]

Ambiguous words include 3a *forswealg* and 6b *swealg* 'swallowed' / 'understood', 4a *pȳstro* 'darkness' / 'ignorance', 4b *cwide* 'utterance' / 'morsel', and 5a *stapol* 'parchment' (i.e. 'foundation of writing') / 'intellectual foundation'. These allow the riddle to develop on two levels, simultaneously describing a moth consuming parchment and a reader failing to gain wisdom. Human qualities are often attributed to animals or objects in the riddles: here it happens gradually during the course of the poem, as the creature moves from *moððe* 'moth' and *wyrm* 'worm, insect' in lines 1a and 3a to *þēof* 'thief' and *stæl-giest* 'thief' in 4a and 5b. All four words are given prominence through alliteration. In addition, *se wyrm* and *þēof in þȳstro* are linked through variation, and *stæl-giest* is particularly striking as a unique compound from *stæl* 'steal' and *giest* 'guest, stranger'. Finally, since *wyrm*, *þēof* and *stæl-giest* are all masculine nouns, the pronoun *hē* 'he' in 6b is both grammatically correct and also completes the transformation of the riddle's subject from insect to person.

In many riddles, the object describes itself in the first person, a device known as 'prosopopoeia'. Here is an example, for which several solutions have been suggested. Read through it, and see if you can work it out.

Ic eom æpelinges	eaxl-gestealla,
I am prince's	*shoulder-companion*
fyrd-rinces gefara,	frēan mīnum lēof,
warrior's comrade	*lord to my dear*
cyninges geselda.	Cwēn mec hwīlum
king's retainer.	*Queen me sometimes*
hwīt-loccedu	hond on legeð,
white-locked	*hand on lays*
eorles dohtor,	þēah hēo æþelu sȳ. 5
nobleman's daughter	*although she noble is*
Hæbbe mē on bōsme	þæt on bearwe gewēox.
Have me in bosom	*what in wood grew*
Hwīlum ic on wloncum	wicge rīde
Sometimes I on proud	*horse ride*
herges on ende.	Heard is mīn tunge.
of army at end	*Harsh is my tongue*
Oft ic wōð-boran	word-lēana sum
Often I minstrel	*reward for words a certain*
āgyfe æfter giedde.	Good is mīn wīse, 10
give after song	*Good is my manner*
ond ic sylfa salo.	Saga hwæt ic hātte.
and I myself dark	*Say what I am called*

[I am a prince's shoulder-companion, a warrior's comrade, dear to my lord, the king's retainer. Sometimes the fair-haired (lit. white-locked) queen, a nobleman's daughter, lays a hand on me, although she is noble. I have in my bosom what grew in the wood. Sometimes I ride on a proud horse at the head of the army. My tongue is harsh. Often I give a reward to the minstrel after a song. My manner is good, and I myself dark. Say what I am called.]

The riddle is usually taken to refer to a horn, described in its dual roles of musical instrument and drinking-vessel; but alternative suggestions include falcon, spear and sword. The description provides a number of clues before challenging the reader with a formula common to many riddles: *Saga hwæt ic hātte* 'Say what I am called'.

The same formula concludes a shorter riddle which attempts to confuse the reader as to whether the subject is human or non-human. Again, see if you can guess the answer before looking at the solution at the end – also, can you see anything wrong with the riddle itself?

Wiht cwōm gongan	þǣr weras sǣton	
Creature came to walk	*where men sat*	
monige on mæðle,	mōde snottre.	
many at assembly	*in mind wise*	
Hæfde ān ēage	ond ēaran twā	
Had one eye	*and ears two*	
ond twēgen fēt,	twelf hund hēafda,	
and two feet	*twelve hundred heads*	
hrycg ond wombe	ond honda twā,	5
back and stomach	*and hands two*	
earmas ond eaxle,	ānne swēoran	
arms and shoulder	*one neck*	
ond sīdan twā.	Saga hwæt ic hātte.	
and sides two	*Say what I am called*	

[A creature came walking where many men sat at assembly, wise in mind. It had one eye and two ears and two feet, twelve hundred heads, a back and stomach and two hands, arms and shoulder, one neck and two sides. Say what I am called.]

The solution is a one-eyed garlic seller, the 'trick' of the riddle being that in the context of vocabulary relating to parts of the body, the reference to twelve hundred heads calls to mind monsters rather than 'heads' of garlic. However, there is a problem in that the riddle is written in the third person but concludes with the customary challenge *Saga hwæt ic hātte* 'Say what I am called' in the first person. A copying error, or confusion of some kind, must have taken place.

Elegiac poetry: *Wulf and Eadwacer*

Although not 'riddles' as such, many other Old English poems use riddling techniques such as word-play and ambiguities for a range of purposes. One of the most enigmatic among several poems in the Exeter Book traditionally referred to as 'elegies' is a short piece often known as *Wulf and Eadwacer*. Like all titles given to Old English poems, this does not appear in the manuscript but is a modern construct. Some editors prefer the title *Wulf*, since it is uncertain whether Wulf and Eadwacer are different characters or the same person, or even whether these are personal names or ordinary words. Since Anglo-Saxon personal names were made up of vocabulary words, and are not capitalised in the manuscripts, it is not always clear how they are being used, and poets could deliberately exploit the ambiguity.

The poem has a female narrator, who presents herself as separated from Wulf and surrounded by hostile people who wish to capture him. The intensity of her longing for Wulf, together with the passion with which she addresses him in lines 13–15, appears to identify him as the lover described in 10–12; but in 16a she goes on to address Eadwacer, implying that he is the father of the child described punningly as a *hwelp* 'whelp' in 16b–17. Some scholars take Eadwacer to be the speaker's husband and Wulf her lover, while others think Eadwacer is the real name of a character nicknamed Wulf. Alternatively, since the literal meaning of Eadwacer is 'guardian' and that of Wulf is 'wolf', it is possible that either or both should be understood as ordinary words rather than as personal names. This would be more consistent with the other elegies, where personal names are generally avoided. On the other hand, *Wulf and Eadwacer* is already unusual among Old English poems in having a more flexible structure, with single half-lines in 3a, 8a, 17a and 19a, and a refrain in 2–3a and 7–8a. At least, this is how they are usually set out in modern editions: the verse is, as always, written consecutively in the manuscript, so it is possible that the Anglo-Saxons may have thought of it differently. Similarly, the use of modern punctuation imposes a choice between capitals and lower-case for the initial letters of *wulf* and *eadwacer*, which in turn imposes an interpretation of personal name or vocabulary word. The manuscript presentation is much more flexible, leaving alternative possibilities open.

Try reading the poem through, and compare the printed text with the opening of the poem on folio 100ᵛ of the Exeter Book (Illustration 13). Most of the letters are fairly similar to their modern counterparts, but the Old English alphabet had no letter *w*, using instead the runic letter 'wynn' (shaped like an angular *p*) which we saw in Chapter 1 (Illustration 5). Notice particularly the almost total lack of manuscript punctuation. The use of commas, exclamation marks, full stops, question marks and so on in printed editions of Old English poetry is modern, and varies from edition to edition.

Lēodum is mīnum
To people is my
Willað hȳ hine āþecgan
Wish they him to capture
Ungelic is ūs.
Unlike is us
Wulf is on īege,
Wulf is on island
fæst is þæt ēg-lond,
fast is the island
Sindon wæl-rēowe
Are bloodthirsty
Willað hȳ hine āþecgan
Wish they him to capture
Ungelic is ūs.
Unlike is us
Wulfes ic mīnes wīd-lāstum
Of Wulf I my far wanderings
þonne hit wæs rēnig weder
then it was rainy weather
þonne mec se beadu-cāfa
when me the warrior
wæs mē wyn tō þon,
was me joy to that
Wulf, min Wulf,
Wulf my Wulf

swylce him mon lāc gife.
as if them one gift might give
gif hē on þrēat cymeð.
if he with a troop comes

ic on ōþerre;
I on another
fenne biworpen.   5
by fen surrounded
weras þǣr on īge.
men there on island
gif hē on þrēat cymeð.
if he with a troop comes

wēnum dogode;
expectations suffered
ond ic rēotugu sæt,   10
and I grieving sat
bōgum bilegde:
with limbs covered
wæs mē hwæþre ēac lāð.
was me however also pain
wēna mē þīne
expectations me your

13   Exeter, Cathedral Library, MS 3501, fol. 110ᵛ (*detail*)

sēoce gedydon,   þīne seld-cymas,
sick made   *your seldom comings*
murnende mōd,   nales mete-līste.   15
mourning mood   *not lack of food*
Gehȳrest þū, Ēadwacer?   Uncerne earmne hwelp
Do you hear Eadwacer   *Our wretched whelp*
bireð wulf tō wuda.
bears wolf to woods
þæt mon ēaþe tōsliteð   þætte næfre gesomnad wæs:
That one easily tears apart   *which never joined was*
uncer giedd geador.
our song together

[It is to my people as if they might be given a gift. They wish to
capture him, if he comes with a troop. We are unlike. Wulf is on one
island, I on another: the island is fast, surrounded by fen. The men
there on the island are bloodthirsty. They wish to capture him, if he
comes with a troop. We are unlike. I suffered with expectations of my
Wulf's far wanderings; then it was rainy weather and I sat grieving,
when the warrior covered me with his limbs: that was joy to me,

however it was also pain to me. Wulf, my Wulf, expectations of your rare visits have caused my sickness, my grieving mood, not lack of food. Do you hear, Eadwacer? A wolf will bear our wretched whelp to the woods. That which was never joined is easily torn apart: our song together.]

A wide range of interpretations have been suggested for the poem as a whole; but as with some of the riddles, no certainty has been reached. Even the narrator's gender is established only by two feminine inflexions in the second half (10b *rēotugu* and 14a *sēoce*), perhaps indicating that the poet intended to maintain ambiguity for as long as possible. Here are some questions to think about:

- Who is Wulf, and why do the narrator's people wish to capture him? One theory is that he may be a Viking raider who has made her pregnant during an earlier attack; another, that all the characters are from Germanic legend, presenting a riddle-like challenge to the reader to identify them. But the poem has also been read literally, as a fable about dogs and wolves.
- What is the *lāc* 'gift' mentioned in line 1b? Suggestions include the speaker's pregnancy, or the prospect of capturing Wulf if he returns for her. However, alternative meanings of the word as 'play' or 'message' – perhaps even 'battle' – cannot be ruled out.
- In what way are Wulf and the narrator *ungelic* 'unlike'? Perhaps in terms of race, if he is a Viking and she is Anglo-Saxon. Alternatively, *ungelic* may have the sense of 'apart', referring to their physical separation. Since the *un-* prefix in Old English occasionally has an intensifying rather than negative force, the meaning may even be 'too much alike', indicating that the lovers have committed incest – a crime taken very seriously in Anglo-Saxon society.
- Is the refrain in lines 3a and 8a supposed to be identical? The ending -*lic* in Old English identifies an adjective, while -*līce* identifies an adverb. Some scholars take the final -*e* in 8a to be a copying error, but others see significance in the movement from an adjective to an adverb. It may be relevant that spelling is not wholly consistent throughout the poem: the word for 'island' (Dative singular) is spelled *īege* in 4a but *īge* in 6b.
- Is the use of *Wulf* as personal name or word consistent throughout the poem? Most editors capitalise the occurrences in lines 4a, 9a and 13a as personal names, but take 17a *wulf* as the noun 'wolf' in

conjunction with 16b *hwelp* 'whelp'. How logical is this – and indeed, might *Hwelp* also be a personal name?

- Why the reference to lack of food in 15b? Is the narrator being starved by her people, or fasting as a penance? Or is she not short of food at all? The statement that her grief is not caused by lack of food leaves it uncertain whether she has plenty of food, or if hunger is trivial in comparison with her other troubles.
- How many direct questions are there in the poem? As we saw in the last chapter, Old English forms questions by reversing the order of Subject and verb, so 16a *Gehȳrest þū* is punctuated with a question mark in modern editions. However, word order is more flexible in poetry than in prose, and the same reversal in 2a and 7a, *Willað hȳ* is usually taken as an ordinary statement. Again, is this logical, or should all be treated in the same way?
- Are events happening in the present or the future? Since Old English verbs have a single form for both tenses, 17a *bireð* may mean 'bears' or 'will bear', indicating either that the narrator knows her child has been taken from her, or that she fears it will be. Similarly 18a *tōsliteð* could be translated 'tears apart' or 'will tear apart'.
- What is the *giedd* of 19a? The literal meaning is 'song' or 'riddle', but here a metaphorical meaning, 'marriage', may be suggested by similarities between line 18 and St Matthew 19:6, 'What therefore God hath joined together, let not man put asunder'.

Much of the attraction of this beautiful poem is its enigmatic quality. Its meaning is partly obscured by the passing of time, but its elusiveness is also a consequence of its poetic design.

Heroic poetry: *Deor*

The possibility that the protagonists of *Wulf and Eadwacer* may be characters from Germanic legend brings us to the final genre to be discussed in this chapter: heroic poetry. Heroic poetry draws on the legend cycles of the early Germanic era, often referring allusively to characters and events that were familiar to the original audience but cannot always be reconstructed by a twenty-first-century readership. An example is the Exeter Book poem *Deor*, of which the first six lines only are reproduced below.

Wēlund him be wurman	wræces cunnade.
Weland him among ???	*persecution endured*
Ān-hȳdig eorl	earfoþa dreag,
Single-minded nobleman	*torments suffered*
hæfde him to gesīþþe	sorge ond longaþ,
had him as companion	*sorrow and longing*
winter-cealde wræce.	Wēan oft onfond
winter-cold suffering	*Hardship often endured*
siþþan hine Nīðhad on	nēde legde, 5
after him Nithhad on	*constraints laid*
swoncre seono-bende	on syllan monn.
supple sinew-bonds	*on better man*

[Weland endured persecution among *wurman*. The single-minded nobleman suffered torments, had as companion sorrow and longing, winter-cold suffering. He often endured hardship after Nithhad had laid constraints on him, supple sinew-bonds on the better man.]

The broad outline of the story is known. Weland was a smith-god who was captured and hamstrung by King Nithhad, and forced to work for him as the royal smith. He subsequently escaped by flying, having taken his revenge by raping Nithhad's daughter and killing his two sons, making their skulls into bowls, their eyeballs into jewels, and their teeth into brooches. The precise details of the Anglo-Saxon version are unclear, however. As in *Wulf and Eadwacer*, the lack of manuscript punctuation makes it impossible to differentiate between names and nouns. Line 1a *wurman* is sometimes taken as a tribal name referring to the Vermar (the people of Värmland in Sweden), and translated 'Weland endured persecution among the Vermar'. Other scholars prefer to associate it with the Old English word *wurma* 'purple', referring to blood. Another suggestion is the word *wyrm*, which becomes *worm* in present-day English but in Old English had a wider range of meaning including 'snake' and, as we shall see in the next chapter, 'dragon'. This raises further possibilities: perhaps Weland was tortured with snakes, or was forced to make rings and other objects resembling snakes in shape; perhaps the reference is to a serpentine pattern on the sword used to hamstring him, or perhaps the worm is metaphorical, reflecting the mental anguish he suffered.

As well as dealing with legendary material, heroic poetry draws on the values of the 'heroic code', a pre-Christian tradition reflecting the

14   Franks Casket (*front panel*)

warrior culture of early Germanic society. Of central importance were the virtues of courage and honour, the duty of loyalty to one's lord, and the maintenance of a good reputation during life and after death. The most famous account of the heroic code is a description of the Germanic tribes in the first century, given by the Roman historian Tacitus in a propaganda piece *Germania*. According to Tacitus, the chief was surrounded by a group of close followers known as his *comitatus*, who owed him total allegiance and swore both to protect his life with their own and to avenge his death. In return, they ate and slept in the chief's hall, and received gifts of land and other valuables. The chief fought at the head of his troops in battle, and if he was killed no member of the *comitatus* could survive him without disgrace.

The surviving corpus of Old English contains only five 'heroic poems' based on the Germanic legend cycles: *Beowulf, Deor, Finnsburh, Waldere* and *Widsith*. However, many other poems make use of the heroic tradition, for instance by depicting the plight of a lordless man, or incorporating the values of the heroic code. In lines 1–3a of the 'Horn' riddle discussed above, the object is personified as a member of its lord's *comitatus*. Part II of this book will include an extract from *Beowulf* as well as an entry from the *Anglo-Saxon Chronicle* and the complete texts of two poems from different genres – narrative and religious – all of which also draw strongly on the heroic tradition.

Finally, it is important to remember that Anglo-Saxon literature forms part of a continuum with other art forms. Interest in the early Germanic legend cycles is evident not only in heroic verse but in surviving artefacts. A scene from the Weland story is carved onto the front panel of the Franks Casket (Illustration 14), an eighth-century whalebone box now in the British Museum. The scene on the left shows Weland at his anvil, with two women and a man (possibly Weland's brother Egill). The body of one of Nithhad's sons is on the ground, and Weland seems to be offering one of the women the bowl made from the boy's skull. On the right is a religious scene, showing the Adoration of the Magi – the visit of the Wise Men to the infant Jesus. This is sometimes regarded as an odd juxtaposition, but it may have seemed no more strange to the Anglo-Saxons than the inclusion of poetry from different genres within a single manuscript, or (as we shall see in Part II, Text D) the use of different genres within a single poem. Indeed, represented on the same panel is another genre that we have looked at in this chapter. Around the edge is an Old English riddle written in runic script. It reads as follows:

Fisc flōdu āhōf   on fergen-berig.
Fish flood cast up   *on mountain-cliff*
Warþ gās-rīc grorn   þǣr hē on greut giswom.
Became terror-king sad   *where he on shingle swam*
Hronæs bān.
Whale's bone

[The flood cast up the fish on the mountain-cliff. The terror-king became sad where he swam on the shingle. Whale's bone.]

The riddle provides its own solution, describing the material the casket is made from: the bone of a beached whale. The casket demonstrates that riddles, religious episodes, and heroic myth could exist side by side in the rich tapestry of Anglo-Saxon culture.

Note

1   Fred C. Robinson, 'Artful Ambiguities in the Old English "Book-Moth" Riddle', in *Anglo-Saxon Poetry: Essays in Appreciation for John C. McGalliard*, ed. Lewis E. Nicholson and Dolores Warwick Frese (Notre Dame, IL: University of Notre Dame Press, 1975), pp. 355–62. The article presents a detailed analysis of the riddle.

7   Translating Old English Poetry: *Beowulf*

In courses on Old English, the desired outcome is usually for students to read, understand and ultimately translate texts from Old English into present-day English. Acquiring the skills and knowledge necessary for accurate and effective translation involves a considerable investment of time and energy, and this book can only be the first step on such a journey. However, with even a rudimentary knowledge of Old English, the interested reader can compare different translations of Old English texts with the originals, and compare the strategies used by the translators. The aim of this chapter is to set various translations of an excerpt from *Beowulf* alongside the Old English source text, and so explore the issues that arise from translation:

- as a zone of contact between past and present cultures
- as a means of teaching and learning.

The focus of the chapter will be on different published translations of a small section of the most famous Old English literary text, *Beowulf.* This long narrative poem falls into three main parts: the hero's fight with the monster Grendel, his further battle with Grendel's witch-like mother, and a final battle against a fire-breathing dragon. Interspersed among these main episodes are 'digressions' which, as J. R. R. Tolkien argued in a famous essay,[1] echo and reinforce the values espoused by the poem.

The plot of *Beowulf*

Beowulf opens with the celebrations of the King of the Danes, Hrothgar, following the construction of Heorot, his great 'mead-hall' or palace. In a practice expected of lords according to the heroic code,

Hrothgar rewards his followers with gifts. However, the celebrations are cut short when a neighbouring monster called Grendel, made jealous by the joyful sounds, begins visiting Heorot, carrying off Hrothgar's followers, and devouring them. These raids last for 12 years, during which time none of Hrothgar's men is strong enough to resist Grendel's terrifying attacks.

Beowulf, a warrior of the Geats, hears of Grendel's attacks on the Danes and of Hrothgar's misery. He sails to Denmark and arrives in Heorot with 14 chosen companions. Hrothgar accepts Beowulf's offer of assistance, and the day is spent drinking beer and talking, before night falls. Hrothgar takes the unprecedented step of leaving Heorot under Beowulf's care and so Beowulf and his companions keep a sleepy watch over the hall.

Grendel comes over the moors to the mead-hall, kills one of the sleeping guardsmen and approaches Beowulf. They engage in a great wrestling match, which ends when Beowulf rips Grendel's arm off. The monster is fatally wounded, and howling in agony, he returns to his lair in the swamp.

The next day the warriors throng Heorot and celebrate Beowulf's victory over Grendel. Hrothgar and his thanes generously distribute gifts to Beowulf and his companions. However, the following night Grendel's mother comes to avenge the death of her son. While Beowulf is sleeping in a separate chamber, she takes and devours one of Hrothgar's favourite counsellors. Beowulf pursues Grendel's mother to the swamp and swims down into the depths. He encounters the creature and she drags him to her lair. There he sees Grendel's body. After another mighty battle, Beowulf finally slays Grendel's mother, and he swims to the surface, bearing Grendel's head.

The victory celebrations recommence in Heorot. Hrothgar rewards Beowulf and his companions with even more gifts. Beowulf leaves Heorot to return home, and he is greeted as a hero by the Geats, and in particular by his uncle Higelac, the King of the Geats. When Higelac dies, Beowulf succeeds him as king, and he rules the kingdom for 50 years. At the end of his reign, his kingdom is harried by a fire-breathing dragon, which the aged Beowulf resolves to kill. In the battle that follows, at the dragon's cave, both the dragon and Beowulf die. The Geats mourn their lost king, and to honour his memory they build a great funeral pyre, on which his body is cremated, and then bury his remains in a tomb so large that it is visible well out to sea.

The poem ends with a tribute to Beowulf's many virtues, including his courage, mercy and generosity.

The origins of *Beowulf*

The importance of *Beowulf* is such that it is still a canonical text in English Literature courses (now usually in modern translation), and its eponymous hero also maintains a presence in popular culture – in comic books, graphic novels, television and film. There have been two recent film productions, *Beowulf and Grendel* (2005), filmed in Iceland, and a big-budget Hollywood version, *Beowulf* (2007).

A verse translation of the poem, by Nobel laureate Seamus Heaney, achieved the distinction of being both critically praised and a *New York Times* bestseller in 2000. Heaney's translation is only one of many that have been made of an epic poem that exists in a single tenth- or eleventh-century manuscript that is now in the British Library (see Chapter 6).

We do not know who wrote *Beowulf* or even when the poem was composed. Colin Chase surveys the last century-and-a-half of theories about the poem's date of composition, and debates continue in scholarly circles, arguing for any time between AD 650 and the period of the only surviving manuscript.[2] The story of *Beowulf* opens at the court of the Danish king, Hrothgar, and situates his reign at the end of the fifth and beginning of the sixth centuries. Given that the poem is set in Scandinavia and sympathetic to Scandinavian heroes, it has been argued that it was written before the start of the Danish invasions of England in the late eighth century, although others have challenged this view. The poem shows evidence of knowledge of Scandinavian legends, such as the story of Grendel's family, and also Germanic figures, such as the Gothic king Ermanaric, mentioned in line 1201. However, there does not seem to be any extensive 'Beowulf legend' in Scandinavia on which this poem is based, and the style of the poem has no parallel elsewhere in northern Europe. The narrator's interest in the ancestry of particular historical families, and the language variety used, suggest an eastern English origin, and the tension between its Christian elements and its heroic ethos suggests either multiple authorship, or a single author who was well versed in both theology and the secular narrative traditions of northern and western Europe. One of the poem's foremost editors, Friedrich

Klaeber, sifts through the many theories of *Beowulf*'s origins, before concluding:

> We may . . . picture to ourselves the author of *Beowulf* as a man connected in some way with an Anglian court, a royal chaplain or abbot of noble birth or, it may be, a monk friend of his, who possessed an actual knowledge of court life and addressed himself to an aristocratic, in fact a royal audience.[3]

This picture can only be speculation, now rather dated in comparison with recent scholarly deliberations, yet it helps new readers to put the poem into some kind of context. We can at least imagine, however tentatively, a monk or another holder of religious office, a member of one of the few literate groups in Anglo-Saxon society, drawing upon the Scandinavian and Germanic stories with which he was familiar, and fashioning from them a new tale, the tale of a man who embodies the heroic virtues valued in leaders of the time, but a tale tempered also by the ethos of the writer's Christian education. It is possible that this tale was written down, in alliterative half-lines, for recitation, perhaps even in episodic 'instalments', at the court of an English king who had familial or ancestral relations with Scandinavia. The 'exotic' Scandinavian setting would also make the supernatural elements of the poem more plausible.

The poem survives in the single manuscript acquired by Sir Robert Cotton in the seventeenth century. In the early 1700s, a scholar of Anglo-Saxon called George Hickes employed Humphrey Wanley to catalogue all the Old English texts that had survived in Britain. It was Wanley who rediscovered the *Beowulf* manuscript in Cotton's library, which was at that time housed in a building in Westminster. The manuscript suffered fire damage in 1731 and further damage in the subsequent rebinding. Wanley's account of the manuscript later attracted the attention of a Danish scholar, G. J. Thorkelin, who had it transcribed in 1786. In 1805, while Thorkelin was working on his translation, Sharon Turner published excerpts from the poem, translated into modern English, in an anthology of Anglo-Saxon relics. But it was Thorkelin who eventually published the first full translation, into Latin, in 1815. A revision of Thorkelin's Latin version, alongside some passages translated into modern English blank verse, was published in J. J. Conybeare's *Illustrations of Anglo-Saxon Poetry* in 1826. Together, these translations sparked off a revival of interest during the nineteenth century, and numerous translations into different languages followed, the earliest full modern English version being a prose rendition by J. M. Kemble in 1833. Other English translations, in prose and verse, appeared at regular intervals, and the *Beowulf* industry has prospered ever since, diversifying into other media, such as comic books, films and at least one rock opera, as Marijane Osborn and Syd Allan have detailed.[4]

Many of the adaptations stray far from the original story, for example *O Monstro do Caim* 'The Monster of Cain', a Brazilian comic-book version from the 1950s (Illustration 15), itself a translation from an Italian original, and Michael Crichton's 'historical' retelling of the legend, *Eaters of the Dead* (1976), subsequently filmed as *The Thirteenth Warrior* (1999).

Beowulf and its translations

The main issue in translating any literary text is that translation cannot be separated from the process of interpretation. *Beowulf*'s translators have consciously or unconsciously rendered the poem in accordance with their view of its cultural significance. Those who believe it is a Scandinavian epic stress its Scandinavian content; those who believe it is Germanic, stress its Germanic characteristics. Those who believe it is Christian foreground those elements; those who believe the Christian features are later additions and corruptions downplay them. Those who see the poem as the founding text of English Literature use their translations to link the poem with later English tradition.

The difficulty in translating even the opening word, 'Hwæt', often reveals the translator's view of the narrator's relationship with his audience. 'Hwæt' in Old English functions as a signal that a poetic narrative, or a major section of such a narrative, is about to begin. This little attention-seeking device has no obvious modern equivalent, and it is variously rendered in modern editions, from the emphatic 'Lo!' of several translators (e.g. Lumsden, 1883; Hall, 1892; Gummere, 1909), or the literal and even more emphatic 'What!' (Morris and Wyatt, 1895, 1898), to the laconic 'So' of Heaney (2000). Edwin Morgan omits the word entirely from his translation, first published in 1952.[5] The emphatic 'Lo!' and 'What!' – and alternatives such as 'What ho!', 'Behold!', 'Hark!' or 'Listen!' – all interpret the

15   *Monstro do Caim*

poem as an old-fashioned epic whose narrator has the bardic authority to command his audience. 'What ho!', as Edwin Morgan
comments acerbically in the introduction to his own translation (p.
xiv), trades authority for a cringe-inducing heartiness. Heaney
describes 'So' as an Hiberno-Irish particle that 'obliterates all previous discourse and narrative, and at the same time functions as an
exclamation calling for immediate attention' (p. xxvii). Yet the use of

'So' gives Heaney's narrator a less hectoring and more conversational tone of voice, a quality sustained throughout his translation.

Translations, then, differ. To illustrate this fact more extensively, let us consider several translations of a passage later in the poem, when the dragon that will eventually kill and be killed by Beowulf, appears in the narrative (lines 2312–23). The Old English text reads as follows:

Ðā se gæst ongan	glēdum spīwan,	
beorht hofu bærnan.	Bryne-lēoma stōd	
eldum on andan:	nō ðǣr āht cwices	
lāð lyft-floga	lǣfan wolde.	2315
Wæs þæs wyrmes wīg	wīde gesȳne,	
nearo-fāges nīð	nēan ond feorran,	
hū se gūð-sceaða	Gēata lēode	
hatode ond hȳnde.	Hord eft gescēat,	
dryht-sele dyrnne,	ǣr dæges hwīle.	2320
Hæfde land-wara	līge befangen,	
bǣle ond bronde.	Beorges getruwode,	
wīges ond wealles:	him sēo wēn gelēah.	

A selection of six of the many different versions of these lines is given below:

Then spued the fiend out flames of fire and burned the dwellings fair;
Baneful to men the lightnings flashed; the hate that winged the air
Willed death to every living thing. Wide was his bitter wrath
And slaughter seen; and far and near that scather of the Goth
Wronged them with hatred – brought them low – and then ere break of day
Betook him to his hoard again in secret hall that lay.
The land-folk had he girt with fire and burning brand and bale,
Trusting his stronghold and his might; him nought did they avail!
(Lumsden, 1883)

The stranger began then to vomit forth fire,
To burn the great manor; the blaze then glimmered
For anguish to earlmen, not anything living
Was the hateful air-goer willing to leave there.
The war of the worm widely was noticed,
The feud of the foeman afar and anear,
How the enemy injured the earls of the Geatmen,

Harried with hatred: back he hied to the treasure.
To the well-hidden cavern ere the coming of daylight.
He had circled with fire the folk of those regions,
With brand and burning; in the barrow he trusted,
In the wall and his war-might: the weening deceived him.

(Hall, 1892)

Began then the guest to spew forth of gleeds,
The bright dwellings to burn; stood the beam of the burning
For a mischief to menfolk; now nothing that quick was
The loathly lift-flier would leave there forsooth;
The war of the Worm was wide to be seen there,
The narrowing foe's hatred anigh and afar,
How he, the fight-scather, the folk of the Geats
Hated and harm'd; shot he back to the hoard,
His dark lordly hall, ere yet was the day's while;
The land-dwellers had he in the light low encompass'd
With bale and with brand; in his burg yet he trusted;
His war-might and his wall: but his weening bewray'd him.

(Morris and Wyatt, 1895/1898)

Then the baleful fiend its fire belched out,
and bright homes burned. The blaze stood high
all landsfolk frighting. No living thing
would that loathly one leave as aloft it flew.
Wide was the dragon's warring seen,
its fiendish fury far and near,
as the grim destroyer those Geatish people
hated and hounded. To a hidden lair
to its hoard it hastened at hint of dawn.
Folk of the land it had lapped in flame,
with bale and brand. In its barrow it trusted,
its battling and bulwarks: that boast was vain!

(Gummere, 1909)

The visitant began then to belch glowing flakes,
To burn the fair courts; the glare of the fire
Struck horror to men; nothing living would escape
If the persecutor flying in the clouds had his will.
The serpent's attack was seen far and wide,
Both at hand and by rumour the enemy's malicework,
How the lawless war-bringer hated and humiliated

The folk of the Geats. He sped back to the hoard,
To his great hidden hall before the light of day.
He had lapped the inhabitants of the land in fire,
In flame, in blaze; he put faith in his cave,
In his war-cunning and his cave-wall: but his trust failed him.

                                                    (Morgan, 1953)

The dragon began to belch out flames
and burn bright homesteads; there was a hot glow
that scared everyone, for the vile sky-winger
would leave nothing alive in his wake.
Everywhere the havoc he wrought was in evidence.
Far and near, the Geat nation
bore the brunt of his brutal assaults
and virulent hate. Then back to the hoard
he would dart before daybreak, to hide in his den.
He had swinged the land, swathed it in flame,
in fire and burning, and now he felt secure
in the vaults of his barrow; but his trust was unavailing.

                                                    (Heaney, 2000)

In discussing *The Seafarer*, an Old English elegy that raises questions similar to those raised by *Beowulf*, Susan Bassnett sums up some of the issues facing translators:

> Should the poem be perceived as having a Christian message as an integral feature, or are the Christian elements additions that sit uneasily over the pagan foundations? Second, once the translator has decided on a clear-cut approach to the poem, there remains the whole question of the form of Anglo-Saxon poetry; its reliance on a complex pattern of stresses within each line, with the line broken into two half-lines and rich patterns of alliteration running through the whole. Any translator must first decide what constitutes the total structure (i.e. whether to omit Christian references or not) and then decide on what to do when translating a type of poetry which relies on a series of rules that are non-existent in the TL [target language].[6]

The same issues haunt *Beowulf*. The description of the dragon sets the scene for the final episode, in which the hero will selflessly sacrifice himself for his people – a faint echo of Christian mythology, strengthened perhaps by the fact that the enemy is portrayed in the form of a dragon, which in biblical lore, along with the serpent, is a traditional manifestation of the devil, in the books of Revelation and Genesis respectively. For example, in Revelation 12:9 we read:

> And the great dragon was cast out, that old serpent, called the Devil, and Satan, which deceiveth the whole world: he was cast out into the earth, and his angels were cast out with him.

One issue for translators of this episode in *Beowulf*, then, is how they will refer to the creature that terrorises the Geats and which the hero ultimately destroys – will they choose to echo biblical language and therefore reinforce a Christian reading of the poem?

The Old English words and phrases used to describe the creature in this extract are various and the translations acknowledge or avoid this variety, as the table below shows.

Beowulf	Lumsden	Hall	Morris & Wyatt	Gummere	Morgan	Heaney
gæst	fiend	stranger	guest	fiend	visitant	dragon
lyft-floga	–	air-goer	lift-flier	–	persecutor	sky-winger
wyrm	–	worm	Worm	dragon	serpent	–
gūð-sceaða	scather	enemy	fight-scather	destroyer	war-bringer	–

The key term here is clearly *wyrm*. Gummere uses the term 'dragon' and Morgan offers the term 'serpent', explicitly echoing biblical terms. Hall, and Morris and Wyatt, prefer the modern descendant of the Old English term *wyrm*, 'worm', but with the original meaning of 'serpent'. Morris and Wyatt capitalise 'Worm', suggesting again a manifestation of the devil. Lumsden and Heaney avoid translating *wyrm* directly, though the latter translates *gæst* as 'dragon', and the former as 'fiend', both of which also suggest the devil.

Gæst is translated in ways that are even more diverse. Because manuscripts of Old English do not differentiate between long and short vowels, the term may represent either of two different words: *gæst* (short vowel), which becomes 'guest' but has a wider range of meanings in Old English including 'visitor' and 'stranger', or *gǣst* (long vowel), which becomes 'ghost' but again has a wider range of meanings in Old English including 'spirit' and 'demon'. Earlier, in line 102, the term may have the latter meaning, since Grendel is there described as *se grimma gǣst*, an apparent paraphrase of *fēond on helle* in the previous line. However, in line 1800 Beowulf himself is described as *gǣst*, evidently meaning a 'visitor' or 'guest'. In line 2312, then, the different translators fall into two camps, depending on whether they think the fire-breathing *gǣst/gǣst* is best described as a 'fiend/dragon' or a 'stranger/guest/visitant'.

A further term used for the creature is *lyft-floga*, one of several compound terms, here a combination of 'air' or 'sky' and 'fly' or 'flyer'. Several of the translators echo this compound, some using the word 'lift', which retains the meaning of 'sky' in language varieties such as Scots: 'air-goer', 'lift-flier', 'sky-winger'. However, the others prefer not to re-create this feature of Old English verse here, and paraphrase the concept instead: 'the hate that winged the air', 'aloft it flew', 'the persecutor flying in the clouds'. A similar pattern recurs with the other compound noun, *gūð-sceaða*, a combination of 'war', 'battle' or 'fight' and 'enemy' or 'someone who does harm'. (The root of this last word survives today in the negative adjective 'unscathed' and – in a figurative sense – in the term 'scathing'.) This compound is variously rendered as 'scather', 'enemy', 'fight-scather', 'destroyer' and 'war-bringer'.

Various translating strategies are evident even in the few examples we have considered so far. First, as noted earlier, translators can invite a particular interpretation of the poem by choosing specific terms to describe concepts that may or may not have had similar associations a thousand years ago: thus Beowulf can be made to battle a 'fiend', 'serpent' or 'dragon', with their echoes in Christian mythology. Alternatively, he can be made to battle a 'stranger', 'worm' or 'foe' – which all have less of a Christian connotation. Translators can also choose to make compound words, like 'war-bringer', and so imitate this characteristic of Old English poetry, or they can choose to paraphrase ideas that are expressed in Old English compounds, as in 'the havoc he wrought'. Unusual compounds, alongside old-fashioned or dialectal expressions, such as 'lift' or 'scather', can be seen as a strategy of defamiliarising or 'making strange' the poem – of acknowledging that it is *not* a modern poem. Critical opinion is divided on this last strategy. Critical praise for Heaney's translation, reprinted in the introductory blurb of the Norton paperback edition of 2001, focused on its 'elegant flowing style', its 'freshness' and a language that is 'startlingly contemporary'. Claire Harman in the *Evening Standard* noted that it makes 'previous versions look slightly flowery and antique by comparison'. Traditionally, translations have been praised for their 'fluency' and the expertise with which they absorb the foreign text into the host language and culture.

Nevertheless, there is a minority, but still influential, view that a translation should indeed 'make visible' the process of translation by introducing archaic and non-standard language to give a flavour of the foreignness of the original text. Of the translations discussed here, Morris and Wyatt's rendition is the most obviously odd. Their old-fashioned and dialectal vocabulary and even stranger grammar ('stood the beam of the burning / For a mischief to menfolk') demand much more of the reader than Heaney's conversational ease ('there was a hot glow / that scared everyone'). Arguably Morris and Wyatt pay a greater respect to the poem by demanding that the reader spend some time wrestling with its elusive meanings; the alternative argument is that Heaney makes a great and neglected text accessible to all. The lesson is that a single translation cannot replace the original; it can only show aspects of it.

Refashioning the past: translating *Beowulf*'s form

A subtle but important question to ask of any Old English translation – as Bassnett indicates in the quotation above – is how it deals with the poetic form, for example, the Old English patterns of alliteration, rhythm and variation. We shall focus here on one of the most obvious features of Anglo-Saxon poetry, the alliterative half-lines with their complex patterns of rhythms. The elemental choice facing the translator here is whether to mimic the ancient ways of making verse, or to opt for something more modern. That decision is not without significance for the overall meaning of the translation, as we shall see.

The alliterative patterns of Old English verse are discussed in greater detail in Chapter 6. To recap, and summarise the *Beowulf* poet's practice briefly:

- The Old English poetic line generally has four strong stresses or beats.
- The line is divided into two halves, each half-line having two stressed syllables.

- The first stressed syllable of the second half-line should alliterate with one or both of the stressed syllables in the preceding half-line.
- The second stressed syllable of the second half-line should *not* alliterate with the stressed syllable immediately before it, but it *can* alliterate with one of the stressed syllables in the first half-line, so long as that is not a syllable that matches the first stressed syllable of the second half-line.
- All vowels alliterate with all other vowels.

Written as a set of rules, the *Beowulf* poet's practice seems more complicated than it is. To give a simple illustration, consider the first four lines of the extract given above. The stressed syllables are printed in bold, with alliteration underlined (double for headstaves).

First half-line	Second half-line	Alliterating syllables
Ðā se **gǣst** on**gan**	**glē**dum spī̄wan,	**gǣst** ... **gan** ... **glē**dum
beorht hofu **bǣr**nan;	**bryne**-lēoma stōd	**beorht** ... **bǣr**nan ... **bryne**
eldum on **and**an;	nō ðǣr **āht** cwices	**eld**um ... **and**an ... **āht**
lāð lyft-floga	**lǣ**fan **wolde**.	**lāð lyft** ... **lǣ**fan

Remember that it is the headstave, that is, the *first* stressed syllable in the *second* half-line, that is the key to the pattern. It must alliterate with one or both of the previous stressed syllables, and must not alliterate with the final stressed syllable. So, in the first line above, **glēd**- alliterates with the preceding stressed syllables **gǣst** and **-gan** and does *not* alliterate with the succeeding stressed syllable **spī**-. It is a complex pattern, difficult to maintain – particularly in modern English – and few modern translators even try.

In his translation of 1883, Lieutenant-Colonel H. W. Lumsden gives himself the considerable task of rendering the alliterative verse in seven-foot iambic couplets:

> Then **spued** the **fiend** out **flames** of **fire** and **burned** the **dwellings fair**;
> **Baneful** to **men** the **light**nings **flashed**; the **hate** that **winged** the **air**

The seven-foot (heptameter) line is unusual in English, and one that is more usually set down as a ballad stanza of alternating tetrameter (4-foot) and trimeter (3-foot) lines, a division here reinforced by the grammatical divisions. Although alliteration is present in many of Lumsden's lines, it is not used systematically to bind lines together, as in the Anglo-Saxon original. Lumsden acknowledges in the introduction to his translation that the 'alliterated rhythmical lines of Anglo-Saxon poetry are, perhaps, more artificial than any modern form of English verse' and that, therefore, the 'common ballad measure has seemed to me on the whole the best fitted to give a close, but I hope a fairly readable, version of a work too little known to English readers' (p. xxvi). As in many ballads, the rhyme in Lumsden's lines, if recast in this form, would be only on the second and fourth lines:

> Then spued the fiend out flames of fire
> And burned the dwellings fair;
> Baneful to men the lightnings flashed;
> The hate that winged the air

The use of the ballad measure, even though partially disguised in the long heptameter lines, gives Lumsden's translation the raciness and narrative pace of the great oral ballads. This quality is substituted in Hall's translation, published in Boston in 1892, by the gravity of an unrhymed, freer, four-beat stress metre that in this respect imitates the Old English form:

> The **stranger** be**gan** then to **vom**it forth **fire**,
> To **burn** the great **man**or; the **blaze** then **glim**mered
> For **ang**uish to **earl**men, not **any**thing **living**
> Was the **hateful air**-goer **will**ing to **leave** there.

Alliteration is also often present, uniting half-lines ('burn . . . blaze', 'earlmen' . . . 'anything') but it is not used systematically. Hall's description of his own practice is worth quoting at length (p. viii):

> The measure used in the present translation is believed to be as near a reproduction of the original as modern English affords. The cadences closely resemble those used by Browning in some of his most striking poems. The four stresses of the Anglo-Saxon verse are retained, and as much thesis and anacrusis is allowed as is consistent with a regular cadence. Alliteration has been used to a large extent; but it was thought that modern ears would hardly tolerate it on every line. End-rhyme has been used occasionally; internal rhyme, sporadically. Both have some warrant in Anglo-Saxon poetry.

Hall allies his verse to the then innovative practice of the Victorian poet Robert Browning, whose dramatic and philosophical verse was stretching the stressed/unstressed beat of regular iambic verse to breaking point and beyond. ('Anacrusis' and 'thesis' refer to the substitution of stressed syllables where regular verse would demand unstressed syllables, and vice versa.) Hall's verse practice, then, turns *Beowulf* into a different kind of poem – an ancient poem, yes, but one that has affinities with the best and most experimental verse of his own contemporaries.

Morris and Wyatt's verse form resembles Hall's in that it is a four-beat stress metre. However, on a closer inspection, there is a greater metrical regularity in their lines, which are anapaestic tetrameter (that is, four feet, each consisting of two unstressed syllables, followed by a stressed syllable, for example 'then the **guest**' and 'forth of **gleeds**') with occasional iambic substitutions (one unstressed syllable followed by a stressed syllable, such as 'be**gan**' and 'to **spew**'):

> Be**gan** then the **guest** to **spew** forth of **gleeds**,
> The bright **dwell**ings to **burn**; stood the **beam** of the **burn**ing
> For a **mis**chief to **men**folk; now **no**thing that **quick** was
> The **loath**ly lift-**fli**er would **leave** there for**sooth**

Alliteration on the strong stresses is very widely used here to link the old half-lines, although not in the strict patterns of Old English poetry. For example, there is often alliteration on the final stressed syllable of the second half-line: '(be)gan . . . guest . . . gleeds', 'burn . . . beam . . . burn(ing)'. Morris and Wyatt do not discuss the rationale for their verse technique but it can be set in the context of their general archaising, or 'making old-fashioned', noted earlier. This is, after all, a partnership that provides its readers with a glossary giving 'The Meaning of Some Words Not Commonly Used Now' (pp. 190–1). The relentless alliteration does not spare modern ears, and the underlying, fairly regular anapaestic beat announces *Beowulf* as a traditional poem – and what is more, a poem higher in register than an oral ballad.

In the past century translations of *Beowulf* have continued to use poetic form as a means of interpreting the text. Francis Gummere's introduction praises Hall's translation and condemns Morris and Wyatt's (pp. 20–1), and like the former finds kinship between Anglo-Saxon poetic practice and modern writers such as Browning; thus he argues for an integrated and whole English verse tradition.

> Then the **baleful fiend** its **fire** belched **out**,
> and **bright** homes **burned**. The **blaze** stood **high**
> all **landsfolk frighting**. No **living thing**
> would that **loathly** one **leave** as a**loft** it **flew**.

Gummere is one of the few translators to attempt to mimic both the alliterative patterns and the stress patterns of the source text. Notice how the third stressed syllable of each line alliterates with at least one of the two preceding stressed syllables but avoids alliterating with the final one:

1	2	3	4
bale	*fiend*	*fire*	out
bright	*burned*	*blaze*	high
lands	fright	*liv-*	thing
loathly	*leave*	*-loft*	flew

Halfway through the twentieth century, Edwin Morgan composed a translation that sought to privilege poetry over philology. He observes of Gummere's rendition that it 'can only be described as painstaking and close to the text: it has no poetic life, and its archaism would not now be tolerated' (p. xiii). Morgan, like Hall, felt the need for a *modern* translation of *Beowulf,* and while Hall appealed to the pioneering example of Robert Browning, Morgan looks to the metrical experiments of T. S. Eliot, W. H. Auden and Christopher Fry – all of whom wrote verse for the stage as well as the page. He also takes inspiration from Richard Eberhart, a twentieth-century American poet who wrote war poetry using forms inspired by Anglo-Saxon verse. Morgan concludes that 'a translation of *Beowulf* for the present period may and perhaps should employ a stress metre and not a syllabic one; and its diction should not be archaic except in the most unavoidable terms of reference' (p. xxviii).

> The **vis**itant be**gan** then to **belch** glowing **flakes**,
> To **burn** the fair **courts**; the **glare** of the **fire**
> Struck **horror** to **men**; nothing **living** would es**cape**
> If the **per**secutor **flying** in the **clouds** had his **will**.

There are here no constraints of rhyme, regular metre or alliteration, and the vocabulary he uses avoids the traditional fairytale diction of dragons and heroes – the dragon is a 'visitant' and a 'persecutor'. All translation is appropriation of one kind or another, and the task that Morgan sets himself here is to wrest *Beowulf* away from the dusty scholars and the backward-gazing romantics, and to reset the poem firmly within the canon of modernist poetry.

A further half-century later, at the dawn of the twenty-first century, Seamus Heaney continues the modernising project set out by Hall and Morgan. Like Gummere, he argues for unity of tradition, noting that his own early poems fell 'naturally' into an Anglo-Saxon pattern. However, like Morgan, he dispenses with traditional forms, particularly where they interfere with his quest to find a 'forthright delivery' (p. xxviii). Therefore, on occasion, Heaney cleaves to the alliterative patterns followed by Gummere, and on other occasions he ignores or breaks the alliterative rules, even alliterating on the forbidden fourth syllable of a line! He sticks, in the main, to the four-beat line:

> The **dragon** be**gan** to **belch** out **flames**
> and **burn** bright **home**steads; there was a **hot glow**
> that **scared** ev**ery**one, for the **vile sky**-winger
> would **leave no**thing a**live** in his **wake**.

In this extract the second and fourth lines conform to the rules of Old English verse, alliterating 'hot' with the preceding 'homesteads', and '(a)live' with 'leave'. The diction is even more commonplace than that of Morgan, though, as we saw earlier, there are nods towards Old English compounds in new-coined expressions like 'sky-winger' (*lyft-floga*), and Heaney takes pleasure in 'Irishing' this English epic by studding the poem here and there with dialect words from his native Ulster. If Morgan's translation is a modernist *Beowulf*, Heaney's is a post-colonial one. He notes (p. xxx):

> Indeed, every time I read that lovely interlude that tells of the minstrel singing in Heorot just before the first attacks of Grendel, I cannot help thinking of Edmund Spenser in Kilcolman Castle, reading the early cantos of *The Faerie Queene* to Sir Walter Raleigh, just before the Irish burned the castle and drove Spenser back to the Elizabethan court.

Heaney acknowledges through this apparently idiosyncratic association, that every reading of the poem, like every translation, is personal, and depends on the complex histories of author, reader, text – and their respective national communities – down the ages. Each translation, like every reading, is a highly nuanced interaction between present and past.

Translation in teaching

It should be clear from the foregoing that the notion of a group of students sitting in a classroom and going through an Anglo-Saxon text like *Beowulf* line by line, pausing on difficult features of language (those tricky expressions that scholars call *cruxes*), is or can be limiting. Of course, if the group is enthusiastic, tight-knit, supportive and prepared to invest considerable time and energy in the process, then line-by-line translation may be a rewarding experience; nevertheless, for less engaged students the experience can be arid.

There is, however, no escaping the hard labour involved in translation. Seamus Heaney gives a vivid account of his own translation practice (pp. xxii–xxiii):

> It was labour-intensive work, scriptorium-slow. I worked dutifully, like a sixth-former at homework. I would set myself twenty lines a day, write out my glossary of hard words in longhand, try to pick a way through the syntax, get the run of the meaning established in my head, and then hope that the lines could be turned into metrical shape and raised to the power of verse.

Heaney translated the poem as a commission from the publisher, W. W. Norton; however, students in seminar rooms are translating for rather different purposes. The task master or mistress in the process is a lecturer, not a publisher, and translation is largely a means by which the lecturer attempts to assess the student's grasp of the language, familiarity with the text, and skill in dealing with textual difficulties. As we have seen in the earlier sections, however, each translation – even a student one – involves an interaction between different cultures.

The use of translation in *teaching* must confront this interaction and encourage reflection on the diverse possible products of the translation process. There are many ways of encouraging reflection on the interaction between past and present cultures, and some rich case studies are gathered together in the Modern Language Association of America's guide, *Approaches to Teaching Beowulf*.[7] In this guide, *Beowulf* is the focus of a hubbub of scholarly conversations and explorations. For example, Howell Chickering asks his students to 'declaim' the Old English lines to get a sense of the 'movement' of the verses, before asking his students to translate them (pp. 40–4); Robert Yeager uses his institutional setting (an agricultural college located near an Indian burial ground) to bring home the immediacy and contemporary relevance of the poem's location and themes (pp. 52–6); others in the guide look at the Old English poem in relation to other texts, from the fourteenth-century poem *Sir Gawain and the Green Knight*, to derivative modern works like Tolkien's *The Lord of the Rings* or John Gardner's novel, told from the perspective of Beowulf's first great enemy, *Grendel* (1971). One class even compared *Beowulf* to Miloš Forman's film of Ken Kesey's *One Flew Over the Cuckoo's Nest* on the grounds that both the Anglo-Saxon poem and Forman's film dramatise the theme of appropriate codes of behaviour in oppressive institutional settings.

A common issue in courses dealing with Anglo-Saxon literature is clearly motivation – how can teachers convince students who are unfamiliar with the language and culture, of the distant and often intangible rewards to be had from working hard at translation? Appeals to contemporary relevance and popular culture can sustain short-term interest and enthusiasm, at least until the students' skills are developed enough and their confidence is sufficiently high to tackle the poem head-on. Looking at and evaluating different translations of key passages can also serve to sustain interest and motivate further exploration, particularly in the early stages of exposure to the original text. The relatively new field of Translation Studies has developed a series of key questions that can be asked of translations, particularly literary translations; for example:

- What is the status of the source text in relation to the target culture?
- How does the translation fit into the target culture's 'literary system'?
- Has the translator attempted to 'make visible' the source text's 'foreignness' or has the translator 'domesticated' the source text, making it largely indistinguishable from an original work in the target culture?

As we have seen, *Beowulf* can be claimed as the 'foundational text' of several cultures, English, Danish and German, and it stands in opposition to the Greek and Latin 'foundational' epics, the *Iliad* and the *Aeneid*. In translation it can fit into the target culture's literary system as a rollicking yarn of heroes and monsters, a Christian allegory of sacrifice and redemption, a modernist fable of values constructed and honoured in a hostile universe, or a post-colonial tale of resistance to oppression. The translator can plunder the whole history of the English language and its literatures to 'make strange' the poem through old-fashioned or dialectal vocabulary, unusual compounds, twisted word order and rhythmic, alliterative verse forms. Or the translator can make the vocabulary strictly contemporary, untwist the word order, and play down the archaic verse techniques in order to deliver a fluent, 'invisible' translation. Students can look critically at the values that are implicit in the choices made by past translators, and so become more reflective practitioners when it comes to making their own translating choices.

Further exploration

Beowulf is not only translated into poetry; there have been numerous prose translations of the poem. Look at the renderings of the passage discussed above into prose by three twentieth-century translators.[8] In view of the above discussion, how would you characterise the choices made by each translator? What is gained and what is lost by translation into prose rather than verse?

> Then the monster began to belch forth flames, to burn the bright dwellings. The flare of the fire brought fear upon men. The loathly air-flier wished not to leave aught living there. The warring of the dragon was widely seen, the onslaught of the cruel foe far and near, how the enemy of the people of the Geats wrought despite and devastation. He hastened back to the hoard, to his hidden hall, ere it was day. He had compassed the dwellers in the land with fire, with flames, and with burning; he trusted in the barrow, in bravery, and the rampart. His hope deceived him.   (R. K. Gordon, 1926; revised in 1956, p. 46)

> The creature began to spew fire and burn dwellings; and while the light of burning filled people with horror, the flying monster spared

no living thing. The onset and devastating vengeance of the Worm, its hatred for and humiliation of the Geats, was to be seen everywhere. Before daybreak it flew back to its secret hide-out, the treasure-hoard, having surrounded the country-folk with fire and flame and burning. It trusted to its own ferocity and in the ramparts of the barrow, yet that faith proved deceptive.

(David Wright, 1956, pp. 81–2)

So this visitant started vomiting fiery gobbets and burning up splendid buildings; the glare of the conflagration was a source of terror to mortals. The malignant creature flying aloft did not mean to leave anything living there. Wide afield, near and far, the reptile's belligerence, the malice of an intransigent foe, was evident, and how the warlike ravager hated and held in contempt the Geatish people. Then back to the hoard he hurried, to his secret princely dwelling before it was time for day. He had surrounded the land's inhabitants with fire, with blazing heap and flaming brand. He put his trust in the burial mound, in combat and in the earthwork: this hope deceived him.

(Bradley, 1982, p. 472)

Reading practice

Try reading the following lines from an earlier episode in *Beowulf*, when Hrothgar first hears of the hero's arrival in his kingdom and relates what he knows about the young warrior (lines 371–84). Make sure you understand the text by answering the comprehension questions, and then make a rough translation of the lines. Finally, seek out two or three published translations of the poem and compare your translation with those.[9] What do the different translations suggest about your interpretation of the lines – and the interpretations of others?

1. When did Hrothgar first know Beowulf?
2. What is the relationship between Beowulf, Ecgtheow and Hrethel the Geat?
3. Who told Hrothgar of Beowulf's more recent exploits? What were they taking to the land of the Geats?
4. How strong is Beowulf reputed to be?
5. Why has God led Beowulf to the West-Danes?

ār-stafum kindness	*heaþo-rōf* brave in battle
cniht-wesende as a youth	*helm* protector
cūðe knew	*holdne* loyal
eafora son	*maþelode* spoke
eald-fæder late father	*mægen-cræft* strength
forgeaf gave	*mund-grip* hand-grip
fyredon brought	*sǣ-līþende* seafarers
gif-sceattas precious gifts	*Ðonne* furthermore
gryre terror	*wēn* expectation
hāten called	*wine* friend
heard strong	

Hrōðgār maþelode,	helm Scyldinga:	
'Ic hine cūðe	cniht-wesende.	
Wæs his eald-fæder	Ecgþēo hāten,	
ðǣm tō hām forgeaf	Hrēþel Gēata	
āngan dohtor.	Is his eafora nū	375
heard hēr cumen,	sōhte holdne wine.	
Ðonne sægdon þæt	sǣ-līþende,	
þā ðe gif-sceattas	Gēata fyredon	
þyder tō þance,	þæt hē þrītiges	
manna mægen-cræft	on his mund-gripe	380
heaþo-rōf hæbbe.	Hine hālig God	
for ār-stafum	ūs onsende,	
tō West-Denum,	þæs ic wēn hæbbe,	
wið Grendles gryre.		

Discussion

In this speech, Hrothgar tells that he knew Beowulf as a youth – his father Ecgtheow married the only daughter of Hrethel of the Geats. Hrothgar has heard tales of Beowulf's more recent exploits from sailors bringing him gifts from the Geats. They claimed that he had the strength of 30 men in his grip. Hrothgar announces that God has led Beowulf to the West-Danes to defend them from the terror of Grendel.

By this point in the book, you should be able, with the help of a good glossary or dictionary, to make some basic sense of a passage of Old English and compare it intelligently with different translations, commenting on why different translation choices might have been made. In Part II of the book, we practise more extensive reading of unsimplified Old English texts.

Notes

1   J. R. R. Tolkien [1936], 'Beowulf: The Monsters and the Critics', Reprinted in *The Monsters and the Critics, and other Essays*, ed. Christopher Tolkien (London: Allen & Unwin, 1983).
2   Colin Chase (ed.), *The Dating of Beowulf* (Toronto: University of Toronto Press, 1981).
3   Friedrich Klaeber (ed.), *Beowulf and the Fight at Finnsburg*, 3rd edn (Boston, MA: D. C. Heath, 1950), p. cxix.
4   Marijane Osborn, 'Translations, Versions, Illustrations,' in *A Beowulf Handbook*, ed. J. D. Niles and R. Bjork (Lincoln: University of Nebraska Press, 1997), pp. 341–82. See also her update at www.asu.edu/clas/acmrs/web_pages/online_resources/online_resources_beowulf_intro.html and Syd Allan's web resource at www.jagular.com/beowulf
5   The translations considered in detail in this chapter are F. B. Gummere, *Beowulf: The Oldest English Epic* (New York, 1909); J. L. Hall, *Beowulf: An Anglo-Saxon Epic Poem* (Boston, MA: D. C. Heath, 1892); Seamus Heaney, *Beowulf, A New Verse Translation* (New York: W. W. Norton, 2000); H. W. Lumsden, *Beowulf: An Old English Poem Translated into Modern Rhymes* (London: Kegan Paul, Trench, 1883); Edwin Morgan, *Beowulf: A Verse Translation in to Modern English* ([1952]; reprinted Manchester: Carcanet, 2002); William Morris and A. J. Wyatt, *The Tale of Beowulf, Sometime King of the Weder Geats* (London, [1895]; revised and reprinted in 1898). Page references are to these editions.
6   Susan Bassnett, *Translation Studies*, 3rd edn (London: Routledge, 2002), p. 98.
7   J. B. Bessinger, Jr, and R. F. Yeager (eds), *Approaches to Teaching Beowulf* (New York: Modern Language Association of America, 1984).
8   S. A. J. Bradley, *Anglo-Saxon Poetry* (London: Dent, 1982); R. K. Gordon, *Anglo-Saxon Poetry* (London: Dent, 1926/1954); David Wright, *Beowulf, A Prose Translation* (Harmondsworth: Penguin, 1956).
9   Various translations are collected on Syd Allan's website: www.jagular.com/beowulf

Part II

Four Old English Texts

Introduction

One reason for studying Old English is to trace the roots of our own language, and provide a historical context for our language today. Another is to gain direct access to the outstanding literature that survives from pre-Conquest England. In this section, we look at four major texts from the Old English literary canon. The first is a prose narrative: an entry from the *Anglo-Saxon Chronicle* recounting an attempt to usurp the throne of Wessex. The other three are poems: an extract from the epic poem *Beowulf* describing the hero's fight with the monster Grendel; a narrative poem, *The Battle of Maldon*, based on an event during the Viking invasions of the late tenth century; and a religious poem, *The Dream of the Rood*.

Some of the vocabulary from each text has been introduced in earlier chapters, and will already be familiar to you. The meanings of many of the other words can be worked out using the skills you learned in Chapter 2. None the less, the vocabulary of Old English is so extensive that there remain a number of words that have no present-day descendants, or are too rare to be worth learning. These are translated for you in the glosses following each section of text, while the words that you can probably work out for yourselves are collected together in a glossary at the end – just in case you get stuck! We have included some basic grammatical information showing which case nouns are in, and whether verbs are singular or plural, but this has been kept to a minimum so that you can focus on reading the texts rather than on deciphering the glossary. The following abbreviations have been used:

n = nominative
a = accusative
g = genitive
d = dative
s = singular

p = plural
j = subjunctive
t = past participle

A note on spelling

Chapters 1–5 have to some extent standardised the spelling of Old English, as it is not helpful for beginners to be faced immediately with inconsistencies between different dialects, and between early and late forms of the language. Now that we have reached this stage, however, there will be a closer adherence to the readings of the actual manuscripts in which the texts are preserved. The main issues affected are as follows:

(i)   Many Anglo-Saxon scribes use ð and þ interchangeably. This means, for instance, that words such as *oþ-þæt* 'until' and *þā* 'then, when, the' are just as likely to be written *oð-ðæt, oð-þæt* or *oþ-ðæt* and *ðā*, and different spellings may appear within the same text. The capital form of ð is Ð.

(ii)   Early West Saxon *īe* developed into *ī* in Late West Saxon, so the pronoun *hīe* 'they, them' appears as *hī* in late texts such as *The Battle of Maldon*, and both forms are used interchangeably in others such as *The Dream of the Rood*.

(iii) Towards the end of the Anglo-Saxon period, the inflexional system began to break down, with originally distinct case endings falling together. This applies particularly to *The Battle of Maldon*, where the subjunctive plural form of verbs appears as *-on* instead of *-en*, and even the distinctive *-um* inflexion of Dative plural nouns is sometimes replaced by *-on*.

Text A
Cynewulf and Cyneheard

One of the most famous episodes in the *Anglo-Saxon Chronicle* is the entry for the year 757. In contrast to the brevity of many of the other early annals drawn up retrospectively when the *Chronicle* was begun in the late ninth century, this is a lengthy account of a power struggle between the West Saxon king Cynewulf and the brother of the former king Sigebryht. The inclusion of direct speech, in the dialogue between the followers of the two main protagonists, suggests that the story may have circulated orally before being written down. Another indication of oral origin is the frequent use of the pronouns *hē* 'he' and *hīe* 'they' without specifying whom they refer to, apparently on the assumption that the original audience would already be sufficiently familiar with the story to know who was doing what. The beginning of the annal in the earliest surviving *Chronicle* manuscript, now held in the Parker Library in Cambridge, is shown in Illustration 10.

Perhaps more than any other Old English text, this narrative provides an illustration of the heroic code in action. It may have been included in the *Chronicle* for this reason. The followers of both Cynewulf and Sigebryht's brother are on different occasions faced with impossible odds, and with a conflict of loyalties to their lord and to their kindred. Both groups make the right choice according to the heroic tradition, putting the ties of lordship above those of kindred, and fighting courageously to the death without hope of success.

We shall look at the text in small sections. Characteristic of early Old English prose is the linking of long sequences of clauses with the conjunction *ond* 'and'. This makes it difficult to break the narrative up into units corresponding to present-day sentences. Here sentence breaks have been introduced largely as a means of navigating through the text, and are numbered for ease of reference.

Section 1

This *Chronicle* entry is unusual in covering a time-span of 31 years, rather than the events of a single year. The first section provides the historical background to Cyneheard's subsequent attempt on the West Saxon throne. Read through it, and see if you can answer the following questions.

- There is an error in the manuscripts at this point. Can you see what it is?
- Who deprived Sigebryht of his kingdom, and why?
- How long did Sigebryht keep Hampshire?
- Where did Cynewulf drive Sigebryht then?
- How long did he stay there?
- Whom did the swineherd avenge?
- Who fought great battles against the Britons?

> 755   [1] Hēr Cynewulf benam Sigebryht his rīces ond West-Seaxna wiotan for unryhtum dǣdum, būton Hamtūn-scīre. [2] Ond hē hæfde þā oþ hē ofslōg þone aldor-mon þe him lengest wunode. [3] Ond hine þā Cynewulf on Andred ādrǣfde. [4] Ond hē þǣr wunade oþ-þæt hine ān swān ofstang æt Pryfetes flōdan. [5] Ond hē wræc þone aldor-mon Cumbran. [6] Ond se Cynewulf oft miclum gefeohtum feaht wiþ Bretwālum.

[1]   *benam* deprived; *wiotan* counsellors; *būton* except; *Hamtūn-scīre* Hampshire
[2]   *þā* it, i.e. Hampshire; *wunode* stayed
[3]   *Andred* Andred Forest (now the Weald); *ādrǣfde* drove
[4]   *wunade* lived; *swān* swineherd; *ofstang* stabbed (to death); *Pryfetes flōdan* Privett's flood
[5]   *wræc* avenged; *Cumbran* Cumbra (personal name inflected for Accusative case)
[6]   *gefeohtum* battles; *Bretwālum* Britons

Discussion

The story is written in quite simple language, so you have probably found it fairly easy to follow. However, the account is deceptively straightforward, leaving many questions unanswered. The opening statement that Cynewulf and the counsellors of the West Saxons deprived Sigebryht of his kingdom because of his unjust deeds may indicate that he was formally deposed; but alternatively it may refer to a successful conspiracy between Cynewulf and some members of the council. We therefore do not know whether the deposition was legal or not. Similarly, the statement that Sigebryht kept Hampshire until he killed the alderman who had stayed with him longest leaves it unclear why Sigebryht should wish to kill his only ally. On the face of it, it seems a bad move. No reason is given for Cynewulf to then drive Sigebryht into the Weald. Perhaps this was a punishment for the murder; but other suggestions are that Cynewulf was in a stronger position to banish Sigebryht once the latter no longer had the alderman's support, or that Sigebryht was more likely to resume his 'unjust deeds' without the alderman's restraining influence.

It is not clear what conclusions are to be drawn from the fact that it was a swineherd who avenged the alderman (now identified by name as Cumbra) by killing Sigebryht. Perhaps this reflects the way in which the duty of vengeance pervades the whole of Anglo-Saxon society down to the lowliest of ranks. Alternatively though, it may illustrate the depths of humiliation to which Sigebryht had sunk. We may also wonder why no one else avenged the alderman. Vengeance for a dead lord or kinsman was one of the most important duties in Anglo-Saxon society, so why was it left to a swineherd? A possible answer is that Cumbra's family would have been legally debarred from avenging him if he had been executed for a crime, so this may suggest that Sigebryht killed him justly rather than as an act of treachery.

As we continue through the narrative, we shall see that it is tightly structured, with close parallels between different sections. Here the reference to Cynewulf's battles against the Britons is probably included to account for the presence later on of a British hostage among his followers.

Due to an error in the original compilation of the *Chronicle*, most entries from the mid-eighth to the mid-ninth century are dated two years too early. Hence the entry for 757 is incorrectly dated 755 in the surviving manuscripts.

Section 2

The time now moves forward 31 years to the main events of the story.

- Who was Cyneheard?
- What was the king doing at Merton?
- Did Cyneheard surround the bed-chamber before or after being discovered by the men who were with the king?

[7] Ond ymb xxxi wintra þæs þe hē rīce hæfde, hē wolde ādræfan ānne æþeling sē was Cyneheard hāten. [8] Ond se Cyneheard wæs þæs Sigebryhtes brōþur. [9] Ond þā geāscode hē þone cyning lȳtle werode on wīf-cȳþþe on Meran-tūne, ond hine þær berād, ond þone būr ūtan be-ēode, ær hine þā men onfunden þe mid þām kyninge wærun.

[7] *ymb* after; *þæs þe* that (year) in which; *ādræfan* to drive out; *hāten* called [9] *geāscode* discovered; *lȳtle werode* with a small troop; *on wīf-cȳþþe* in the company of a woman; *on Meran-tūne* in Merton; *berād* rode up to; *būr* chamber; *ūtan* outside; *be-ēode* surrounded

Discussion

Again, the sequence of events is clear, but the motivation of the characters is not. No reason is given for Cynewulf to wish to exile Sigebryht's brother Cyneheard 31 years after taking over the kingdom, nor for Cyneheard to then mount an ambush while Cynewulf was spending the night with a woman at Merton. Perhaps Sigebryht's death had left Cyneheard in a strong position to challenge for the kingship, or with a duty to avenge him, so that Cynewulf decided to take pre-emptive action. Does the ambush represent Cyneheard's response to the attempt to exile him, or was he planning it anyway? And how was he able to surround the bed-chamber before being discovered by the king's followers? It has been suggested that this points to negligence on their part; but since no criticism is levelled at them within the account itself, it is difficult to know whether or not this was the chronicler's view.

Section 3

In the next section, the king discovers that he is under attack, and the fighting begins.

* Where did King Cynewulf go to defend himself?
* What did he do when he saw Cyneheard?
* Why was this a mistake?

[10] Ond þā ongeat se cyning þæt, ond hē on þā duru ēode, ond þā unhēanlīce hine werede oþ hē on þone æþeling lōcude, ond þā ūt

ræsde on hine ond hine miclum gewundode. [11] Ond hīe alle on
þone cyning wærun feohtende oþ-þæt hīe hine ofslægenne hæfdon.

[10]   *ongeat* perceived; *unhēanlīce* bravely; *hine* himself; *werede* defended; *on . . . lōcude*
      looked at, caught sight of; *ræsde* rushed

Discussion

Despite being outnumbered, Cynewulf defended himself bravely in the
doorway of the room, managing to hold off his attackers until he caught
sight of Cyneheard and rushed out at him. Having lost the protection of
the doorway, he was then quickly overwhelmed and killed. The rash
action leading to his death is a heroic motif that we shall see again in
The Battle of Maldon. Indeed, it has been suggested that since the room
was dark and all the potential witnesses except the woman were dead
by the next day, this detail must have been invented in order to present
Cynewulf in a heroic light. There is at any rate no doubt of the chronicler's approval. Within a text otherwise devoid of comment on the characters' actions, the adverb *unhēanlīce* 'nobly' stands out in sharp
contrast to the impartial style of the rest of the account.

Section 4

At this point, the king's followers hear the commotion and hurry to
the scene, arriving too late to save him.

• What did Cyneheard offer to the king's followers?
• How many of them accepted his offer?
• What did they do instead?
• How many of them remained alive at the end of the battle?

> [12] Ond þā on þæs wīfes gebærum onfundon þæs cyninges þegnas þā
> unstilnesse, ond þā þider urnon, swā hwelc swā þonne gearo wearþ
> ond radost. [13] Ond hiera se æþeling gehwelcum feoh ond feorh
> gebēad, ond hiera nænig hit geþicgean nolde. [14] Ac hīe simle feoht-
> ende wæran oþ hīe alle lægon būtan ānum Bryttiscum gīsle, ond sē
> swīþe gewundad wæs.

[12]   *gebærum* outcries; *unstilnesse* disturbance; *urnon* ran; *swā hwelc swā* whoever; *gearo*
      ready; *radost* quickest
[13]   *gehwelcum* to each; *feoh* money; *gebēad* offered; *geþicgean* accept
[14]   *simle* always; *Bryttiscum* British; *gīsle* hostage

Discussion

The men whom Cynewulf had taken with him to Merton were hopelessly outnumbered by Cyneheard's followers. Cyneheard offered
them money and safe conduct, but they refused to compromise their
loyalty in order to save their lives. Not one of them would accept his
offer: instead, they kept fighting until they were all dead except one
British hostage, and even he was severely wounded. Through their
actions, they displayed two virtues central to the heroic code: loyalty
and courage.

Section 5

The tables are turned the following morning when the main body of
the king's retainers hear what has happened at Merton.

- What did the king's retainers do when they heard that he had been
  killed?
- Name two of the king's retainers who had been left behind.
- Whom did they meet in the stronghold where the king lay dead?
- What had been done to the gates?
- What two inducements did Cyneheard offer to the king's retainers
  if they would grant him the kingdom?

> [15] Þā on morgenne gehīerdun þæt þæs cyninges þegnas, þe him be-
> æftan wærun, þæt se cyning ofslægen wæs. [16] Þā ridon hīe þider,
> ond his aldor-mon Ōsrīc, ond Wīferþ his þegn, ond þā men þe hē be-
> æftan him lǣfde ǣr, ond þone æþeling on þǣre byrig mētton þǣr se
> cyning ofslægen læg (ond þā gatu him tō belocen hæfdon) ond þā
> þǣrtō ēodon. [17] Ond þā gebēad hē him hiera āgenne dōm fēos ond
> londes, gif hīe him þæs rīces ūþon, ond him cȳþde þæt hiera mǣgas
> him mid wǣron, þā þe him from noldon.

[16]   byrig stronghold; him tō against them; belocen locked
[17]   gebēad offered; āgenne own; fēos of money; ūþon would grant; cȳþde informed

Discussion

When the retainers who had been left behind on the king's visit to
Merton heard that he had been killed, they rode there under the lead-
ership of alderman Osric and retainer Wiferth, and met Cyneheard.
Now it was Cyneheard's men who were outnumbered, and had locked

the gates against the new arrivals. But Cyneheard had not yet given up. He tried to bargain with Cynewulf's men, offering them money and land (literally 'their own judgement of money and land') if they would grant him the kingdom, and pointing out that many of them had relatives among his own followers who would be killed in the fighting. The latter in particular would be a strong inducement, since loyalty to kindred was second only to loyalty to one's lord in Anglo-Saxon society.

Section 6

The next section concludes the account of the hostilities.

* How did the king's retainers respond to Cyneheard's offer?
* What counter-offer did they make to their relatives among Cyneheard's followers?
* How did their relatives respond?
* Where did the fighting take place?
* How many of Cyneheard's followers remained alive at the end of the battle?

> [18] Ond þā cwǣdon hīe þæt him nǣnig mǣg lēofra nǣre þonne hiera hlāford, ond hīe nǣfre his banan folgian noldon. [19] Ond þā budon hīe hiera mǣgum þæt hīe gesunde from ēodon. [20] Ond hīe cwǣdon þæt tæt ilce hiera gefērum geboden wǣre þe ǣr mid þām cyninge wǣrun. [21] þā cwǣdon hīe þæt hīe hīe þæs ne onmunden 'þon mā þe ēowre gefēran þe mid þām cyninge ofslǣgene wǣrun'. [22] Ond hīe þā ymb þā gatu feohtende wǣron, oþ-þæt hīe þǣr-inne fulgon, ond þone æþeling ofslōgon ond þā men þe him mid wǣrun, alle būtan ānum, sē wæs þæs aldor-monnes god-sunu. [23] Ond hē his feorh generede, ond þēah hē wæs oft gewundad.

[18] *banan* slayer; *folgian* follow
[19] *budon* offered; *gesunde* unhurt
[20] *tæt ilce* the same; *geboden wǣre* had been offered
[21] *hīe hīe þæs ne onmunden* they would take no heed of that; *þon mā þe* any more than
[22] *ymb* around; *fulgon* burst
[23] *generede* saved

Discussion

Like their comrades before them, the main body of the king's retainers refused Cyneheard's offer, replying that no kinsman was dearer to them than their lord, and that they would never follow his killer. They did, however, offer safe conduct to any of their relatives among Cyneheard's men who wished to leave before the fighting started. But Cyneheard's followers had no intention of behaving in a less heroic way than the king's guard, who had turned down a similar offer of safe conduct the previous night. They too refused the offer and were killed in the ensuing fighting around the gates – again, all except one (alderman Osric's godson), who was severely wounded.

The formal patterning of the narrative is very evident in the parallels between the two battles. Both involve a small force outnumbered by a larger force, both are preceded by offers of safe conduct, and both conclude with the slaughter of all except one from the losing side.

Section 7

The account (though not the annal itself) concludes with some historical information.

- How long did Cynewulf's reign last?
- Where is he buried?
- Where is Cyneheard buried?
- How far can their genealogy be traced?

> [24] Ond se Cynewulf rīcsode xxxi wintra, ond his līc līþ æt Wintanceastre, ond þæs æþelinges æt Ascan-mynster. [25] Ond hiera ryhtfæderen-cyn gǣþ tō Cerdice.

[24]   *rīcsode* reigned; *līþ* lies; *Wintan-ceastre* Winchester; *Ascan-mynster* Axminster
[25]   *ryht-fæderen-cyn* direct paternal ancestry; *gǣþ* goes

Discussion

The statement that Cynewulf ruled for 31 years is probably incorrect, as his death is recorded in the *Anglo-Saxon Chronicle* entry dated 784: 29 years after 755. The mistake may have arisen through a reversal of the last two digits of the Roman numeral: xxxi (31) instead of xxix (29).

It is worth noting that in addition to its importance as a historical document, the *Chronicle* also contains some of the earliest forms of English place-names, including Winchester and Axminster, the burial places of Cynewulf and Cyneheard. The statement that their direct paternal ancestry goes back to Cerdic, the founder of the West Saxon dynasty, reflects an emphasis on genealogy characteristic of Anglo-Saxon documents. The same theme continues later in the annal, which goes on to mention several West Mercian kings and to trace the genealogy of one of them (Offa) back to the god Woden.

Glossary of common or familiar words

ac 14   'but'
aldor-mon (as) 2, 5; (ns) 16; aldor-monnes (gs) 22   'alderman' (i.e.
    king's representative)
alle (np) 11, 14; (ap) 22   'all'
ān (ns) 4; ānne (as) 7; ānum (ds) 14, 22   'one, a'
ǣr 9, 16, 20   'before'
æt 4, 24   'at'
æþeling (as) 7, 10, 16, 22; (ns) 13; æþelinges (gs) 24   'prince'
be-æftan 15, 16   'behind'
brōþur (ns) 8   'brother'
būtan 14, 22   'except'
cwǣdon (p) 18, 20, 21   'said'
cyning (as) 9, 11; (ns) 10, 15, 16; cyninge (ds) 20, 21; cyninges (gs) 12,
    15   'king'
dǣdum (dp) 1   'deeds'
dōm (as) 17   'judgement'
duru (as) 10   'door'
ēode (s) 10; ēodon (p) 16; (pj) 19   'went'
ēowre (p) 21   'your'
feaht (s) 6   'fought'
feohtende 11, 14, 22   'fighting'
feorh (as) 13, 23   'life'
for 1   'because of'
from 17, 19   'from'
gatu (ap) 16, 22   'gates'
gefēran (np) 21; gefērum (dp) 20   'comrades'
gehīerdun (p) 15   'heard'
gewundad (t) 14, 23   'wounded'
gewundode (s) 10   'wounded'
gif 17   'if'

god-sunu (ns) 22   'godson'

hæfde (s) 2, 7; hæfdon (p) 11, 16   'had'

hē (ns) 2, 4, 5, etc.   'he'

hēr 1   'here, at this time'

hīe (np) 11, 14, 16, etc.   'they'

hiera (gp) 13 'of them'; 17, 18, 19, 20, 25   'their'

him (ds) 2, 15, 16, 17, 22   'him'

him (dp) 17, 18   'them'

hine (as) 3, 4, 9, 10, 11   'him'

his (gs) 1, 16, 18, 23, 24   'his'

hit (as) 13   'it'

hlāford (as) 18   'lord'

kyninge (ds) 9   'king'

lǣfde (s) 16   'left'

læg (s) 16; lǣgon (p) 14   'lay (dead)'

lengest 2   'longest'

lēofra 18   'dearer'

līc (ns) 24   'body'

londes (gs) 17   'land'

mǣg (ns) 18; mǣgas (np) 17; mǣgum (dp) 19   'kinsman'

men (np) 9, 16; (ap) 22   'men'

mētton (p) 16   'met'

miclum 6 'great'; 10   'greatly'

mid 9, 17, 20, 21, 22   'with'

morgenne (ds) 15   'morning'

nǣfre 18   'never' (ne + ǣfre)

nǣnig (ns) 13, 18   'none' (ne + ǣnig)

nǣre (sj) 18   'was not' (ne + wǣre)

nolde (s) 13; noldon (p) 17, 18   'would not' (ne + wolde/woldon)

ofslægen (t) 15, 16; ofslægene 21; ofslægenne 11   'killed'

ofslōg (s) 2; ofslōgon (p) 22   'killed'

oft 6, 23   'often'

on 3   'into'; 10   'to'; 10   'at'; 11   'against'; 12   'from'; 15, 16   'in'

ond 1, 2, 3, etc.   'and'

onfunden (pj) 9; onfundon (p) 12   'discovered'

oþ 2, 10, 14   'until'

oþ-þæt 4, 11, 22   'until'

rīce (as) 7; rīces (gs) 1, 17   'kingdom'

ridon (p) 16   'rode'

se (ns) 6, 8, 24   'this'

se (ns) 10, 13, 15, 16   'the'
sē (ns) 7, 22   'who'
sē (ns) 14   'he'
swīþe 14   'greatly'
tō 25   'to'
þā 3, 9, 10, 12, 15, 16, 17, 18, 19, 21, 22   'then'
þā 9, 10, 12, 16, 22   'the'
þā þe 17   'who'
þām (ds) 9, 20, 21   'the'
þǣr 4, 9   'there'
þǣr 16   'where'
þǣre (ds) 16   'the'
þǣr-inne 22   'there-in, inside'
þǣr-tō 16   'to there, in that direction'
þæs (gs) 8   'this'
þæs (gs) 12, 15, 17, 22, 24   'the'
þæt 10, 15, 17, 18, 19, 20, 21   'that'
þe 2, 9, 15, 16, 20, 21, 22   'who'
þēah 22   'nevertheless'
þegn (ns) 16; þegnas (np) 12, 15   'retainer'
þider 12, 16   'thither, in that direction'
þone (as) 2, 5, 9, etc.   'the'
þonne 12   'then'
þonne 18   'than'
unryhtum (dp) 1   'unjust'
ūt 10   'out'
was (s) 7   'was'
wǣran (p) 14; wǣron (p) 17, 22; wǣrun (p) 9, 11, 15, 21, 22; (pj) 20
    'were'
wæs (s) 8, 14, 15, 22, 23   'was'
wearþ (s) 12   'was, became'
West-Seaxna (gp) 1   'West Saxons'
wīfes (gs) 12   'woman'
wintra (gp) 7, 24   'years'
wiþ 6   'against'
wolde (s) 7   'wanted'

Text B
Beowulf, lines 710–836

Our second text is an extract from the epic poem *Beowulf*, which has already been introduced in Chapters 4 and 7. In Chapter 4, we looked at Henry Sweet's prose adaptation of the Grendel fight, the first of the three battles undertaken by the hero Beowulf during the course of the poem. It is more exciting – though more difficult – to read the original poetry. As the manuscript was badly damaged in the fire of 1731, the text is no longer fully legible, and some readings have been supplied from transcripts made after the fire by scholars who realised that the pages would continue to deteriorate.

Lines 710–719

The poem is divided into sections known as 'fitts'. The account of Beowulf's fight with Grendel comprises fitts 11 and 12, beginning in line 710 with an atmospheric description of Grendel's journey *of mōre* 'from the swamp'.

- Whose anger did Grendel bear (711b)?
- Where was he going?
- The importance of what is emphasised through variation in 714–715?
- Was this the first time that Grendel had sought out Hrothgar's home?
- What had he never found before or after?

      XI
    Ðā cōm of mōre   under mist-hleoþum   710
    Grendel gongan.   Godes yrre bær.
    Mynte se mān-scaða   manna cynnes

sumne besyrwan
Wōd under wolcnum,
gold-sele gumena,
fǣttum fāhne.
þæt hē Hrōþgāres
Nǣfre hē on aldor-dagum,
heardran hǣle

in sele þām hēan.
tō þæs þe hē wīn-reced,
gearwost wisse,   715
Ne wæs þæt forma sīð
hām gesōhte.
ǣr ne siþðan,
heal-ðegnas fand.

710 *mist-hleoþum* misty slopes
711 *gongan* walking
712 *Mynte* intended; *mān-scaða* enemy
713 *sumne* one; *besyrwan* to ensnare; *hēan* high
714 *Wōd* advanced; *wolcnum* clouds; *þæs þe* where
715 *gearwost* most readily; *wisse* knew
716 *fǣttum* with ornaments; *fāhne* decorated; *forma* first; *sīð* time
718 *aldor-dagum* days of his life
719 *hǣle* outcome

Discussion

Although set in the pre-Christian past, the poem was written for a Christian audience, and contains many Biblical allusions. Grendel has previously been introduced as a member of the race of Cain, an Old Testament character cursed by God for killing his brother: here the poet reminds us that he 'bore God's anger' (711b). He was making his way to Heorot, the great hall built by the Danish king Hrothgar and the scene of much of the action in the first part of the poem. Since the hall was the organisational centre of heroic society – the place where retainers gathered to make vows of allegiance to their lord, to receive gifts from him, and to feast – Grendel's attacks on it were in effect attacks on civilised society. Its importance is emphasised through variation (*wīn-reced* 'wine-hall' 714b, *gold-sele gumena* 'gold-hall of men' 715a).

At this point in the poem, Grendel has been terrorising the hall of Heorot for twelve years, killing anyone he finds there at night. The poet's comment 'that was not the first time that he had sought out Hrothgar's home' (716b–717) is therefore an example of ironic understatement or 'litotes', a common device in Old English poetry. So too the laconic statement that 'never in the days of his life, before or after, did he find hall-retainers with harsher outcome' (718–719) is loaded with irony when we realise that the 'harsher outcome' alluded to is his death.

Lines 720–730a

When Grendel arrives at Heorot, he immediately goes inside.

- How is Grendel described in this passage?
- How did he gain access to the hall?
- What shone from his eyes?
- How are the men whom he saw in the hall described?

Cōm þā tō recede	rinc sīðian,	720
drēamum bedǣled.	Duru sōna onarn,	
fȳr-bendum fæst,	syþðan hē hire folmum gehrān.	
On-brǣd þā bealo-hȳdig,	ðā hē gebolgen wæs,	
recedes mūþan.	Raþe æfter-þon	
on fāgne flōr	fēond treddode,	725
ēode yrre-mōd.	Him of ēagum stōd	
ligge gelīcost	lēoht unfæger.	
Geseah hē in recede	rinca manige,	
swefan sibbe-gedriht	samod æt-gædere,	
mago-rinca hēap.		730

720 *sīðian* travelling
721 *drēamum bedǣled* deprived of joys; *onarn* sprang open
722 *fȳr-bendum* bars forged in fire (lit. fire-bars); *hire* it (the door); *gehrān* touched
723 *On-brǣd* opened; *bealo-hȳdig* intending harm; *gebolgen* enraged
724 *Raþe* quickly
725 *fāgne* decorated
726 *stōd* shone
727 *ligge* fire; *gelīcost* most like; *unfæger* horrible
729 *swefan* sleep; *sibbe-gedriht* troop of kinsmen; *samod æt-gædere* together
730 *hēap* band

Discussion
Part of Grendel's menace is that he is never clearly described. The poet maintains an ambivalence as to whether he is man or monster, here using the same term *rinc* 'warrior' both for Grendel (720b) and for the troop of men whom he saw in the hall (728b, 730a). Human attributes are also suggested by the formula *drēamum bedǣled* 'deprived of joys' (721a), a reminder that he was cut off from God as a descendant of Cain; while *fēond* (725b) survives as 'fiend' but could simply mean 'enemy' in Old English. On the other hand, Grendel has monstrous strength, as the hall door sprang open at the

touch of his hands (721b–722), and the horrible light, most like fire, that shone from his eyes (726b–727) is clearly non-human.

Lines 730b–749

- Was Grendel sad or happy?
- What did he intend to do?
- Who was watching him?
- What did he do to the sleeping warrior at the first opportunity?
- Whom did he seize next?

	Þā his mōd āhlōg.	730
Mynte þæt hē gedǣlde,	ǣr-þon dæg cwōme,	
atol āglǣca,	ānra gehwylces	
līf wið līce,	þā him ālumpen wæs	
wist-fylle wēn.	Ne wæs þæt wyrd þā gēn,	
þæt hē mā mōste	manna cynnes	735
ðicgean ofer þā niht.	Þrȳð-swȳð behē old	
mǣg Higelā ces	hū se mā n-scaða	
under fǣr-gripum	gefaran wolde.	
Ne þæt se āglǣca	yldan þōhte,	
ac hē gefēng hraðe	forman sīðe	740
slǣpendne rinc,	slā t unwearnum,	
bā t bā n-locan,	blōd ēdrum dranc,	
syn-snǣdum swealh.	Sōna hæfde	
unlyfigendes	eal gefeormod,	
fēt ond folma.	Forð nē ar æt-stōp,	745
nam þā mid handa	hige-þīhtigne	
rinc on ræste.	Rǣhte ongē an	
fēond mid folme.	Hē onfē ng hraþe	
inwit-þancum	ond wið earm gesæt.	

730　*āhlōg* exulted
731　*Mynte* intended; *gedǣlde* would separate
732　*atol* terrible; *ānra gehwylces* of each one
733　*ālumpen* come about
734　*wist-fylle wēn* expectation of feasting; *wyrd* fate; *þā gēn* still
735　*mōste* would be allowed
736　*ðicgean* devour; *ofer* after; *Þrȳð-swȳð* mighty
737　*mā n-scaða* enemy
738　*fǣr-gripum* sudden attack; *gefaran* act
739　*yldan* to delay

740	*gefēng* seized; *hraðe* quickly; *forman* first; *sīðe* opportunity
741	*slāt* tore; *unwearnum* unrestrainedly
742	*bāt* bit; *ēdrum* from veins
743	*syn-snǣdum* huge gobbets; *swealh* swallowed
744	*gefeormod* devoured
745	*ǣt-stōp* stepped
746	*nam* seized; *hige-þīhtigne* stout-hearted
747	*ræste* bed; *Rǣhte* reached; *ongēan* towards
748	*onfēng* realised; *hraþe* quickly
749	*inwit-þancum* hostile intention

Discussion

The way Grendel exulted in spirit (730b) at the sight of his prey is again clearly monstrous: he intended to kill (lit. 'separate life from body') each of the men before day came (731–733a). Watched by Beowulf (the 'mighty kinsman of Hygelac' 736b–737a), he seized a sleeping warrior (740–741a), tore him unrestrainedly (741b), bit his muscles (742a), drank blood from his veins (742b), and swallowed huge gobbets (743a) until he had completely consumed the lifeless man, feet and hands (743b–745a). Then he stepped nearer to Beowulf himself (the 'stout-hearted warrior on his bed', 746b–747a) and reached out for him with his hand (747b–748a). However, Beowulf realised what he intended to do, and sat up against Grendel's arm (748b–749).

Lines 750–766

- What did Grendel immediately realise?
- How had his mood changed?
- Where did he wish to flee to?
- What did Beowulf do?
- Which part of the body was the focus of the struggle?

Sōna þæt onfunde	fyrena hyrde,	750
þæt hē ne mētte	middan-geardes,	
eorþan scēata	on elran men	
mund-gripe māran.	Hē on mōde wearð	
forht on ferhðe.	Nō þȳ ǣr fram meahte.	
Hyge wæs him hin-fūs,	wolde on heolster flēon,	755
sēcan dēofla gedræg.	Ne wæs his drohtoð þǣr	
swylce hē on ealder-dagum	ǣr gemette.	
Gemunde þā se gōda	mǣg Higelāces	

æfen-spræce,	up-lang āstōd
ond him fæste wið-fēng.	Fingras burston. 760
eoten wæs ūt-weard.	Eorl furþur stōp.
Mynte se mæra,	þær hē meahte swā,
wīdre gewindan	ond on weg þanon
flē on on fen-hopu.	Wiste his fingra geweald
on grames grāpum.	Þæt wæs gēocor sīð 765
þæt se hearm-scaþa	tō Heorute ātēah.

750 *fyrena* of wicked deeds; *hyrde* guardian
752 *scēata* regions; *elran* another
753 *mund-gripe* hand-grip; *māran* greater
754 *forht* afraid; *ferhðe* spirit; *Nō þy ǣr* none the sooner
755 *Hyge* heart; *hin-fūs* eager to get away; *heolster* darkness
756 *gedrǣg* company; *drohtoð* experience
757 *swylce* such as; *ealder-dagum* days of life; *gemette* encountered
758 *Gemunde* remembered
759 *æfen-sprǣce* evening speech
760 *wið-fēng* seized
761 *eoten* giant; *ūt-weard* striving to escape (lit. outward)
762 *Mynte* intended
763 *wīdre* further off; *gewindan* escape; *on weg* away; *þanon* from there
764 *fen-hopu* fen retreats; *Wiste* knew; *geweald* power
765 *grames* of a hostile (one); *grāpum* grasps; *gēocor* sad; *sīð* journey
766 *hearm-scaþa* enemy; *ātēah* taken

Discussion

Grendel, the 'guardian of wicked deeds' (750b), immediately realised that he had met his match – or, as the poet puts it, 'that he had not met a greater handgrip in another man in the world, in the regions of the earth' (751–754a). Now afraid and desperate to escape Beowulf's grasp, he wanted to flee into the darkness (755b), but Beowulf stood up and held onto him firmly (759b–760a). The two combatants are contrasted in line 761 through the alliteration of *eoten* 'giant' and *eorl* 'nobleman'; and the poet focuses on their fingers – those of Beowulf were bursting with the effort (760b), while those of Grendel were in the grasps of a hostile enemy (765a).

Lines 767–782a

- Who or what is the focus of attention in these lines?
- How does the presentation of Beowulf and Grendel change here?
- What was the only means by which the hall could be destoyed?

Dryht-sele dynede.	Denum eallum wearð,	
ceaster-būendum,	cēnra gehwylcum,	
eorlum ealu-scerwen.	Yrre wǣron bē gen,	
rēþe ren-weardas.	Reced hlynsode.	770
Þā wæs wundor micel,	þæt se wīn-sele	
wið-hæfde heaþo-dēorum,	þæt hē on hrūsan ne fēol,	
fæger fold-bold;	ac hē þæs fæste wæs	
innan ond ūtan	īren-bendum	
searo-þoncum besmiþod.	Þǣr fram sylle ā bē ag	775
medu-benc monig,	mīne gefrǣge,	
golde geregnad,	þǣr þā graman wunnon.	
Þæs ne wēndon ǣr	witan Scyldinga,	
þæt hit ā mid gemete	manna ǣnig	
betlic ond bān-fāg	tō-brecan meahte,	780
listum tō-lūcan,	nymþe līges fæþm	
swulge on swaþule.		

767 *dynede* resounded
768 *ceaster-būendum* to the fortress-dwellers; *cēnra* of the brave; *gehwylcum* to each
769 *ealu-scerwen* ale-serving
770 *rēþe* fierce; *ren-weardas* hall-guardians; *hlynsode* resounded
772 *wiðhæfde* withstood; *heaþo-dēorum* those bold in battle; *hrūsan* ground
773 *fold-bold* building; *þæs* so
775 *searo-þoncum* skilfully; *besmiþod* forged; *sylle* floor; *ābēag* gave way
776 *mīne gefrǣge* as I heard
777 *geregnad* adorned; *graman* fierce ones; *wunnon* contended
778 *wēndon* thought; *witan* wise men; *Scyldinga* of the Scyldings
779 *mid gemete* by any means
780 *betlic* excellent; *bān-fāg* adorned with bone; *tō-brecan* break up
781 *listum* with skill; *tō-lūcan* destroy; *nymþe* unless; *līges* of fire; *fæþm* embrace
782 *swulge* should swallow; *swaþule* flame

Discussion

Here the hall of Heorot becomes almost an actor in the drama, as the poet breaks off from the account of the fight to describe the effects on its surroundings. Beowulf and his adversary no longer appear distinct but are linked together as *rēþe ren-weardas* 'fierce hall-guardians' (770a), *heaþo-dēorum* 'those bold in battle' (772a) and *þā graman* 'the fierce ones' (777b), while attention focuses on the way the hall resounded with the affray. Amazingly, the hall remained standing despite its mead-benches being wrenched from the floor, leading to the conclusion that it could not be destroyed other than by the embrace of fire – an ironic comment in view of hints earlier in the poem that Heorot would indeed eventually be burned.

The compound *ealu-scerwen* (769a) is problematic, as the first
element may mean either 'ale' or 'good fortune', and the second
either 'dispensation' or 'deprivation'. In connection with the mead-
hall, a reference to ale may seem appropriate, used figuratively to
refer either to the joy about to be experienced by the Danes when
Grendel was defeated, or to their fear on hearing the sounds of
combat. A possible interpretation of 767b–769a is: 'that was a dispensation of sweet/bitter ale towards all the Danes, the fortress-dwellers,
each of the brave warriors'.

Lines 782b–790

- From whose perspective are the events now presented?
- Were they confident or fearful?
- Who was wailing a song of defeat?
- What was Beowulf doing?

	Swēg up āstāg	
nīwe geneahhe.	Norð-Denum stōd	
atelic egesa	ānra gehwylcum	
þāra þe of wealle	wōp gehȳrdon,	785
gryre-lēoð galan	Godes andsacan,	
sige-lēasne sang,	sār wānigean	
helle hæfton.	Hē old hine fæste	
sē þe manna wæs	mægene strengest	
on þǣm dæge	þysses līfes.	790

782   *swēg* noise; *āstāg* rose
783   *geneahhe* often; *stōd* came upon
784   *atelic* terrible; *egesa* fear; *ānra gehwylcum* to each one
785   *wōp* wailing
786   *gryre-lēoð* song of despair; *galan* sing; *andsacan* adversary
787   *sige-lēasne* defeated (lit. victory-less); *sār* pain; *wānigean* lament
788   *hæfton* captive
789   *mægene* in strength
790   *on þǣm dæge* at that time (lit. on that day)

Discussion

At the close of fitt 11, the poet heightens the tension by moving
outside the hall to the North-Danes listening by the wall, trying to
work out what is going on from the noise. A terrible fear came upon

them as they heard the sound of Grendel ('God's adversary', 786b) wailing. Beowulf still held him firmly.

Lines 791–808

- How are Beowulf and Grendel described in these lines?
- What did Beowulf's men do?
- Why were they unsuccessful?
- Can you find a formula (an often-repeated 'stock phrase'; see Chapter 6) in this passage?

XII

Nolde eorla hlēo	ǣnige þinga	
þone cwealm-cuman	cwicne forlǣtan,	
ne his līf-dagas	lēoda ǣnigum	
nytte tealde.	Þǣr genehost brægd	
eorl Bēowulfes	ealde lāfe,	795
wolde frēa-drihtnes	feorh ealgian,	
mǣres þēodnes,	ðǣr hīe meahton swā.	
Hīe þæt ne wiston,	þā hīe gewin drugon,	
heard-hicgende	hilde-mecgas,	
ond on healfa gehwone	hēawan þōhton,	800
sāwle sēcan:	þone syn-scaðan	
ǣnig ofer eorþan	īrenna cyst,	
gūð-billa nān	grētan nolde,	
ac hē sige-wǣpnum	forsworen hæfde,	
ecga gehwylcre.	Scolde his aldor-gedāl	805
on ðǣm dæge	þysses līfes	
earmlic wurðan,	ond se ellor-gāst	
on fēonda geweald	feor sīðian.	

791 *hlēo* protector (lit. helmet)
792 *cwealm-cuman* deadly comer; *forlǣtan* to let go
793 *lēoda* people
794 *nytte* of use; *tealde* considered; *genehost* most often; *brægd* brandished
795 *lāfe* heirloom
796 *ealgian* to protect
798 *wiston* knew; *gewin* strike; *drugon* undertook
799 *heard-hicgende* stout-hearted; *hilde-mecgas* warriors
800 *healfa gehwone* each side; *hēawan* to strike
801 *syn-scaðan* enemy
802 *īrenna* of iron swords; *cyst* best
803 *gūð-billa* of battle-swords; *grētan* harm

804   *sige-wǣpnum* victory-weapons; *forsworen* foresworn (i.e. bewitched)
805   *gehwylcre* each; *aldor-gedāl* parting from life
807   *earmlic* wretched; *wurðan* would be; *ellor-gāst* alien spirit
808   *geweald* power; *sīðian* travel

Discussion

It is characteristic of the poet's style that Beowulf and Grendel are generally referred to not by name, but circuitously as in 791–792: 'the protector of warriors (i.e. Beowulf) did not intend for anything to let the deadly visitor (i.e. Grendel) go alive'. Similarly, Beowulf is described as 'lord' (796a) and 'famous lord' (797a), and Grendel as 'enemy' (801b) and 'alien spirit' (807b). When Beowulf's name does appear in 795a, it is within a circumlocution referring to the men who had accompanied him on his mission, and had just woken up to what was going on: 'there most often a warrior of Beowulf brandished an ancient heirloom' (794b–795). Their swords could not harm Grendel, who seemed to have magical abilities rendering weapons useless; but his parting from life would none the less be wretched 'at that time in this life' (806) – a formula echoing the same phrase used of Beowulf in 790, just as the formula 'if they could' (797b) echoes 'if he could' used of Grendel in 762b.

Lines 809–818a

- What did Grendel realise?
- In which part of the body was he wounded?

Ðā þæt onfunde	sē þe fela ǣror	
mōdes myrðe	manna cynne,	810
fyrene gefremede	– hē fāg wið God –	
þæt him se līc-homa	lǣstan nolde,	
ac hine se mōdega	mǣg Hygelāces	
hæfde be honda.	Wæs gehwæþer ōðrum	
lifigende lāð.	Līc-sār gebād	815
atol ǣglǣca.	Him on eaxle wearð	
syn-dolh sweotol,	seonowe on-sprungon,	
burston bān-locan.		

810   *myrðe* afflictions
811   *fyrene* wicked deeds; *gefremede* carried out; *fāg* at feud
812   *lǣstan* serve

814   *gehwæþer* each
815   *Līc-sār* body-pain; *gebād* experienced
816   *atol* terrible
817   *syn-dolh* huge wound; *sweotol* visible

Discussion

Again, instead of naming the two protagonists, the poet describes Grendel as 'he who had carried out many wicked deeds, heartfelt afflictions, against mankind – he at feud against God' (809b–811) and 'terrible enemy' (816a, repeating 732a), and describes Beowulf as 'the brave kinsman of Hygelac' (813, partly repeating 737a). Grendel realised that his body would no longer serve him (809a, 812), but Beowulf had him by the hand (813–814a). Each was hateful to the other living (814b–815a). Grendel was wounded in the shoulder (816b–817a): his sinews sprang apart (817b), and his muscles burst (818a).

Lines 818b–836

- To whom was victory in battle granted?
- Who had to flee, mortally wounded, under the fen slopes?
- What did he leave behind?
- What did Beowulf do with it?

	Bēowulfe wearð	
gūð-hrēð gyfeþe.	Scolde Grendel þonan	
feorh-sēoc flēon	under fen-hleoðu,	820
sēcean wyn-lēas wīc.	Wiste þē geornor,	
þæt his aldres wæs	ende gegongen,	
dōgera dæg-rīm.	Denum eallum wearð	
æfter þām wæl-ræse	willa gelumpen.	
Hæfde þā gefælsod	sē þe ǣr feorran cōm,	825
snotor ond swȳð-ferhð,	sele Hrōðgāres,	
genered wið nīðe.	Niht-weorce gefeh,	
ellen-mǣrþum.	Hæfde Ēast-Denum	
Gēat-mecga lēod	gilp gelǣsted.	
Swylce oncȳþðe	ealle gebētte,	830
inwid-sorge,	þe hīe ǣr drugon	
ond for þrēa-nȳdum	þolian scoldon,	
torn unlȳtel.	Þæt wæs tācen sweotol,	

```
syþðan hilde-dēor          hond ālegde,
earm ond eaxle             – þǣr wæs eal geador        835
Grendles grāpe –           under gēapne hrōf.
```

819   gūð-hrēð victory in battle; gyfeþe granted; þonan from there
820   feorh-sēoc mortally wounded (lit. life-sick); fen-hleoðu fen-slopes
821   wyn-lēas joyless; wīc dwelling; Wiste knew; þē geornor the more surely
822   aldres of life; gegongen reached
823   dōgera of days; dæg-rīm life-span (lit. number of days)
824   wæl-rǣse deadly combat; gelumpen come about
825   gefǣlsod cleansed
826   snotor wise; swȳð-ferhð stout-hearted
827   genered saved; nīðe affliction; gefeh rejoiced
828   ellen-mǣrþum courageous deeds
829   Gēat-mecga of the Geatish people; lēod prince; gilp boast; gelǣsted fulfilled
830   Swylce also; oncȳþðe grief; gebētte remedied
831   inwid-sorge sorrow caused by malice; drugon endured
832   for þrēa-nȳdum through necessity; þolian endure
833   torn affliction; sweotol clear
834   hilde-dēor bold in battle; ālegde laid
835   eal geador altogether
836   grāpe grasp; gēapne spacious

Discussion

Religious references in the poem are often ambiguous, and the statement that victory in battle was granted to Beowulf (818b–819a – the personal name has a Dative singular -e inflexion) leaves open the question of whether it was granted by God or by fate. Grendel had to flee to the fens in the knowledge that his life was over (819b–823a). Beowulf – again circuitously described as 'he who had come from far, wise and stout-hearted' (825b–826a), 'prince of the Geatish people' (829a), and '(the one) bold in battle' (834) – had cleansed Hrothgar's hall (825a, 826b), and in so doing fulfilled his heroic boast to the East-Danes (828b–829). At the end of the fitt, we discover that Grendel had escaped only by leaving behind his arm, which Beowulf placed as a token under the roof of Heorot (834–836).

Glossary of common or familiar words

ā 779 'ever'
ac 740, 773, 804, 813 'but'
āglǣca (ns) 732, 739, 816 'enemy'
āstōd (s) 759 'stood'

æfter 824   'after'
æfter-þon 724   'afterwards'
ænig (ns) 779, 802; ænige (ds) 791; ænigum (dp) 793   'any'
ǣr 718, 757, 778, 825, 831   'before'
ǣror 809   'previously'
ǣr-þon 731   'before'
bān-locan (ap) 742; 818 (np)   'muscles'
bær (s) 711   'bore'
be 814   'by'
bēgen 769   'both'
behēold (s) 736   'beheld, watched'
blōd (as) 742   'blood'
burston (p) 760, 818   'burst'
cōm (s) 710, 720, 825; cwōme (sj) 734   'came'
cwicne (as) 792   'alive'
cynne (ds) 810; cynnes (gs) 712, 735   'kind, race'
dæg (ns) 731; dæge (ds) 790, 806   'day'
Denum (dp) 767, 823   'Danes'
dēofla (gp) 756   'devils'
dranc (s) 742   'drank'
dryht-sele (ns) 767   'lordly hall'
duru (ns) 721   'door'
ēagum (dp) 726   'eyes'
eal 744   'all, entirely'
ealde (as) 795   'old'
ealle (as) 830; eallum (dp) 767, 823   'all'
earm (as) 749, 835   'arm'
eaxle (ds) 816; (as) 835   'shoulder'
ecga (gp) 805   'edges, blades'
ende (ns) 822   'end'
ēode (s) 726   'went'
eorl (ns) 761, 795; eorla (gp) 791; eorlum (dp) 769   'nobleman,
   warrior'
eorþan (gs) 752; (as) 802   'earth'
fand (s) 719   'found'
fæger 773   'fair, beautiful'
fæst 722   'firm'
fæste 760, 773, 788   'firmly'
fela 809   'many'
fēol (s) 772   'fell'

fēond (ns) 725, 748; fēonda (gp) 808   'fiend, enemy'
feor 808   'far'
feorh (as) 796   'life'
feorran 825   'from afar'
fēt (ap) 745   'feet'
fingra (gp) 764; fingras (np) 760   'fingers'
flēon 755, 764, 820   'to flee'
flōr (as) 725   'floor'
folma (ap) 745; folme (ds) 748; folmum (dp) 722   'hand'
forð 745   'forward'
fram 754, 775   'from'
frēa-drihtnes (gs) 796   'lord'
furþur 761   'further'
gehȳrdon (p) 785   'heard'
gesæt (s) 749   'sat'
geseah (s) 728   'saw'
gesōhte (s) 717   'sought out'
gōda (ns) 758   'good'
God (as) 811; Godes (gs) 711, 786   'God'
golde (ds) 777   'gold'
gold-sele (as) 715   'gold-hall'
gumena (gp) 715   'men'
hām (as) 717   'home'
handa (ds) 746   'hand'
hæfde (s) 742, 804, 814, 825, 828   'had'
hē (ns) 714, 717, 718, 722, etc.   'he'
hē (ns) 772, 773   'it'
heal-ðegnas (as) 719   'hall-retainers'
heardran 719   'harsher'
helle (gs) 788   'hell'
hēold (s) 788   'held'
hīe (np) 797, 798, 831   'they'
him (ds) 726, 733, 755, 816; (as) 760, 812   'him'
hine (as) 788, 813   'him'
his (gs) 730, 756, 764, 793, 805, 822   'his'
hit (as) 779   'it'
hond (as) 834; honda (ds) 814   'hand'
hrōf (as) 836   'roof'
hū 737   'how'
in 713, 728, 782   'in'

innan 774 'inside'

īren-bendum (dp) 774 'iron bands'

lāð 815 'hateful' ('loathe')

lēoht (ns) 727 'light'

līce (ds) 733 'body'

līc-homa (ns) 812 'body'

līf (as) 733; līfes (gs) 790, 806 'life'

līf-dagas (ap) 793 'life-days'

lifigende 815 'living'

mā 735 'more'

mago-rinca (gp) 730 'warriors'

manige (ap) 728 'many'

manna (gp) 712, 735, 779, 789, 810 'men'

mǣg (ns) 737, 758, 813 'kinsman'

mǣra (ns) 762; mǣres (gs) 797 famous (one)

meahte (s) 754, 762, 780; meahton (p) 797 'could'

medu-benc (ns) 776 'mead-bench'

men 752 (ds) 'man'

mētte (s) 751 'met'

micel 771 'great'

mid 746, 748 'with'

middan-geardes (gs) 751 'in the world'

mōd (ns) 730; mōde (ds) 753; mōdes (gs) 810 'mind'

mōdega 813 'brave'

monig 776 'many'

mōre (ds) 710 'moor, swamp'

mūþan (as) 724 'mouth' (i.e. door)

nān (ns) 803 'none'

nǣfre 718 'never'

ne 716, 734, 739, 751, etc. 'not'

ne 718 'nor'

nēar 745 'nearer'

niht (as) 736 'night'

niht-weorce (ds) 827 'night's work'

nīwe 783 'new'

nolde 791, 803, 812 'did not intend, would not' (ne + wolde)

of 710, 726, 785 'from'

ofer 802 'over'

on 718, 752, 753, 754, 757, 765, 808 'in'; 725 'onto'; 746, 790, 800, 806, 816 'on'; 755, 764, 772 'to'

ond 745, 749, 760, 763, etc.   'and'
onfunde (s) 750, 809   'discovered'
on-sprungon (p) 817   'sprang apart'
ōðrum (ds) 814   'other'
reced (ns) 770; recede (ds) 720, 728; recedes (gs) 724   'hall'
rinc (ns) 720; (as) 741, 747; rinca (gp) 728   'warrior'
sang (as) 787   'song'
sāwle (as) 801   'soul'
scolde (s) 805, 819; scoldon (p) 832   'had to, must' ('should')
se (ns) 712, 737, 739, 758, etc.   'the'
sē (ns) 789, 809, 825   'he'
sēcan 756, 801, sēcean 821   'to seek'
sele (ds) 713; (as) 826   'hall'
seonowe (np) 817   'sinews'
siþðan 718, syþðan 722, 834   'after, when'
slǣpendne (as) 741   'sleeping'
sōna 721, 742, 750   'immediately'
stōp (s) 761   'stepped'
strengest 789   'strongest'
swā 762, 797   'so'
tācen (ns) 833   'token'
tō 714, 720, 766   'to'
treddode (s) 725   'trod'
þā, ðā 710, 720, 723, 730, 746, 758, 771, 825   'then'
þā, ðā 723, 733, 798, 809   'when'
þā (as) 736; (ap) 777   'the'
þām (ds) 713, 824   'the'
þāra (gp) 785   'of those'
ðǣm (ds) 790, 806   'that'
þǣr 756, 775, 794, 835   'there'
þǣr 762, 797   'if'
þǣr 777   'where'
þæs (gs) 778   'of the'
þæt 716, 717, 731, 734, 735, etc.   'that'
þe 785, 789, 809, 825   'who'
þe 831   'which'
þēodnes (gs) 797   'lord'
þinga (gp) 791   'thing'
þōhte (s) 739; þōhton (p) 800   'thought, intended'
þone (as) 792, 801   'the'

þysses (gs) 790, 806   'of this'
under 710, 714, 738, 820, 836   'under'
unlyfigendes (gs) 744   'lifeless (one)'
unlӯtel 833   'great'
up 782   'up'
up-lang 759   'upright'
ūtan 774   'outside'
wǣron (p) 769   'were'
wæs (s) 716, 723, 733, 734, etc.   'was'
wealle (ds) 785   'wall'
wearð (s) 753, 761, 767, 816, 818, 823   'was, became'
willa (ns) 824   'will, desire'
wīn-reced (as) 714   'wine-hall'
wīn-sele (ns) 771   'wine-hall'
wið 733, 827   'from'; 749, 811   'against'
wolde (s) 738, 755, 796   'wanted, intended'
wundor (ns) 771   'wonder, marvel'
yrre (as) 711   'anger, ire'
yrre 769   'angry'
yrre-mōd 726   'angry'

Text C
The Battle of Maldon

The Battle of Maldon is a narrative poem commemorating a battle that took place near the town of Maldon in south-east England during the Scandinavian invasions of the late tenth century (see Illustration 3). The *Anglo-Saxon Chronicle* records that in 991, Ipswich was ravaged, and Alderman Byrhtnoth was killed at Maldon. Little more is known from historical sources of the battle in which he lost his life, but the poem provides a very detailed account, setting out the words and actions not only of Byrhtnoth himself but of many other members of the English army. To what extent the account is factually accurate, and to what extent it reflects poetic licence, is uncertain. One aspect of the presentation is certainly fictional. The events of the poem are set not in tenth-century England but within the framework of an earlier heroic society, presenting Byrhtnoth as a Germanic warlord and the English army as his loyal followers or *comitatus*. This has two main effects. First, Byrhtnoth and his men are elevated above their actual roles in contemporary society to the status of legendary heroes such as Beowulf. Secondly, the outcome of the battle becomes less important. The test of success is not victory against the Vikings, but how well the members of the English army live up to the ideals of the heroic code. The poem has an enduring appeal because of the way it turns the story of a defeat into a moral victory, celebrating the heroism of Byrhtnoth and of the men who died with him.

Lines 1–16

The opening lines have been lost, and the surviving poem begins with the English army preparing for battle beside the River Pante, now known as the Blackwater. The initial focus is on two individuals. One is named Eadric (11a), but the other is identified less directly as *Offan mǣg* 'Offa's kinsman' (5a), a recurrent formula within the poem, describing protagonists as 'X's kinsman/son/etc.' As with most formulas, it is not merely decorative but serves a thematic purpose, emphasising the solidarity of English society and the importance of kinship ties.

- What type of animals were the warriors ordered to drive away in line 2?
- What type of bird did Offa's kinsman let fly from his hands to the wood in lines 7–8b?
- Name three items of equipment carried by Eadric.
- The English leader Byrhtnoth is mentioned several times within this passage, although not by name. Can you find three references to him?

...	brocen wurde.	
Hēt þā hyssa hwæne	hors forlǣtan,	
feor āfӯsan,	and forð gangan,	
hicgan tō handum	and tō hige gōdum.	
Þā þæt Offan mǣg	ǣrest onfunde,	5
þæt se eorl nolde	yrhðo geþolian,	
hē lēt him þā of handon	lēofne flēogan,	
hafoc wið þæs holtes,	and tō þǣre hilde stōp:	
be þām man mihte oncnāwan	þæt se cniht nolde	
wācian æt þām wīge,	þā hē tō wǣpnum fēng.	10
Ēac him wolde Ēadrīc	his ealdre gelǣstan,	
frēan tō gefeohte,	ongan þā forð beran	
gār tō gūþe.	Hē hæfde gōd geþanc	
þā hwīle þe hē mid handum	healdan mihte	
bord and brād swurd;	bēot hē gelǣste	15
þā hē æt-foran his frēan	feohtan sceolde.	

1 *brocen wurde* became broken (what this refers to is unknown)
2 *hyssa hwæne* each of the warriors; *forlǣtan* to abandon
3 *āfӯsan* to drive away
4 *hicgan tō* to be intent on; *handum* deeds of hand; *hige* courage
6 *yrhðo* cowardice; *geþolian* tolerate
8 *hafoc* hawk; *holtes* wood
9 *be þām* by that means; *oncnāwan* perceive; *cniht* youth
10 *wācian* weaken; *tō . . . fēng* took up
11 *Ēac* also, as well as; *gelǣstan* to serve
13 *geþanc* intention
14 *þā hwīle þe* as long as
15 *gelǣste* carried out

Discussion

Perhaps not much of the poem has been lost, as the surviving fragment opens with Byrhtnoth arraying his men for battle, ordering them to drive their horses away and to advance, intent on deeds of hands and on good courage. As yet he may be a stranger to some of the troops: this at least appears to be the implication of the statement in 5–6 that Offa's kinsman 'first discovered that the nobleman would not tolerate cowardice', after which he let his beloved hawk fly from his hands to the wood and advanced to the battle. Eadric seems to be both better prepared and better equipped, bringing not a hawk but a spear (13a), shield and broad sword (15a).

The poetic fiction of an early heroic society is already evident in this opening passage. The English leader Byrhtnoth is not described according to his actual status as a tenth-century land-owner, but as *eorl* 'nobleman' (6a), *ealdor* 'lord' (Dative singular *ealdre*, 11b) and *frēa* 'lord' (Dative singular *frēan*, 12a and 16a). All are terms drawn from the traditional heroic vocabulary used of Germanic warlords: compare for instance the use of *eorl* in the 'Horn' riddle and *Deor* in Chapter 6, and in the *Beowulf* extract in Text 2, where it also has a more general sense 'warrior', used of Beowulf's men. The statement that Edward 'carried out his vow when he had to fight before his lord' (15b–16) is a reference to the vow of allegiance made by each follower to his lord in heroic society.

Lines 17–24

The focus now turns to Byrhtnoth himself.

- Was Byrhtnoth on horseback or on foot?
- Which item of equipment did he instruct his men how to hold?
- What did he tell them not to do?

Ða þær Byrhtnōð ongan	beornas trymian,
rād and rǣdde,	rincum tǣhte
hū hī sceoldon standan	and þone stede healdan,
and bæd þæt hyra rand	an-rihte hēoldon, 20
fæste mid folman,	and ne forhtedon nā.
Þā hē hæfde þæt folc	fægere getrymmed,
hē līhte þā mid lēodon	þær him lēofost wæs,
þær hē his heorð-werod	holdost wiste.

17   *trymian* to array
18   *rædde* instructed; *tæhte* directed
19   *stede* position
20   *rand* shield; *anrihte* correctly
21   *ne forhtedon* not to be afraid
22   *fægere* properly; *getrymmed* arrayed
23   *līhte* dismounted; *mid lēodon* among the people
24   *heorð-werod* group of retainers; *holdost* most loyal; *wiste* knew

Discussion

Once the other members of the army had driven away their horses, Byrhtnoth was the only person on horseback. This will be important later in the poem when cowards take his horse to flee from the battle, giving the impression that Byrhtnoth himself is in retreat. He appears to be a good leader, showing his men how they should stand and hold the position (19), and instructing them on how to hold their shields firmly in their hands, and not to be afraid (20–21). The statement that he dismounted 'among the people where it was most pleasing to him, where he knew his group of retainers to be most loyal' (23–24) is ironic, as this group probably included the cowards who were later to betray his trust. The compound *heorð-werod* literally means 'hearth-troop' (24a): another heroic term presenting the members of the English army as an early Germanic *comitatus*, the chosen followers of a warlord.

Lines 25–41

The Vikings have previously sailed up the River Pante, or Blackwater, and landed on the Island of Northey, directly opposite the English army on the mainland. This means that the two armies are unable to join battle, but can communicate with each other by shouting across the river. The next section of the poem is a dialogue between a Viking messenger standing on one bank of the river, and Byrhtnoth on the opposite bank.

- Which poetic device is prominently represented in lines 25–27?
- Which group of people sent the messenger (29b)?
- What were the Vikings prepared to establish in exchange for gold (35)?
- In 41b, the masculine noun *friþ* 'peace' is the Direct Object of the

verb *healdan* 'to keep'. Which grammatical case would you expect it to be in? Which case is actually represented by the form *friþes*?

Þā stōd on stæðe,	stīðlīce clypode 25
wīcinga ār,	wordum mælde,
sē on bēot ābēad	brim-līþendra
ærænde tō þām eorle,	þǣr hē on ōfre stōd:
'Mē sendon tō þē	sǣ-men snelle,
hēton ðē secgan	þæt þū mōst sendan raðe 30
bēagas wið gebeorge;	and ēow betere is
þæt gē þisne gār-rǣs	mid gafole forgyldon,
þon wē swā hearde	hilde dǣlon.
Ne þurfe wē ūs spillan,	gif gē spēdaþ tō þām;
wē willað wið þām golde	grið fæstnian. 35
Gyf þū þæt gerǣdest	þe hēr rīcost eart,
þæt þū þīne lēoda	lȳsan wille,
syllan sǣ-mannum	on hyra sylfra dōm
feoh wið frēode,	and niman frið æt ūs,
wē willaþ mid þām sceattum	ūs tō scype gangan, 40
on flot fēran,	and ēow friþes healdan.'

25 *stæðe* shore; *stīðlīce* harshly; *clypode* called
26 *ār* messenger
27 *on bēot* threateningly; *ābēad* announced; *brim-līþendra* of the seafarers
29 *snelle* bold
30 *mōst* must; *raðe* quickly
31 *bēagas* rings; *gebeorge* defence
32 *gafole* tribute; *forgyldon* buy off
33 *þon* than; *dǣlon* deal out
34 *þurfe* need; *ūs* each other; *spillan* destroy; *spēdaþ* prosper; *tō þām* sufficiently
35 *grið* truce; *fæstnian* establish
36 *gerǣdest* decide; *rīcost* most powerful
37 *lēoda* people; *lȳsan* to ransom
38 *syllan* to give; *on hyra sylfra dōm* according to their own judgement
39 *feoh* property; *frēode* peace; *niman* to accept; *frið* peace
40 *sceattum* tributes
41 *flot* sea; *fēran* to go; *friþes* peace; *healdan* to keep

Discussion

The Viking messenger's speech is given a big build up through the use of variation, the poetic device whereby a single idea is expressed more than once. The phrases *stīðlīce clypode* 'harshly called out' (25b), *wordum mælde* 'spoke with words' (26b) and *on bēot ābēad* 'threateningly announced' (27a) all have the same basic meaning, so they heighten the dramatic tension without advancing the narrative. 'Bold sailors' (29b) have sent the messenger to demand tribute as the price of peace. Attempting to unnerve the English army by implying that they cannot defeat the Vikings, he offers to 'establish a truce in exchange for the gold' (35), after which the invaders 'are willing to embark with the tributes, to sail away and keep peace with you' (40–41).

The dialogue preceding the battle belongs to a literary tradition known as 'flyting'. Flyting is a verbal contest, a battle of wits rather than of physical strength, and is a common motif in heroic literature. The flyting match in *The Battle of Maldon* may also represent the earliest use of literary dialect in English. The messenger is a Scandinavian, and several aspects of his speech suggest Scandinavianisms rather than standard Old English. The compound *gār-rǣs* 'spear-attack, battle' (32a) and the phrase *hilde dǣlon* 'deal out battle' (33b) are unrecorded elsewhere in Old English, but have equivalents in Old Norse. The usual Old English word for 'than' is *þonne* (as in 195b and 213a), so *þon* (33a) may be intended as an imperfect translation of Old Norse *þan*. The phrase *gif gē spēdaþ tō þām* 'if you prosper sufficiently' (34b) sounds awkward and may suggest a lack of fluency, while *grið* 'truce' (35b) is a Scandinavian loanword not previously recorded in Old English. Finally, it is unclear why *friþes* 'peace' (41b) is in the Genitive case (identified by the *-es* inflexion) rather than the Accusative normally used for Direct Objects. Perhaps the poet intended to portray a non-native speaker having trouble with his inflexional endings.

Lines 42–61

The second half of the flyting match is Byrhtnoth's reply to the Vikings' threats, in which he refutes their claims of superiority and emphasises the determination of the English army to fight and win.

- Can you identify two poetic devices in lines 42–44?
- What were the English willing to give as tribute (46–48)?
- What religion were the Vikings (55a)?
- Can you find any parallels between the two speeches in the flyting match?

Byrhtnōð maþelode,   bord hafenode,
wand wācne æsc,   wordum mælde,
yrre and ānræd   āgeaf him andsware:
'Gehȳrst þū, sǣ-lida,   hwæt þis folc segeð?   45
Hī willað ēow tō gafole   gāras syllan,
ǣttrynne ord   and ealde swurd,
þā here-geatu   þe ēow æt hilde ne dēah.
Brim-manna boda,   ābēod eft ongēan,
sege þīnum lēodum   miccle lāþre spell,   50
þæt hēr stynt unforcūð   eorl mid his werode,
þe wile gealgean   ēþel þysne,
Æþelrēdes eard,   ealdres mīnes,
folc and foldan.   Feallan sceolon
hǣþene æt hilde.   Tō hēanlic mē þinceð   55
þæt gē mid ūrum sceattum   tō scype gangon
unbefohtene,   nū gē þus feor hider
on ūrne eard   in becōmon.
Ne sceole gē swā sōfte   sinc gegangan;
ūs sceal ord and ecg   ǣr gesē man,   60
grim gūð-plega,   ǣr wē gofol syllon.'

42 *maþelode* spoke; *hafenode* raised
43 *wand* brandished; *wācne* slender
44 *ānræd* resolute
45 *Gehȳrst* hear; *sǣ-lida* sailor; *segeð* says
46 *tō gafole* as tribute; *syllan* to give
47 *ǣttrynne* deadly
48 *here-geatu* armour; *dēah* avail
49 *Brim-manna* of the sailors; *boda* messenger; *ābēod* announce; *eft ongēan* in reply
50 *sege* say; *lēodum* people
51 *stynt* stands; *unforcūð* honourable
52 *gealgean* defend; *ēþel* homeland
55 *hēanlic* humiliating; *mē þinceð* it seems to me
56 *sceattum* tributes
57 *unbefohtene* unopposed
58 *becōmon* have come
59 *sōfte* easily; *sinc* treasure; *gegangan* obtain
60 *gesē man* arbitrate between
61 *gofol* tribute; *syllon* pay

Discussion

Again the speech is introduced through variation, with *maþelode* 'spoke' (42a), *wordum mælde* 'spoke with words' (43b) and *āgeaf him andsware* 'gave him answer' (44b) all expressing the same idea. Comparison with 26b shows that *wordum mælde* is a formula. (It will appear again in 210b.) Byrhtnoth's reply to the Vikings is laced with irony. Since they have demanded tribute, he declares that his people will pay it, but in the form of deadly weapons: 'they are willing to give you spears as tribute, deadly spear and old swords, armour that will not avail you in battle' (46–48). In 48a, *here-geatu* is doubly ironic, for as well as meaning 'armour' this was also a tax, a tribute paid to an Anglo-Saxon lord on the death of a tenant.

Variation appears again in 52–54a, with Byrhtnoth's statement that he 'intends to defend this homeland, the homeland of Æthelred, my lord's people and land'. The three references to homeland (*ēþel, eard* and *foldan*) emphasise the theme of patriotism which is prominent throughout the poem, and the reference to the king, Æthelred II (968–1016), may serve the same purpose. The alliterative emphasis on *hǣþene* (55a) – 'the heathens must fall in battle' – reinforces the contrast between the Christian English and the pagan Vikings.

There are many verbal echoes between the two speeches, where Byrhtnoth is playing on words used by his Viking opponent. In line 32, the messenger associated battle with tribute through the alliteration of *gār-rǣs* and *gafole*. Byrhtnoth picks this up in line 46 but reverses both the order and the meaning: *gafole gāras*. In line 40, the messenger said, 'we are willing to go with the tributes', but Byrhtnoth changes this into a subjunctive form to make it more hypothetical: 'It seems to me too humiliating that you should go with our tributes' (56). Finally, in lines 59–61, he says: 'You must not obtain treasure so easily: first spear and sword' (literally 'point and edge') 'must arbitrate between us, fierce battle, before we pay tribute'. Here his *swā softe* 'so easily' (59a) echoes the Viking's *swā hearde* 'so fiercely' (33a), again reversing the effect of his opponent's speech. Byrhtnoth's display of verbal dexterity leaves him the clear winner of the flyting match, despite his lack of success in the subsequent battle.

Lines 62–71

The Pante is a tidal river, cutting off the Island of Northey from the mainland at high tide. Both armies have to wait for the tide to go out before they can join battle.

- Where did Byrhtnoth order his men to stand?
- Did the time seem long or short until they could join battle?

• What type of weapon could be used at this point?

Hēt þā bord beran,	beornas gangan,
þæt hī on þām ēa-steðe	ealle stōdon.
Ne mihte þǣr for wætere	werod tō þām ōðrum:
þǣr cōm flōwende	flōd æfter ebban; 65
lucon lagu-strēamas.	Tō lang hit him þūhte,
hwænne hī tōgædere	gāras bēron.
Hī þǣr Pantan strēam	mid prasse be-stōdon,
Ēast-Seaxena ord	and se æsc-here;
ne mihte hyra ǣnig	ōþrum derian, 70
būton hwā þurh flānes flyht	fyl genāme.

63   *ēa-steðe* river-bank
65   *flōd* flood-tide; *ebban* ebb-tide
66   *lucon* joined; *lagu-strēamas* tidal waters; *þūhte* seemed
67   *hwænne* until
68   *prasse* proud array; *be-stōdon* stood around
69   *ord* vanguard; *æsc-here* naval force
70   *derian* injure
71   *būton* unless; *flānes* arrow's; *fyl* death; *genāme* received

Discussion

The river plays a crucial part in the poem, preventing the armies from meeting until low tide. In the meantime, Byrhtnoth ordered his men to stand on the river-bank (62–63). Neither side could get to the other because of the water, and they grew impatient: 'it seemed too long to them, until they could bear spears together against each other' (66b–67). With both armies lining the River Pante, neither was able to injure the other, unless someone received death through the flight of an arrow (70–71).

Lines 72–83

At low tide, the Island of Northey is linked to the mainland by a raised causeway, referred to in the poem by the term *bricg*. The following lines describe what happened when the tide went out, making it possible for the Vikings to cross to the mainland.

• Were the Vikings eager for battle or reluctant?

- Name the three English warriors responsible for defending the causeway.
- What weapon did Wulfstan use to kill the first Viking who stepped onto the causeway?

Se flōd ūt gewāt.	Þā flotan stōdon gearowe,
wīcinga fela,	wīges georne.
Hēt þā hæleða hlēo	healdan þā bricge
wigan wīg-heardne,	sē wæs hāten Wulfstān, 75
cāfne mid his cynne:	þæt wæs Cēolan sunu,
þe þone forman man	mid his francan ofscēat
þe þær baldlīcost	on þā bricge stōp.
þær stōdon mid Wulfstāne	wigan unforhte,
Ælfere and Maccus,	mōdige twēgen, 80
þā noldon æt þām forda	flēam gewyrcan,
ac hī fæstlīce	wið ðā fȳnd weredon,
þā hwīle þe hī wæpna	wealdan mōston.

72 *flōd* flood-tide; *gewāt* went; *flotan* sailors; *gearowe* ready
73 *wīges* for battle
74 *hlēo* protector
75 *wīg-heardne* battle-hard; *hāten* named
76 *cāfne* brave; *cynne* family
77 *forman* first; *francan* spear; *ofscēat* killed
78 *stōp* stepped
79 *unforhte* unafraid
81 *þā* who; *flēam gewyrcan* take flight
82 *hī* themselves; *weredon* defended
83 *þā hwīle þe* as long as; *mōston* were able

Discussion

As the tide went out, the Vikings stood ready, eager for battle (72–73). The English army was now in a good position. They could stop the Vikings from reaching the mainland by picking them off as they filed over the narrow causeway. Byrhtnoth ordered an experienced ('battle-hard') warrior called Wulfstan to hold the causeway (74–75). He killed with his spear the first Viking to step onto it (77–78). Two brave warriors, Ælfere and Maccus, stood with Wulfstan (79–80): they would not take flight from the ford, but resolutely defended themselves against the enemy as long as they were able to wield weapons (81–83).

Lines 84–95

Realising that they are at a disadvantage, the Vikings ask for safe passage to the mainland to join battle.

- Did Byrhtnoth agree to the Vikings' request or not?
- What reason does the poet give for his decision?
- What type of phrase is *Byrhtelmes bearn* (92a)?
- According to Byrhtnoth, who alone knew who would win the battle (lit. be allowed to control the battlefield)?

Þā hī þæt ongēaton	and georne gesāwon	
þæt hī þǣr bricg-weardas	bitere fundon,	85
ongunnon lytegian þā	lāðe gystas:	
bǣdon þæt hī ūp-gangan	āgan mōston,	
ofer þone ford faran,	fēþan lǣdan.	
Ðā se eorl ongan	for his ofer-mōde	
ālȳfan landes tō fela	lāþere ðēode.	90
Ongan ceallian þā	ofer cald wæter	
Byrhtelmes bearn	(beornas gehlyston):	
'Nū ēow is gerȳmed.	Gāð ricene tō ūs,	
guman tō gūþe.	God āna wāt	
hwā þǣre wæl-stōwe	wealdan mōte.'	95

84 *ongēaton* perceived
85 *bricg-weardas* causeway-defenders; *bitere* fierce
86 *lytegian* to bargain; *gystas* strangers (lit. guests)
87 *ūp-gangan* passage (to land); *āgan* have
88 *faran* to go; *fēþan* foot solders
89 *ofer-mōde* pride, over-confidence
90 *ālȳfan* to allow; *ðēode* people
91 *ceallian* to call
92 *gehlyston* listened
93 *gerȳmed* granted passage; *gāð* go; *ricene* quickly
94 *wāt* knows
95 *wæl-stōwe* battle-field; *wealdan* to control

Discussion

In lines 89–90, the poet states that Byrhtnoth 'began to allow too much land to the hateful people because of his *ofer-mōde*'. The compound *ofer-mōd* (here inflected for Dative case) usually means 'pride', and it has been taken to indicate that Byrhtnoth was to blame for a serious error of judgement. However, some scholars consider an alternative translation 'over-confidence' to be more consistent with his presentation elsewhere in the poem, and with the Christian humility (rather than sinful pride) of his comment, 'God alone knows who may be allowed to control the battlefield' (84b–95). With hindsight, Byrhtnoth's decision led to the defeat of the English army; but this may have seemed the best chance to confront the Vikings rather than leaving them to sail off and attack an undefended part of the English coast. Possibly Byrhtnoth's action is to be seen as rash but heroic, like that of Cynewulf in leaving the protection of the doorway in order to rush out at Cyneheard in the 757 *Chronicle* annal.

Byrhtnoth is not referred to by name in this passage. Instead the heroic term *eorl* 'nobleman' (89a) is used, with the formula *Byrhtelmes bearn* 'Byrhtelm's son' (92a) emphasising his family connections.

Lines 96–105

The Vikings now cross the causeway to the mainland.

- What type of compound is *wæl-wulfas* (96a)?
- What is the effect of the variation in lines 96–99?
- What is the effect of the alliteration in line 101?
- What was Byrhtnoth's battle strategy?

Wōdon þā wæl-wulfas,	for wætere ne murnon,
wīcinga werod,	west ofer Pantan,
ofer scīr wæter	scyldas wēgon,
lid-men tō lande	linde bǣron.
Þǣr ongēan gramum	gearowe stōdon 100
Byrhtnōð mid beornum.	Hē mid bordum hēt
wyrcan þone wī-hagan,	and þæt werod healdan
fæste wið fēondum.	Þā wæs feohte nēh,
tīr æt getohte:	wæs sēo tīd cumen
þæt þǣr fæge men	feallan sceoldon. 105

96   *Wōdon* advanced; *wæl-wulfas* slaughter-wolves; *murnon* cared
98   *scīr* shining; *wēgon* carried
99   *lid-men* sailors; *linde* shields
100 *ongēan* against; *gramum* fierce ones; *gearowe* ready
102 *wyrcan* to make; *wī-hagan* shield-wall
104 *tīr* glory; *getohte* battle
105 *þæt* when; *fæge* doomed

Discussion

This is one of the most atmospheric passages of the poem. The term *wæl-wulfas*, literally 'slaughter-wolves' (96a), is an effective kenning (or metaphor) for the Vikings, and the use of variation in 96–99 gives a sense of inexorable advance. The Vikings are referred to three times (96a, *wæl-wulfas* 'slaughter-wolves'; 97a, *wīcinga werod* 'troop of Vikings'; 99a, *lid-men* 'sailors'), and the poet says twice that they came across the water (97b, *west ofer Pantan* 'west over the Pante'; 98a, *ofer scīr wæter* 'across the shining water'), and twice that they carried shields (98b, *scyldas wēgon* 'carried shields'; 99b, *linde bǣron* 'carried shields'). The sense of relentless progress is heightened by the alliteration, with three consecutive lines (95–97) alliterating on /w/, followed by sibilants and liquids in 98–99. This advance is abruptly halted by the harsh /b/ sounds of *Byrhtnōð, beornum* and *bordum* (101), as Byrhtnoth instructed his men to form a wall with their shields, and to hold it firmly against the enemies. This strategy depended on everyone working together. If the shield-wall was broken, the English defence would collapse; and hence the defection of the cowards later in the poem would have devastating results.

Lines 106–129

Now battle commences, with slaughter on both sides.

- What types of birds were circling round?
- Who was the first named member of the English army to be killed?
- What relation was he to Byrhtnoth?
- Who avenged him?

Þær wearð hrēam āhafen.   Hremmas wundon,
earn æses georn.   Wæs on eorþan cyrm.
Hī lēton þā of folman   fēol-hearde speru,
grimme gegrundene   gāras flēogan.
Bogan wæron bysige,   bord ord onfēng.   110
Biter wæs se beadu-rǣs.   Beornas fēollon
on gehwæðere hand,   hyssas lāgon.
Wund wearð Wulfmær,   wæl-ræste gecēas,
Byrhtnōðes mǣg;   hē mid billum wearð,
his swuster-sunu,   swīðe forhēawen.   115

Þær wærð wīcingum	wiþer-lēan āgyfen:
gehȳrde ic þæt Ēadweard	ānne slōge
swīðe mid his swurde,	swenges ne wyrnde,
þæt him æt fōtum fēoll	fǣge cempa.
Þæs him his ðēoden	þanc gesǣde, 120
þām būr-þēne,	þā hē byre hæfde.
Swā stemnetton	stīð-hicgende
hysas æt hilde,	hogodon georne
hwā þær mid orde	ǣrost mihte
on fǣgean men	feorh gewinnan, 125
wigan mid wǣpnum.	Wæl fēol on eorðan.
Stōdon stæde-fæste.	Stihte hī Byrhtnōð,
bæd þæt hyssa gehwylc	hogode tō wīge
þe on Denon wolde	dōm gefeohtan.

106 *hrēam* uproar; *āhafen* raised; *Hremmas* ravens; *wundon* circled round
107 *earn* eagle; *æses* carrion; *cyrm* uproar
108 *fēol-hearde* file-hard
109 *grimme* cruelly; *gegrundene* sharpened
110 *ord* spear; *onfēng* received
111 *biter* fierce
112 *gehwæðere* either; *hyssas* warriors
113 *wæl-ræste* death in battle; *gecēas* chose
114 *billum* swords
115 *swīðe* fiercely; *forhēawen* cut down
116 *wiþer-lēan* requital; *āgyfen* given
117 *gehȳrde* heard; *slōge* struck
118 *swīðe* fiercely; *swenges* blow; *wyrnde* withheld
119 *fǣge* doomed; *cempa* warrior
120 *þæs* for that
121 *būr-þēne* chamberlain; *byre* opportunity
122 *stemnetton* stood firm; *stīð-hicgende* stout-hearted
123 *hysas* warriors; *hogodon* were intent
125 *on* from; *fǣgean* doomed; *men* man; *gewinnan* take
126 *Wæl* the slain
127 *Stihte* encouraged
128 *hyssa gehwylc* each of the warriors; *hogode* should be intent
129 *dōm* glory; *gefeohtan* to win

Discussion

Birds of battle are a recurrent motif in Old English poetry, gathering to feast on the corpses of the slain. The ravens (106b) and eagle (107a) are often accompanied by a wolf, represented here by the earlier description of the Vikings as *wæl-wulfas* 'slaughter-wolves' (96a). The formulaic echo of line 7 in the phrase *Hī lēton . . . of folman . . . flēogan* 'they let fly from their hands' (108–109) also reminds us of the hawk let fly by the unnamed young man at the beginning of the surviving poem; but here the sport has been replaced by deadly battle.

The scene is at first one of generalised combat – spears flew, bows were busy, shield received shaft, men fell dead on both sides – before the focus turns to two individual members of the English army. Wulfmær, Byrhtnoth's nephew, was fiercely cut down with swords (113–115), and Edward, the chamberlain, avenged him by killing a Viking (116–119). Byrhtnoth thanked him for that (120), and encouraged each of the warriors to be intent on battle who wished to win glory against the Danes (127b–129).

Lines 130–148

Byrhtnoth himself is in the thick of the fighting, again identified not by name but as *beorn* 'warrior' (131b), *eorl* 'nobleman' (132b, 146b), *wigena hláford* 'lord of warriors' (135b), *se gūð-rinc* 'the warrior' (138a), *fyrd-rinc* 'warrior' (140a) and *mōdi man* 'brave man' (147a).

- What type of weapon was Byrhtnoth wounded by?
- What did Byrhtnoth do with it?
- What did he do next?
- Whom did Byrhtnoth thank for the day's work?

Wōd þā wīges heard,	wǣpen ūp āhōf,	130
bord tō gebeorge,	and wið þæs beornes stōp.	
Ēode swā ānrǣd	eorl tō þām ceorle:	
ǣgþer hyra ōðrum	yfeles hogode.	
Sende ðā se sǣ-rinc	sūþerne gār,	
þæt gewundod wearð	wigena hláford.	135
Hē scēaf þā mid ðām scylde,	þæt se sceaft tō-bærst,	
and þæt spere sprengde,	þæt hit sprang ongēan.	
Gegremod wearð se gūð-rinc:	hē mid gāre stang	
wlancne wīcing,	þe him þā wunde forgeaf.	
Frōd wæs se fyrd-rinc:	hē lēt his francan wadan	140
þurh ðæs hysses hals;	hand wīsode	
þæt hē on þām fǣr-sceaðan	feorh gerǣhte.	
Ðā hē ōþerne	ofstlīce scēat,	
þæt sēo byrne tō-bærst:	hē wæs on brēostum wund	
þurh ðā hring-locan;	him æt heortan stōd	145
ǣtterne ord.	Se eorl wæs þē blīþra:	

hlōh þā mōdi man,   sǣde Metode þanc
ðæs dæg-weorces   þe him Drihten forgeaf.

130   *wōd* advanced; *wīges heard* one fierce in battle (i.e. a Viking); *āhōf* raised
131   *tō gebeorge* in defence
132   *ānrǣd* resolute
133   *yfeles hogode* intent on harm
136   *scēaf* thrust, *tō-bærst* shattered
137   *sprengde* broke; *ongēan* back
138   *gegremod* enraged; *stang* stabbed
139   *wlancne* proud; *forgeaf* gave
140   *francan* spear; *wadan* go
141   *hysses* warrior's; *wīsode* guided
142   *fǣr-sceaðan* enemy; *gerǣhte* wounded
143   *ofstlīce* quickly; *scēat* shot
144   *byrne* corselet; *tō-bærst* shattered
145   *hring-locan* corselet of ringmail
146   *ætterne* deadly; *þē blīþra* the more pleased
147   *hlōh* laughed
148   *forgeaf* gave

Discussion

A Viking advanced towards Byrhtnoth, and wounded him with a 'southern spear' (134b): possibly a spear thrown from the south, but more probably one of southern make. Byrhtnoth's courage and fighting skills are displayed as he thrust with his shield in such a way that the shaft shattered and the spear broke and sprang back (136–137). Enraged, Byrhtnoth then used his own spear to stab the Viking who gave him the wound (138–139). Then he quickly shot another Viking, so that his corselet shattered and the deadly spear stood at his heart (143–146a). Byrhtnoth was the more pleased: he laughed, and thanked God for the day's work that the Lord had given him (146b–148).

Lines 149–171

So far, the two armies appear to be fairly evenly matched, and neither side has the advantage. The turning point comes with Byrhtnoth's death at the hands of at least three Vikings.

- What did the first Viking throw at Byrhtnoth?
- Who threw it back?
- Why did another Viking approach Byrhtnoth?

- What did Byrhtnoth do to defend himself?
- Why did Byrhtnoth drop his sword?
- What could Byrhtnoth no longer do?

Forlēt þā drenga sum
flēogan of folman,
þurh ðone æþelan
Him be healfe stōd
cniht on gecampe,
brǣd of þām beorne
Wulfstānes bearn,
forlēt forheardne
Ord in gewōd,
þe his þēoden ǣr
Ēode þā gesyrwed
hē wolde þæs beornes
rēaf and hringas
Þā Byrhtnōð brǣd
brād and brūn-eccg,
Tō raþe hine gelette
þā hē þæs eorles
Fēoll þā tō foldan
ne mihte hē gehealdan
wǣpnes wealdan.
hār hilde-rinc,
bǣd gangan forð
Ne mihte þā on fōtum leng

daroð of handa,
þæt sē tō forð gewāt   150
Æþelrēdes þegen.
hyse unweaxen,
sē full cāflīce
blōdigne gār,
Wulfmǣr se geonga;   155
faran eft ongēan.
þæt sē on eorþan læg
þearle gerǣhte.
secg tō þām eorle;
bēagas gefecgan,   160
and gerēnod swurd.
bill of scēðe,
and on þā byrnan slōh.
lid-manna sum,
earm āmyrde.   165
fealo-hilte swurd;
heardne mēce,
Þā gȳt þæt word gecwæð
hyssas bylde,
gōde gefēran.   170
fæste gestandan.

149 *Forlēt* let; *drenga sum* one of the warriors; *daroð* spear
150 *forð* deeply; *gewāt* went
152 *healfe* side; *hyse* warrior; *unweaxen* not fully grown
153 *cniht* youth; *on gecampe* in battle; *cāflīce* quickly
154 *brǣd* pulled
156 *forlēt* let; *forheardne* very hard (thing); *faran* go; *eft ongēan* back again
157 *gewōd* went
158 *þearle* severely; *gerǣhte* wounded
159 *gesyrwed* armed; *secg* warrior
160 *bēagas* rings; *gefecgan* to carry off
161 *rēaf* armour; *gerēnod* ornamented
162 *brǣd* drew; *bill* sword
163 *brūn-eccg* bright-edged; *byrnan* corselet; *slōh* struck
164 *raþe* quickly; *gelette* prevented; *lid-manna sum* one of the sailors
165 *āmyrde* injured
166 *fealo-hilte* yellow-hilted
167 *mēce* sword

168   *þā gȳt* still
169   *hār* hoary (i.e. grey-haired); *hyssas* warriors; *bylde* encouraged
171   *leng* longer

Discussion

A Viking threw a spear which wounded Byrhtnoth but was then thrown back by a youth standing by his side (Wulfmær the young, son of Wulfstan), with sufficient force to kill the Viking himself (149–158). A second Viking then approached Byrhtnoth to steal his weapons and armour (159–161). Byrhtnoth drew his sword to defend himself and struck him on the corselet (162–163), but a third Viking disabled his arm (164–165), so that the sword fell to the ground (166) with Byrhtnoth unable to hold it (167–168a). Byrhtnoth still continued to encourage his men (168b–170), even though he was no longer able to stand firmly on his feet (171). His behaviour was clearly heroic: also prominent are the themes of loyalty, reflected in Wulfmær's behaviour, and of patriotism, reflected in the description of Byrhtnoth as 'the noble retainer of Æthelred' (151).

Lines 172–184

Byrhtnoth's dying speech takes the form of a prayer, reinforcing the theme of religion which runs through the poem.

- What did Byrhtnoth thank God for?
- What did he request?
- How does the poet describe the Vikings who cut Byrhtnoth down?
- Name the two members of the English army who were standing next to Byrhtnoth and were cut down with him.
- Can you identify two lines within this passage that do not conform to the standard conventions of Old English poetry?

Hē tō heofenum wlāt:
'Ic geþancie þē,   ðē oda Waldend,
ealra þǣra wynna   þe ic on worulde gebād.
Nū ic āh, milde Metod,   mǣste þearfe   175
þæt þū mīnum gāste   gōdes geunne,
þæt mīn sāwul tō ðē   sīðian mōte
on þīn geweald,   þē oden engla,

mid friþe ferian.
þæt hī hel-scēaðan
Ðā hine hē owon
and bē gen þā beornas
Ælfnōð and Wulmǣr
ðā onemn hyra frēan

Ic eom frymdi tō þē
hȳnan ne mōton.'   180
hǣðene scealcas
þe him big stōdon,
bē gen lāgon,
feorh gesealdon.

172 *wlāt* looked
173 *ðēoda* of nations
174 *wynna* joys; *gebād* experienced
175 *āh* have; *milde* gracious; *þearfe* need
176 *gōdes geunne* should grant grace
177 *sīðian* to travel
178 *geweald* power
179 *friþe* protection; *ferian* travel; *ic eom frymdi tō þē* I entreat you
180 *hī* it (i.e. the soul); *hel-scēaðan* devils; *hȳnan* to injure
181 *hēowon* cut down; *scealcas* warriors
184 *onemn* alongside; *gesealdon* gave up

Discussion

The idea of a supernatural struggle between angels and devils for a dying person's soul is a common theme in early writings, and some critics believe that its effect here is to elevate Byrhtnoth to the status of martyr or saint. He begins by thanking God for all the joys that he has experienced in the world (173–174), goes on to express a need that God will grant grace to his spirit (175–176), so that his soul may journey to God in peace (177–179a), and concludes by asking that devils may not be allowed to injure it (179b–180). Significantly, the Vikings who cut him down are described as *hæðene scealcas* 'heathen warriors' (181b), with emphasis on *hæðene* as the headstave of the line.

The only surviving manuscript of *The Battle of Maldon* was destroyed in the same fire that damaged the *Beowulf* manuscript. A transcript which had been made a few years earlier is the basis for all modern editions. Inevitably, it contains errors, some of which may already have been present in the manuscript itself. Here line 172 comprises a single half-line, indicating that the b-verse has probably been lost. Line 183 has no alliteration, possibly because the copyist has mistakenly repeated the word *bēgen* 'both' from the preceding line. The headstave of line 183 should alliterate with the name of one of the warriors who were killed with Byrthnoth: Ælfnoth or Wulmær.

Lines 185–201

The immediate result of Byrhtnoth's death is that some cowardly members of the English army run away.

- Which of Odda's sons left the battlefield on Byrhtnoth's horse?
- What were the names of his brothers who fled with him?
- Who had warned Byrhtnoth at the council meeting earlier in the day that many there spoke boldly who would not hold out in time of need?

Hī bugon þā fram beaduwe	þe þǣr bēon noldon.	185
Þǣr wurdon Oddan bearn	ǣrest on flēame.	
Godrīc fram gūþe,	and þone gōdan forlēt	
þe him mænigne oft	mēarh gesealde.	
Hē gehlēop þone eoh	þe āhte his hlāford,	
on þām gerǣdum	þe hit riht ne wæs,	190
and his brōðru mid him	bēgen ǣr-ðon,	
Godwine and Godwīg,	gūþe ne gȳmdon,	
ac wendon fram þām wīge	and þone wudu sōhton,	
flugon on þæt fæsten	and hyra fēore burgon,	
and manna mā	þonne hit ǣnig mǣð wǣre,	195
gyf hī þā geearnunga	ealle gemundon	
þe hē him tō duguþe	gedōn hæfde.	
Swā him Offa on dæg	ǣr āsæde	
on þām meþel-stede,	þā hē gemōt hæfde,	
þæt þǣr mōdelīce	manega sprǣcon	200
þe eft æt þearfe	þolian noldon.	

185 *bugon* fled
186 *flēame* flight
187 *forlēt* abandoned
188 *mēarh* horse; *gesealde* gave
189 *gehlēop* leaped upon; *eoh* horse; *āhte* owned
190 *gerǣdum* trappings
192 *gȳmdon* cared about
193 *wendon* turned
194 *flugon* fled; *fæsten* place of safety; *burgon* saved
195 *manna mā* more men; *þonne hit ǣnig mǣð wǣre* than was at all fitting
196 *geearnunga* favours; *gemundon* remembered
197 *him tō duguþe* for their benefit
199 *meþel-stede* meeting-place; *gemōt* council
200 *mōdelīce* boldly
201 *eft* afterwards; *þearfe* (time of) need; *þolian* hold out

Discussion

The first to leave the battlefield were Odda's sons Godric, Godwine and Godwig. Godric's action had particularly serious consequences, since he took Byrhtnoth's horse, causing confusion among the English ranks. His treachery is underlined by the poet's comment that he 'left the good man who had often given him many a horse' (187b–188). This is dramatically effective but not literally true, as the giving of horses to loyal retainers belongs in the legendary world of Germanic warrior society, not in the contemporary world of tenth-century England. Again it is part of the imagery through which the poet places the battle within the heroic tradition. The council meeting at which Offa had warned Byrhtnoth not to rely on the bold speeches made by some of his men (198–201) may have been described in the lost opening of the poem.

Lines 202–229

Weakened by the flight of the cowards and the resulting collapse of the shield-wall formation, the English army now represents a small force hopelessly outnumbered by a larger one, as in the two battles described in the *Anglo-Saxon Chronicle* entry for 757. Like the followers of Cynewulf and Cyneheard, Byrhtnoth's men show total allegiance to their lord, resolving to avenge his death at the cost of their own lives rather than leave the battlefield on which he has been killed. They express their determination through a series of stirring speeches, the first of which is by Ælfric.

- Was Ælfric young or old?
- Was he of high or low birth?
- What were the names of his father and grandfather?
- Which part of England was he from?
- Why did he have a strong obligation to avenge Byrhtnoth?

Þā wearð āfeallen þæs folces ealdor,
Æþelrēdes eorl. Ealle gesāwon
heorð-genēatas þæt hyra heorra læg.
Þā ðǣr wendon forð wlance þegenas,   205
unearge men efston georne:
hī woldon þā ealle ōðer twēga,
līf forlǣtan oþðe lēofne gewrecan.

Swā hī bylde forð
wiga wintrum geong,
Ælfwine þā cwæð
'Gemunu þā mælaþe.
þonne wē on bence
hæleð on healle,
nū mæg cunnian
Ic wylle mīne æþelo
þæt ic wæs on Myrcon
wæs mīn ealda fæder
wīs ealdor-man,
Ne sceolon mē on þǣre þēode
þæt ic of ðisse fyrde
eard gesēcan,
forhēawen æt hilde.
hē wæs ǣgðer mīn mǣg
Þā hē forð ēode,
þæt hē mid orde
flotan on þām folce,
forwegen mid his wǣpne.
frȳnd and gefēran,

bearn Ælfrīces,
wordum mǣlde,   210
(hē on ellen sprǣc):
Wē oft æt meodo sprǣcon,
bēot āhōfon,
ymbe heard gewinn:
hwā cēne sȳ.   215
eallum gecȳþan,
miccles cynnes;
Ealhelm hāten,
woruld-gesǣlig.
þegenas æt-wītan   220
fēran wille,
nū mīn ealdor ligeð
Mē is þæt hearma mǣst:
and mīn hlāford.'
fǣhðe gemunde,   225
ānne gerǣhte
þæt sē on foldan læg
Ongan þā winas manian,
þæt hī forð ēodon.

204 *heorð-genēatas* retainers; *heorra* lord
205 *wendon* went; *wlance* proud
206 *unearge* undaunted; *efston* hastened
207 *ōðer twēga* one of two things
208 *forlǣtan* to give up; *gewrecan* to avenge
209 *bylde* encouraged
211 *on ellen* courageously
212 *Gemunu* I remember; *mǣlaþe* discourse; *æt meodo* over mead; *sprǣcon* spoke
213 *þonne* when; *āhōfon* raised
214 *ymbe* about; *gewinn* battle
215 *mæg cunnian hwā cēne sȳ* it is possible to test who is brave
216 *æþelo* lineage; *gecȳþan* make known
217 *Myrcon* Mercians; *miccles cynnes* of a great family
218 *ealda fæder* grandfather; *hāten* named
219 *woruld-gesǣlig* prosperous
220 *þēode* people; *æt-wītan* reproach
221 *fyrde* army; *fēran* to depart
223 *forhēawen* cut down; *hearma* grief
224 *ǣgðer* both
225 *fǣhðe gemunde* mindful of hostility
226 *gerǣhte* wounded
227 *flotan* sailor
228 *forwegen* killed; *winas* friends; *manian* encourage
229 *frȳnd* friends

Discussion

Again the term *heorð-genēatas*, literally 'hearth-companions' (204a), refers directly to a Germanic *comitatus*; and Ælfric's subsequent speech draws extensively on the heroic tradition used as the framework for the poem. He began by reminding his comrades of the vows they had made in earlier times: 'We often spoke over mead, when we raised vows on the bench, warriors in the hall, about fierce battle' (212b–214). Like the earlier allusion to Byrhtnoth giving horses to his followers, the references to mead-benches and vows are anachronistic, but form part of the poetic fiction of a warrior-society whose lives were focused on the mead-hall – as with the hall of Heorot in *Beowulf*. The importance of reputation within the heroic ethos is reflected in Ælfric's concern that 'the retainers among that people will not have to reproach me, that I am willing to depart from this army, seek my homeland, now that my lord lies dead, cut down in battle' (220–223a). He had an obligation to avenge Byrhtnoth, as 'both my kinsman and my lord' (224). As reflected in the *Chronicle* extract, the two strongest bonds in society were kinship and the relationship between lord and follower. Where the two were combined, through the lord being a member of the kin group, the tie was particularly strong.

Ælfwine was the son of Ælfric (209b) and grandson of Ealhelm (218). He is presented as young (210a), of noble birth (217b), and from Mercia (217a). Other members of the army will be described as old, of low birth, or from other areas of England. This seems to be a deliberate patterning, making them representative of all ages and ranks of English society. This in turn has implications for the historical accuracy of the account, as it seems unlikely that the army would actually have comprised such a cross-section of the population.

Lines 230–243

The next speech is by Offa, a senior member of the army and possibly Byrhtnoth's second in command.

- Which weapon did Offa brandish as he spoke?
- What was it necessary for them all to do now that their lord lay dead?
- Why did Godric's flight have such devastating consequences?

Offa gemǣlde,   æsc-holt āscēoc: 230
'Hwæt, þū, Ælfwine,   hafast ealle gemanode,
þegenas tō þearfe.   Nū ūre þēoden līð,
eorl on eorðan,   ūs is eallum þearf
þæt ūre ǣghwylc   ōþerne bylde,
wigan tō wīge,   þā hwīle þe hē wǣpen mæge   235
habban and healdan,   heardne mēce,
gār and gōd swurd.   Ūs Godrīc hæfð,
earh Oddan bearn,   ealle beswicene:
wēnde þæs formoni man,   þā hē on mēare rād,
on wlancan þām wicge,   þæt wǣre hit ūre hlāford;   240
for-þan wearð hēr on felda   folc tō-twǣmed,
scyld-burh tō-brocen.   Ābrēoðe his angin,
þæt hē hēr swā manigne   man āflȳmde.'

230 *æsc-holt* spear; *āscēoc* shook
231 *gemanode* encouraged
232 *tō þearfe* in (time of) need
233 *þearf* need
234 *ūre ǣghwylc* each of us; *bylde* should encourage
235 *þā hwīle þe* as long as; *mæge* is able to
236 *habban* have; *mēce* sword
237 *earh* cowardly; *beswicene* betrayed
239 *wēnde þæs formoni man* very many a man thought; *mēare* horse
240 *wlancan* proud; *wicge* steed
241 *for-þan* therefore; *tō-twǣmed* divided
242 *scyld-burh* shield-defence; *Ābrēoðe his angin* may his action fail
243 *āflȳmde* put to flight

Discussion

Offa brandished his spear (230) and commended Ælfric's speech (231–232a), declaring that now their lord lay dead, it was necessary for each of them to encourage the other to battle for as long as he was able to hold a weapon (232b–237a). He blamed Godric for betraying them all (237b–238): when he rode away on Byrhtnoth's horse, many men mistook him for Byrhtnoth himself, so that the army fell into disarray and the shield-wall was broken (239–242a).

Lines 244–259

The next two speeches are by Leofsunu and Dunnere.

• What did Leofsunu raise as he spoke?

- What vow did he make?
- What did Leofsunu and Dunnere have in common with Ælfwine?
- In what ways were they unlike him?

Lēofsunu gemǣlde,	and his linde āhōf,
bord tō gebeorge;	hē þām beorne on-cwæð: 245
'Ic þæt gehāte,	þæt ic heonon nelle
flēon fōtes trym,	ac wille furðor gān,
wrecan on gewinne	mīnne wine-drihten.
Ne þurfon mē embe Stūrmere	stede-fæste hælæð
wordum æt-wītan,	nū mīn wine gecranc, 250
þæt ic hlāford-lēas	hām sīðie,
wende fram wīge;	ac mē sceal wǣpen niman,
ord and īren.'	Hē ful yrre wōd,
feaht fæstlīce,	flēam hē forhogode.
Dunnere þā cwæð,	daroð ācwehte, 255
unorne ceorl,	ofer eall clypode,
bæd þæt beorna gehwylc	Byrhtnōð wrǣce:
'Ne mæg nā wandian	sē þe wrecan þenceð
frēan on folce,	ne for fēore murnan.'

244 *linde* shield; *āhōf* raised
245 *tō gebeorge* in defence; *on-cwæð* answered
246 *gehāte* vow; *heonon* from here; *nelle* do not intend
247 *flēon* to flee; *trym* length; *gān* to go
248 *wrecan* to avenge; *gewinne* battle
249 *þurfon* need; *embe* around
250 *æt-wītan* to reproach; *gecranc* fell in battle
251 *sīðie* should travel
252 *wende* turn; *niman* take
253 *īren* iron sword; *wōd* advanced
254 *fæstlīce* resolutely; *flēam* flight; *forhogode* scorned
255 *daroð* spear; *ācwehte* brandished
256 *unorne* simple; *clypode* called out
257 *gehwylc* each; *wrǣce* should avenge
258 *mæg* is able; *wandian* to draw back; *wrecan* to avenge; *þenceð* intends
259 *murnan* to care about

Discussion

Leofsunu raised his shield as he answered Offa (244–245), vowing that he would not flee the length of a foot, but intended to advance further, to avenge in battle his beloved lord (246–248). Like Ælfric, he was concerned with reputation: 'Steadfast warriors around Sturmer need not reproach me with words, now my friend has fallen in battle, that I lordless should travel home, should turn away from the battle, but a weapon must take me, spear and sword' (249–253a). Sturmer is a village in northern Essex, indicating that Leofsunu was from a different part of England from Ælfric; while the description of Dunnere as a 'simple peasant' (256a) identifies him as a member of the lower classes. The patterning mentioned above is very much in evidence here, presenting the members of the army as a microcosm of English society. All shared a determination to avenge Byrhtnoth.

Lines 260–272

The remaining members of the English army advance, regardless of their lives.

- Who eagerly began to help them in line 265?
- Where was he from?

Þā hī forð ēodon.	Fēores hī ne rōhton.	260
Ongunnon þā hīred-men	heardlīce feohtan,	
grame gār-berend,	and God bǣdon	
þæt hī mōston gewrecan	hyra wine-drihten	
and on hyra fēondum	fyl gewyrcan.	
Him se gȳsel ongan	geornlīce fylstan;	265
hē wæs on Norðhymbron	heardes cynnes,	
Ecglāfes bearn,	him wæs Æscferð nama.	
Hē ne wandode nā	æt þām wīg-plegan,	
ac hē fȳsde forð	flān genehe;	
hwīlon hē on bord scēat,	hwīlon beorn tǣsde,	270
æfre embe stunde	hē sealde sume wunde,	
þā hwīle ðe hē wæpna	wealdan mōste.	

260   *rōhton* cared about
261   *hīred-men* warriors
262   *grame* fierce; *gār-berend* spear-bearers
263   *gewrecan* to avenge
264   *fyl* death; *gewyrcan* bring about
265   *gȳsel* hostage; *fylstan* to help
266   *Norðhymbron* Northumbrians; *heardes cynnes* of a fierce family
268   *wandode* drew back
269   *fȳsde* shot; *flān* arrow; *genehe* frequently
270   *hwīlon* sometimes; *scēat* shot; *tǣsde* lacerated
271   *æfre embe stunde* repeatedly; *sealde* gave; *sume* a
272   *þā hwīle ðe* as long as

Discussion

As in the Cynewulf and Cyneheard episode, the army includes a hostage who fights no less loyally than the other men under Byrhtnoth's command. Again this shows the poet's policy of selecting representatives from different areas of England, as Æscferth was from Northumbria, the most northerly of the Anglo-Saxon kingdoms. There also seems to be deliberate patterning in the progression from men with the strongest motivation for loyalty to men with least. Ælfric, the first member of the army to declare his intention to avenge Byrhtnoth, had the greatest obligation to do so, as Byrhtnoth was both his kinsman and his lord. Offa, the next to speak, was a close friend of Byrhtnoth, perhaps his second in command. Leofsunu was an ordinary member of the army, while the peasant Dunnere and the hostage Æscferth had still less obligation to carry on fighting. The sequence of speeches appears to be organised to emphasise the theme of loyalty by showing how even the men with the least obligation towards Byrhtnoth were determined to die with him.

Lines 273–294

The catalogue of honour continues, as further members of the English army give their lives to avenge Byrhtnoth.

- Name three members of the English army who die in this section.
- Can you find any references to the heroic tradition?

> Þā gȳt on orde stōd
> gearo and geornful;
> þæt hē nolde flēogan
> ofer bæc būgan,
> Hē bræc þone bord-weall
> oð-þæt hē his sinc-gyfan
> wurðlīce wrec,
> Swā dyde Æþerīc,
> fūs and forð-georn,
> Sībyrhtes brōðor,
> clufon cellod bord,
> Bærst bordes lærig,
> gryre-lēoða sum.

> Ēadweard se langa,
> gylp-wordum spræc,
> fōt-mæl landes,   275
> þā his betera leg.
> and wið þā beornas feaht,
> on þām sǣ-mannum
> ǣr hē on wæle lǣge.
> æþele gefēra,   280
> feaht eornoste,
> and swīðe mænig ōþer
> cēne hī weredon.
> and sēo byrne sang
> Þā æt gūðe slōh   285

Offa þone sǣ-lidan,
and ðǣr Gaddes mǣg
Raðe wearð æt hilde
hē hæfde ðē ah geforþod
swā he bē otode ǣr
þæt hī sceoldon bē gen
hāle tō hāme,
on wæl-stōwe
Hē læg ðegenlīce

þæt hē on eorðan fē oll,
grund gesōhte.
Offa forhē awen:
þæt hē his frē an gehē t,
wið his bē ah-gifan   290
on burh rīdan,
oððe on here crincgan,
wundum sweltan.
ðē odne gehende.

273   þā gȳt still; orde vanguard; langa tall
274   gearo ready; gylp-wordum boasting words
275   fōt-mǣl foot-length
276   ofer bǣc away; būgan turn
277   brǣc broke
278   sinc-gyfan treasure-giver
279   wrec avenged; wæle the slain
281   fūs eager; eornoste zealously
282   swīðe very
283   clufon split; cellod decorated; cēne bravely; hī themeslves; weredon defended
284   bærst burst open; lærig rim; byrne corselet
285   gryre-lēoða terrible song; sum a; slōh struck
286   sǣ-lidan sailor
288   raðe quickly; forhēawen cut down
289   geforþod accomplished; gehēt promised
290   bēotode vowed; bēah-gifan ring-giver
291   on burh to the stronghold
292   hāle unhurt; here battle; crincgan fall in battle
293   wæl-stōwe battle-field; sweltan die
294   ðegenlīce as befits a retainer; gehende beside

Discussion

This section describes the deaths of Edward, Æþeric and Offa, placing them firmly within the heroic tradition through the use of vocabulary and imagery. The heroic boast is represented in the *gylp-wordum* 'boasting words' (274b) uttered by Edward, 'that he would not flee a foot's length of land, flee away, when his better lay dead' (275–276), and in the vow previously made by Offa, 'that they must both ride unhurt home to the fortification or die in battle, die with wounds on the battle-field' (291–293). Similarly, the compounds *sinc-gyfa* 'treasure-giver' (278a) and *bēah-gifa* 'ring-giver' (290b) applied to Byrhtnoth are conventional terms used of Germanic war-lords whose role included the distribution of treasure to their followers.

Lines 295–308

The Vikings advance, with yet more slaughter.

• Can you identify a kenning in line 297?
• How many Vikings did Wistan kill?
• Who was his father?
• What relation were Oswold and Eadwold to each other?

Ðā wearð borda gebræc.	Brim-men wōdon,	295
gūðe gegremode.	Gār oft þurh-wōd	
fǣges feorh-hūs.	Forð ðā ēode Wīstān,	
Þurstānes sunu,	wið þās secgas feaht.	
Hē wæs on geþrange	hyra þrēora bana,	
ǣr him Wīgelines bearn	on þām wæle lǣge.	300
Þǣr wæs stīð gemōt.	Stōdon fæste	
wigan on gewinne.	Wīgend cruncon,	
wundum wērige.	Wæl fēol on eorþan.	
Ōswold and Ēadwold	ealle hwīle,	
bēgen þā gebrōþru,	beornas trymedon,	305
hyra wine-māgas	wordon bǣdon	
þæt hī þǣr æt ðearfe	þolian sceoldon,	
unwāclīce	wǣpna nēotan.	

295 gebræc crash; brim-men sea-men; wōdon advanced
296 gegremode enraged; þurh-wōd went through
297 fǣges of a doomed (one); feorh-hūs body (lit. life-house)
298 secgas warriors
299 geþrange throng; þrēora of three; bana slayer
300 wæle slain (ones)
301 stīð fierce; gemōt encounter
302 gewinne battle; wīgend warriors; cruncon fell in battle
303 wæl the slain
304 ealle hwīle all the time
305 trymedon encouraged
306 wine-māgas dear kinsmen
307 ðearfe (time of) need; þolian persevere
308 unwāclīce boldly; nēotan make use of

Discussion

Wistan, the next to die, killed three Vikings before being killed himself (299–300). Oddly, he appears to be described as the son of both Thurstan (298a) and Wigelin (300a). It is uncertain whether there is a copying error at this point, or if Wigelin is the name of Wistan's mother despite the masculine Genitive singular -es inflexion. An alternative suggestion is that *bearn* (300a) may have the sense 'grandchild' rather than 'child'.

A recurrent theme in the second half of the poem is the encouragement given by members of the English army to each other, reflected here in the words spoken by the brothers Oswold and Eadwold. The compound *feorh-hūs* (297a) is a kenning, as the literal meaning 'life-house' functions as a condensed metaphor for the body.

Lines 309–325

The final speech of the surviving poem is by an old man called Byrhtwold.

* Where have you seen the same formula as in line 309?
* How is the device of variation used in Byrhtwold's speech?

Byrhtwold maþelode,	bord hafenode	
(sē wæs eald genēat),	æsc ācwehte;	310
hē ful baldlīce	beornas lǣrde:	
'Hige sceal þē heardra,	heorte þē cēnre,	
mōd sceal þē māre,	þē ūre mægen lȳtlað.	
Hēr līð ūre ealdor	eall forhēawen,	
gōd on grēote.	Ā mæg gnornian	315
sē ðe nū fram þis wīg-plegan	wendan þenceð.	
Ic eom frōd fēores.	Fram ic ne wille,	
ac ic mē be healfe	mīnum hlāforde,	
be swā lēofan men,	licgan þence.'	
Swā hī Æþelgāres bearn	ealle bylde,	320
Godrīc tō gūþe.	Oft hē gār forlēt,	
wæl-spere windan	on þā wīcingas,	
swā hē on þām folce	fyrmest ēode,	
hēow and hȳnde,	oð-þæt hē on hilde gecranc.	
Næs þæt nā se Godrīc	þe ðā gūðe forbēah. . . .	325

309   *maþelode* spoke; *hafenode* raised
310   *genēat* retainer; *ācwehte* brandished
311   *lǣrde* exhorted
312   *hige* mind; *cēnre* braver
313   *mōd* courage; *māre* greater; *mægen* strength; *lȳtlað* diminishes
314   *forhēawen* cut down

315 *grēote* dust; *Ā* for ever; *mæg gnornian* will be able to mourn
316 *wendan* to go; *penceð* intends
318 *healfe* side
319 *men* man; *pence* intend
320 *bylde* encouraged
321 *forlēt* let go
322 *wæl-spere* deadly spear; *windan* to fly
323 *fyrmest* foremost
324 *hēow* killed; *hȳnde* injured; *gecranc* fell in battle
325 *forbēah* fled from

Discussion

Line 309 repeats line 42, substituting Byrhtwold for Byrhtnoth. This may be intended to point to a parallel between the two men, especially as their names begin with the same element.

Byrhtwold is described as *genēat* 'retainer', another term drawn fom the heroic tradition, and his speech expresses the essence of the heroic code: 'Mind must be the firmer, heart the braver, courage the greater, as our strength diminishes' (312–313). The first three of these half-lines all have the same basic meaning, using poetic variation to reinforce the theme of courage in the face of impossible odds.

This is not the end of the original poem, but it is the end of the surviving text. It is uncertain how much has been lost: possibly not much, as the final defeat is now inevitable. The ending as we have it presents a dramatic contrast between the cowardly Godric who caused the English defeat by fleeing from the battle on Byrhtnoth's horse, and the brave Godric who fights on to the death.

Glossary of common or familiar words

ac 82, 193, 247, 252, 269, 318   'but'
āfeallen 202 (t)   'fallen (dead)'
āgeaf (s) 44   'gave'
āna 94   'alone'
and 3, 4, 8, 15, 18, 19, etc.   'and'
andsware (as) 44   'answer'
ānne (as) 117, 226   'one'
āsæde (s) 198   'said'
æfter 65   'after'
ægþer 133   'each'
ænig (ns) 70   'any'

ǣr 60   'first'

ǣr 61, 158, 198, 279, 290, 300   'before'

ǣrænde (as) 28   'message'

ǣrest 5, 186, ǣrost 124   'first'

ǣr-ðon 191   'before'

æsc (as) 43, 310   'spear (made of ash)'

æt 10, 48, 55, 104, 123, 201, 223, 285, 288, 307   'in'; 39, 81, 268
     'from'; 119, 145   'at'

æt-foran 16   'before'

æþelan (as) 151; æþele (ns) 280   'noble'

baldlīce 311   'boldly'

baldlīcost 78   'most boldly'

bæd (s) 20, 128, 170, 257; bǣdon (p) 87, 262, 306   'ordered, asked'

bǣron (p) 99   'bore'

be 152, 318, 319   'by'

beadu-rǣs (ns) 111   'battle-rush'

beaduwe (ds) 185   'battle'

bearn (ns) 92, 155, 209, 238, 267, 300, 320; (np) 186   'son'

bēgen 182, 183, 191, 291, 305   'both'

bence (ds) 213   'bench'

bēon 185   'to be'

beorn (as) 270; beorna (gp) 257; beornas (ap) 17, 62, 182, 277, 305, 311;
     (np) 92, 111; beorne (ds) 154, 245; beornes (gs) 131, 160; beornum
     (dp) 101   'warrior'

bēot (as) 15; (ap) 213   'vow'

beran 12, 62   'to bear, carry'

bēron (pj) 67   'bore'

betere 31, betera 276   'better'

big 182   'by'

blōdigne (as) 154   'bloody'

bogan (np) 110   'bows'

bord (as) 15, 42, 62, 131, 245, 270, 283, 309; (ns) 110; borda (gp) 295;
     bordes (gs) 284; bordum (dp) 101   'shield'

bord-weall (as) 277   'shield-wall'

brād 15, 163   'broad'

brēostum (ds) 144   'breast'

bricge (as) 74, 78   'causeway'

brōðor (ns) 282; brōðru (np) 191   'brother'

bysige 110   'busy'

cald 91   'cold'

ceorl (ns) 256; ceorle (ds) 132   'churl, peasant'
cōm (s) 65   'came'
cumen (t) 104   'come'
cwæð (s) 211, 255   'said'
dæg (as) 198   'day'
dæg-weorces (gs) 148   'day's work'
Denon (dp) 129   'Danes'
Drihten (ns) 148   'Lord'
dyde (s) 280   'did'
eald (ns) 310; ealde (ap) 47   'old'
ealdor (ns) 202, 222, 314; ealdre (ds) 11; ealdres (gs) 53   'lord'
ealdor-man 219 (ns)   'nobleman'
eall (as) 256; (np) ealle 63, 196, 203, 207; (ap) 231, 238, 320; eallum (dp)
   216, 233; ealra (gp) 174   'all'
eall 314   'all, completely'
eard (as) 53, 58, 222   'homeland'
earm (as) 165   'arm'
eart (s) 36   'are'
Ēast-Seaxena (gp) 69   'East Saxons'
ecg (ns) 60   'edge, sword'
engla (gp) 178   'angels'
ēode (s) 132, 159, 225, 297, 323; ēodon (pj) 229; (p) 260   'went'
eom (s) 179, 317   'am'
eorl (ns) 6, 51, 89, 132, 146, 203, 233; eorle (ds) 28, 159; eorles (gs) 165
   'nobleman' (i.e. Byrhtnoth)
eorþan, eorðan (ds) 107, 157, 233; (as) 126, 303, 286   'earth, ground'
ēow (dp) 31, 41, 46, 48, 93   'you'
fæste 21, 103, 171, 301   'firmly'
fæstlīce 82   'firmly'
feaht (s) 254, 277, 281, 298   'fought'
feallan 54, 105   'to fall'
fela 73   'many'; 90   'much'
felda (ds) 241   '(battle-)field'
feohtan 16, 261   'to fight'
feohte (ns) 103   'battle'
fēol (s) 126, 303; fēoll (s) 119, 166, 286; fēollon (p) 111   'fell'
fēondum (dp) 103, 264   'enemies'
feor 3, 57   'far'
feorh (as) 125, 142, 184; (ds) fēore 194, 259; fēores (gs) 260, 317   'life'
flēogan 7, 109, 150   'to fly'; 275   'to flee'

flōwende 65   'flowing'

flyht (as) 71   'flight'

folc (as) 22, 54; (ns) 45, 241; folce (ds) 227, 259, 323; folces (gs) 202
   'folk, people'

foldan (as) 54; (ds) 166, 227   'earth, ground'

folman (ds) 21, 108, 150   'hand'

for 64, 89, 96   'because of'

ford (as) 88; forda (ds) 81   'ford'

forð 3, 12, 170, 205, etc.   'forth'

forð-georn 281   'eager to go forth'

fōtes (gs) 247; fōtum (dp) 119, 171   'foot'

fram 185, 187, 193, 252, 316, 317   'from'

frēan (ds) 12, 16, 184, 289; (as) 259   'lord'

frōd 140, 317   'old, experienced'

ful 253, 311, full 153   'very'

fundon (p) 85   'found'

furðor 247   'further'

fȳnd (ap) 82   'enemies'

fyrd-rinc (ns) 140   'warrior'

gangan 3, 40, 62, 170   'to go'

gangon (pj) 56   'go'

gār (as) 13, 134, 154, 237, 321; (ns) 296; gāras (ap) 46, 67; (np) 109; gāre
   (ds) 138   'spear'

gār-ræs (as) 32   'battle'

gāste (ds) 176   'spirit' ('ghost')

gē (np) 32, 34, 56, 57, 59   'you'

gebrōþru (np) 305   'brothers'

gecwæð (s) 168   'said'

gedōn (t) 197   'done'

gefeohte (ds) 12   'battle'

gefēra (ns) 280; gefēran (ap) 170, 229   'comrade'

gehealdan 167   'to hold'

gemælde (s) 230, 244   'spoke'

geong 210; geonga 155   'young'

georn (ns) 107; georne (np) 73   'eager'

georne 84, 123, 206   'eagerly'

geornful 274   'eager'

geornlīce 265   'eagerly'

gesāwon (p) 84, 203   'saw'

gesæde (s) 120   'said'

gesēcan 222   'to seek'
gesōhte (s) 287   'sought'
gestandan 171   'to stand'
geþancie (s) 173   'thank'
gewundod (t) 135   'wounded'
gif 34   'if'
God (ns) 94   'God'
gōd (as) 13, 237; gōde (ap) 170; gōdum (ds) 4   'good'
gōd (ns) 315; gōdan (as) 187   'good (man)'
golde (ds) 35   'gold'
grim (ns) 61   'grim, fierce'
grund (as) 287   'ground'
guman (np) 94   'men'
gūþe, gūðe (ds) 13, 94, 187, 285, 296, 321; (gs) 192; (as) 325   'battle'
gūð-plega (ns) 61   'battle-play'
gūð-rinc (ns) 138   'warrior'
gyf 36, 196   'if'
hafast (s) 231   'have'
hals (as) 141   'neck'
hām (as) 251; hāme (ds) 292   'home'
hand (as) 112   'side'
hand (ns) 141; handa (ds) 149; handon (dp) 7; handum (dp) 4, 14
    'hand'
hæfde (s) 13, 22, 121, 197, 199, 289   'had'
hæfð (s) 237   'has'
hæleð (np) 214; hælæð (np) 249; hæleða (gp) 74   'warriors'
hæþene (np) 55, 181   'heathen'
hē (ns) 7, 10, 13, 14, 15, 16, 22, etc.   'he'
healdan 14, 19, 74, 102, 236   'to hold'
healle (ds) 214   'hall'
heard (as) 214; heardne (as) 167, 236   'hard, fierce'
hearde 33   'fiercely'
heardlīce 261   'fiercely'
heardra 312   'harder, firmer'
heofenum (dp) 172   'heavens'
hēoldon (pj) 20   'hold'
heortan (ds) 145; heorte (ns) 312   'heart'
hēr 36, 51, 241, 243, 314   'here'
hēt (s) 2, 62, 74, 101; hēton (p) 30   'ordered'
hī (np) 19, 46, 63, 67, 68, 83, 84, 85, 87, 108, 185, 196, 207, 229, 260,

263, 271, 307   'they'
hī (ap) 127, 209, 320   'them'
hider 57   'hither'
hilde (ds) 8, 48, 55, 123, 223, 288, 324; (as) 33   'battle'
hilde-rinc (ns) 169   'warrior'
him (ds) 7, 11, 23, 44, 119, 120, 139, 145, 148, 152, 182, 188, 191, 198,
   267, 300   'him'
him (dp) 66, 265   'them'
hine (as) 164, 181   'him'
his (gs) 11, 16, 24, 51, etc.   'his'
hit (ns) 66, 137, 190, 195, 240   'it'
hlāford (ns) 135, 189, 224, 240; hlāforde (ds) 318   'lord'
hlāford-lēas (ns) 251   'lordless'
hors (as) 2   'horse'
hringas (ap) 161   'rings'
hū 19   'how'
hwā (ns) 71   'anyone'
hwā 95, 124, 215   'who'
hwæt 45   'what'
hwæt 231   'lo'
hyra (gp) 20, 38, 184, 194, 204, 263, 264, 306   'their'; 70, 133, 299   'of
   them'
ic 117, 173, 174, 175, 179, etc.   'I'
in 58, 157   'in'
is 31, 93, 223, 233   'is, will be'
lāgon (p) 112, 183   'lay (dead)'
lande (ds) 99; landes (gs) 90, 275   'land'
lang 66   'long'
lāðe 86; lāþere 90   'hateful' ('loathe')
lāþre 50   'more hateful'
lǣdan 88   'to lead'
læg (s) 157, 204, 227, 294, leg 276; lǣge (sj) 279, 300   'lay (dead)'
lēofan (ds) 319   'dear'
lēofne (as) 7, 208   'dear (one)'
lēofost 23   'dearest, most pleasing'
lēt (s) 7, 140   'let'; lēton (p) 108   'let'
licgan 319   'to lie (dead)'
līf (as) 208   'life'
ligeð (s) 222, līð 232, 314   'lies (dead)'
man (ns) 9   'one'

man (as) 77, 243, (ns) 147   'man'

manigne (as) 243   'many'

mǣg (ns) 5, 114, 224, 287   'kinsman'

mǣlde (s) 26, 43, 210   'spoke'

mǣnig (ns) 282; mǣnigne (as) 188; manega (np) 200   'many'

mǣst, 223 mǣste 175   'most, greatest'

mē (as) 29, 252; (ds) 55, 220, 223, 249, 318   'me'

men (np) 105, 206   'men'

Metod (ns) 175; Metode (ds) 147   'God'

miccle 50   'much'

mid 14, 21, 32, 40, 51, etc.   'with'

mihte (s) 9, 14, 64, 70, 124, 167, 171   'could'

mīn (ns) 177, 218, 222, 224, 250; mīne (as) 216; mīnes (gs) 53; mīnne
    (as) 248; mīnum (ds) 176, 318   'my'

mōdi (ns) 147; mōdige (np) 80   'brave'

mōste (s) 272   'was allowed'

mōte (sj) 95, 177; mōston (pj) 87, 263; mōton (pj) 180   'be allowed'

nā 21, 258, 268, 325   'not'

nama (ns) 267   'name'

nǣs (s) 325   'was not' (ne + wǣs)

ne 21, 34, 48, 59, etc.   'not'

nēh 103   'near'

nolde (s) 6, 9, 275; noldon (p) 82, 185, 201   'would not' (ne +
    wolde/woldon)

nū 57, 93, 175, 215, etc.   'now'

of 7, 108, 149, 150, 154, 162, 221   'from'

ofer 88, 91, 97, 98, 256   'over'

ōfre (ds) 28   'river-bank'

oft 188, 212, 296, 321   'often'

on 25, 28, 41, 63, 107, 112, 142, 144, 157, 163, 171, 189, 213, 227, 233,
    239, 240, 241, 264, 278, 293   'on'; 58, 194, 270, 322   'into'; 78, 126,
    303   'onto'; 129   'against'; 174, 178, 186, 198, 199, 214, 248, 273,
    292, 299, 302, 315, 324   'in'; 217, 220, 227, 259, 266, 279, 300, 323
    'among'

onfunde (s) 5   'discovered'

ongan (s) 12, 17, 89, 91, 228, 265; ongunnon (p) 86, 261   'began'

ord (as) 47, 110; (ns) 60, 146, 157, 253; orde (ds) 124, 226   'spear'

ōþer (ns) 282; ōþerne (as) 143, 234; ōðrum (ds) 64, 70, 133   'other'

oð-þæt 278, 324   'until'

oððe 208, 292   'or'

rād (s) 18, 239 'rode'
rīdan 291 'to ride'
riht 190 'right'
rincum (dp) 18 'warriors'
sang (s) 284 'sang'
sāwul (ns) 177 'soul'
sǣde (s) 147 'said'
sǣ-mannum (dp) 38, 278; sǣ-men (np) 29 'sailors'
sǣ-rinc (ns) 134 'sailor'
sceaft (ns) 136 'shaft'
sceal (s) 60, 252, 312, 313 'must'
sceolde (s) 16; sceoldon (p) 19, 105, 291, 307 'had to, must' ('should')
sceole (p) 59; sceolon (p) 54, 220 'must'
scēðe (ds) 162 'sheath'
scyldas (ap) 98; scylde (ds) 136 'shield'
scype (ds) 40, 56 'ship'
se (ns) 6, 9, 69, 72, etc. 'the'
sē (ns) 27, 75, 153 'who'
sē (ns) 150 'it'
sē (ns) 157, 227, 258, 310, 316 'he'
secgan 30 'to say'
sendan 30 'to send'
sende (s) 134; sendon (p) 29 'sent'
sēo (ns) 104, 144, 284 'the'
sōhton (p) 193 'sought'
spell (as) 50 'message'
spere (ns) 137; speru (ap) 108 'spear'
sprang (s) 137 'sprang'
sprǣc (s) 211, 274; sprǣcon (p) 200, 212 'spoke'
standan 19 'to stand'
stæde-fæste (np) 127; stede-fæste (np) 249 'steadfast'
stōd (s) 25, 28, 145, 152, 273; stōdon (p) 63, 72, 79, 100, 127, 182, 301
   'stood'
stōp (s) 8, 131 'stepped, advanced'
strēam (as) 68 'river'
sunu (ns) 76, 298 'son'
sūþerne (as) 134 'southern'
swā 33, 59, 122,132, 198, 209, 243, 280, 319, 320, 323 'so'
swā 290 'as'
swurd (as) 15, 161, 237; (ns) 166; (ap) 47; swurde (ds) 118 'sword'

swuster-sunu (ns) 115 'nephew' ('sister's son')
tīd (ns) 104 'time'
tō 8, 13, 28, 29, 40, 56, 64, 93, 94, 99, 132, 159, 166, 172, 177, 179, 235,
    286, 292, 321 'to'; 12 'in'; 55, 66, 90, 150, 164 'too'; 128 'on'
tō-brocen (t) 242 'broken'
tōgædere (np) 67 'together'
twēgen 80 'two'
þā, ðā 2, 7, 12, 17, 23, 25, 62, 74, 85, 89, 91, 96, 103, 130, 134, 136, 143,
    147, 149, 159, 162, 166, 171, 181, 185, 202, 205, 207, 211, 225, 228,
    255, 260, 285, 295, 297 'then'
þā 5, 10, 16, 22, 84, 121, 165, 184, 199, 239, 276 'when'
þā, ðā (ap) 48, 82, 145, 182, 196, 277, 322; (np) 72, 261, 305; (as) 74, 78,
    139, 163, 212, 325 'the'
þām (ds) 10, 28, 35, 63, 64, 81, 121, 132, 136, 142, 154, 159, 193, 199,
    227, 240, 245, 268, 300, 323; (dp) 40, 190, 278 'the'
þanc (as) 120, 147 'thanks'
þās (ap) 298 'these'
þǣr, ðǣr 17, 64, 65, 68, 78, 79, 85, 100, 105, 106, 116, 124, 185, 186, 200,
    205, 287, 301, 307 'there'
þǣr 23, 24, 28 'where'
þǣra (gp) 174; þǣre (ds) 8, 220; (gs) 95 'the'
ðæs (gs) 8, 131, 141, 148, 160, 165, 202 '(of) the'
þæt 5, 6, 9, 20, 30, 32, 36, 37, 51, 56, 76, 84, 85, 87, 117, 128, 176, 180,
    200, 204, 217, 221, 229, 234, 240, 243, 246, 251, 257, 263, 275, 291,
    307, 325 'that'
þæt (as) 22, 102, 168, 194; (ns) 137, 223 'the'
þæt 63, 119, 135, 136, 137, 142, 144, 150, 157, 177, 226, 227, 286 'so
    that'
pæt 289 'that which'
þe 36, 48, 52, 77, 78, etc. 'who, which'
þē, ðē (ds) 29, 30, 173, 177, 179 'you'
þē 312, 313 'the'
ðēah 289 'however'
þegen (as) 151; þegenas (np) 205, 220; (ap) 232 'retainer'
þēoden, ðēoden (ns) 120, 178, 232; (as) 158; ðēodne (ds) 294 'lord'
þīn (as) 178; þīne (ap) 37; þīnum (dp) 50 'your'
þis (ns) 45; (as) 316; ðisse (ds) 221; þisne (as) 32 'this'
þone, ðone (as) 19, 77, 88, 102, 151, 187, 189, 193, 277, 286 'the'
þū (ns) 30, 36, 37, 45, 176, 231 'you'
þurh 71, 141, 145, 151 'through'

þus 57 'thus'

þysne (as) 52   'this'

ūp 130 'up'

ūre (ns) 232, 240, 313, 314; ūrne (as) 58; ūrum (dp) 56   'our'

ūs (dp) 39, 40, 93, 233; (ap) 60, 237   'us'

ūt 72 'out'

wǣpen (as) 130, 235; (ns) 252; wǣpna (gp) 83, 272, 308; wǣpne (ds)
    228; wǣpnes (gs) 168; wǣpnum (dp) 10, 126   'weapon'

wǣre (sj) 240   'was'

wǣron (p) 110   'were'

wæs (s) 23, 75, 76, 103, etc.   'was'

wæter (as) 91, 98; wætere (ds) 64, 96   'water'

Waldend (as) 173   'Lord'

wē (np) 33, 34, 35, 40, 61, 212, 213   'we'

wealdan 83, 168, 272   'to wield'

wearð (s) 106, 113, 114, 116, etc.   'was, became'

wērige (np) 303   'weary'

werod (ns) 64, 97; (as) 102; werode (ds) 51   'troop'

west 97   'west'

wīcing (as) 139; wīcinga (gp) 26, 73, 97; wīcingas (ap) 322; wīcingum
    (dp) 116   'viking'

wiga (ns) 210; wigan (as) 75; (np) 79, 126, 302; (ap) 235; wigena (gp)
    135   'warrior'

wīge (ds) 10, 128, 193, 235, 252   'battle'

wīg-plegan (ds) 268; (as) 316   'battle-play'

wile (s) 52   'intends'

willað, willaþ (p) 35, 40, 46   'are willing'

wille (s) 37   'are willing'

wille (s) 221, 247, 317   'am willing'

wine (ns) 250   'lord'

wine-drihten (as) 248, 263   'dear lord'

wintrum (dp) 210   'years' ('winters')

wīs (ns) 219   'wise'

wið 31, 35, 39   'in exchange for'; 82, 103, 277, 298   'against'; 8, 131
    'towards'; 290   'to'

wolde (s) 11, 129, 160; woldon (p) 207   'wished'

word (as) 168; wordon (dp) 306; wordum (dp) 26, 43, 210, 250   'word'

worulde (ds) 174   'world'

wudu (as) 193   'wood'

wund (t) 113, 144   'wounded'
wunde (as) 139, 271; wundum (dp) 293, 303   'wound'
wurdon (p) 186   'were'
wurðlīce 279   'worthily'
wylle (s) 216   'wish'
yrre 44, 253   'angry'

Text D
The Dream of the Rood

The Dream of the Rood is widely regarded as the greatest of all Old English religious poems. It is unusual in many ways, not least in surviving in more than one version. The full text as we know it is preserved in the Vercelli Book, but sections of the poem, or a closely related poem, are also inscribed on a monumental stone cross at Ruthwell in Dumfries and Galloway, probably dating from the late seventh or early eighth century (see illustrations 4 and 8). On the north and south faces of the Ruthwell Cross are panels containing scenes from the Bible, while the east and west faces contain plant scrolls with birds and beasts.

In the margins of these panels are extracts from *The Dream of the Rood* written in runes in the Northumbrian dialect of Old English. The runic alphabet was probably used in preference to Roman script because its angular lines are easier to cut into stone. Two lines from *The Dream of the Rood* are also inscribed, in Roman letters, on the softer silverwork of the Brussels Cross, a small wooden cross made in England during the late tenth or eleventh century but now in the Cathedral of Saints Michael and Gudule in Brussels.

The Dream of the Rood takes the form of a dream vision in which the story of the crucifixion is told by the Cross. While we shall look at the poem in smaller stages, it is helpful to know that overall it falls into four main sections:

- Lines 1–26: the opening vision. The dreamer sees a marvellous tree, splendidly adorned with gold and jewels yet at the same time drenched with blood.
- Lines 27–77: the account of the crucifixion. The Cross describes how it was cut down as a living tree and made into an instrument of death, suffering alongside Christ at the crucifixion.
- Lines 78–121: the exhortation to the dreamer. The Cross urges the

dreamer to prepare mankind for the Second Coming of Christ by telling them of the vision.

- Lines 122–155: the dreamer's reaction. The dreamer resolves to focus his thoughts and prayers on the Cross in order to attain salvation.

Lines 1–26

In the opening section, the narrator introduces his dream and sets the scene. Look at the first twelve lines and read them through several times. Try reading them aloud, emphasising the alliteration and the rhythm of each line. Then answer the following questions, referring if necessary to the glossary below:

- What time did the dream occur?
- Where did the tree appear?
- What precious metals and stones could the dreamer see?
- How many gems were on the cross-beam?
- Name two groups that accompanied the tree.
- Why does the dreamer deny that this is a *fracodes gealga*?
- Which lines do not have the usual four-beat rhythm? How many beats do they have?

Hwæt! Ic swefna cyst	secgan wylle	
hwæt mē gemǣtte	tō midre nihte	
syðþan reord-berend	reste wunedon.	
Þūhte mē þæt ic gesāwe	syllicre trēow	
on lyft lǣdan,	lēohte bewunden,	5
bēama beorhtost.	Eall þæt bēacen wæs	
begoten mid golde.	Gimmas stōdon	
fægere æt foldan scēatum.	Swylce þǣr fīfe wǣron	
uppe on þām eaxle-gespanne.	Behēoldon þǣr engel Dryhtnes ealle	
fægere þurh forð-gesceaft.	Ne wæs ðǣr hūru fracodes gealga,	10
ac hine þǣr behēoldon	hālige gāstas,	
men ofer moldan	ond eall þēos mǣre gesceaft.	

1 *swefna* of dreams; *cyst* best
2 *mē gemǣtte* I dreamed (lit. it dreamed to me)
3 *reord-berend* people (lit. voice-bearers); *reste wunedon* were at rest
4 *þūhte mē* it seemed to me; *syllicre* marvellous
5 *lyft* air; *bewunden* wound round

7   *begoten* sprinkled
8   *scēatum* surfaces; *Swylce* also
9   *eaxle-gespanne* cross-beam (lit. shoulder-span)
10 *forð-gesceaft* creation; *hūru* certainly; *fracodes* criminal's
12 *moldan* earth; *mǣre* glorious; *gesceaft* creation

In the second half of the introductory section, the dreamer dwells on the contrasting glory and sorrow of the cross, and meditates on the state of his own soul. The contradictory nature of the cross is very powerful in this passage.

- How does the dreamer describe himself?
- How does the description of himself contrast with his description of the tree?
- What does the dreamer feel as he sees this vision of the tree?
- In what way does the vision change its appearance?
- In the final line of this section, what surprising event occurs?

Syllic wæs se sige-bēam
forwunded mid wommum.
wǣdum geweorðode,
gegyred mid golde.
bewrigene weorðlīce
Hwæðre ic þurh þæt gold
earmra ǣr-gewin,
swǣtan on þā swīðran healfe.
Forht ic wæs for þǣre fægran
   gesyhðe.
wendan wǣdum ond blēom.

beswyled mid swātes gange,
Hwæðre ic þǣr licgende
behēold hrēow-cearig
oð-ðæt ic gehŷrde

ond ic synnum fāh,
Geseah ic wuldres trēow,
wynnum scīnan,   15
Gimmas hæfdon
wealdes trēow.
ongytan meahte
þæt hit ǣrest ongan
Eall ic wæs mid sorgum gedrēfed. 20
Geseah ic þæt fūse bēacen

Hwīlum hit wæs mid wǣtan
   bestēmed,
hwīlum mid since gegyrwed.
lange hwīle
Hǣlendes trēow,   25
þæt hit hlēoðrode.

13 *Syllic* marvellous; *sige-bēam* victory-beam; *fāh* stained, guilty
14 *forwunded* wounded; *wommum* sins, stains
15 *wǣdum* with clothes; *geweorðode* adorned; *wynnum* with joys
16 *gegyred* adorned
17 *bewrigene* covered; *weorðlīce* worthily; *wealdes* of the forest, of power
18 *ongytan* perceive
19 *earmra* of wretched ones; *ǣr-gewin* ancient conflict; *ǣrest* first
20 *swǣtan* to bleed; *swīðran* right; *healfe* side; *gedrēfed* troubled
21 *Forht* afraid; *fūse* doomed

22 *wendan* change; *wǣdum* clothes; *blēom* colours; *wǣtan* moisture; *bestēmed* made wet
23 *beswyled* drenched; *swātes* of blood; *gange* flow; *since* treasure; *gegyrwed* adorned
24 *licgende* lying; *lange hwīle* for a long while
25 *hrēow-cearig* sorrowful; *Hǣlendes* Saviour's
26 *hlēoðrode* spoke

Discussion

The poem derives much of its dramatic impact through first-person narrative, by the dreamer in sections 1 and 4, and by the Cross in sections 2 and 3. Drawing on the Old English riddle tradition, the initial description of the Cross uses ambiguities to delay recognition of what it actually is. It is first described as a *trēow* 'tree' (4b), then as a *bēam* 'beam' (6a) and a *bēacen* 'beacon' (6b). It then becomes a *sige-bēam* 'victory-beam' (13a), *wuldres trēow* 'tree of glory' (14b) and *wealdes trēow* 'tree of the forest' (17b); and only in 25b is it identified as *Hǣlendes trēow* 'tree of the Saviour'. Another riddling clue is the reference to clothing in 15a, probably alluding to the church ritual of shrouding crosses on Good Friday.

When the vision first appears to the dreamer in the opening lines, he does not know what it is, so the reader shares in his gradual realisation that the tree towering up into the air is the one on which Christ was crucified, and in his surprise when it speaks. It is important to remember that manuscripts of Old English poetry do not contain titles, so no expectations have been set up in the mind of the reader. The alternating descriptions of the tree as adorned with gold and jewels, and drenched with blood and inspiring fear, are a dramatic evocation of the paradoxical view of the crucifixion popular in the Middle Ages. Christ's death was terrible because it signified man's killing of God's son; it was simultaneously glorious because it signi-fied man's salvation. The dreamer's vision alternates between the terror and the glory, and he is made conscious of his own state, *synnum fāh* 'stained with sins' (13b).

The poem echoes the riddles also in that the description makes extensive use of word-play. Old English *weald* can mean either 'forest' or 'power', so 17b *wealdes trēow* 'tree of the forest' or 'tree of power' may be intended to evoke both senses, perhaps also with an allusion to the similar word *wealdend* 'God'. Old English *bēam*, like its present-day descendant 'beam', can refer either to wood or to light, and again both senses are relevant in 6a, *bēama beorhtost* 'brightest of trees' or 'brightest of rays of light'. The verb *stōdon* (7b), the plural of *stōd*, means 'stood' as in present-day English, implying that the *gimmas* 'gems' were fixed in position. In Old English, however, the same verb also means 'shone' (as in *Beowulf*, 726b), and this too is appropriate in combination with *gimmas*. Old English *fāh* (13b) can mean either 'stained' or 'guilty', presenting both a visual and a moral contrast between the dreamer and the Cross, and there is a similar ambiguity in 14a, where *mid wommum* can mean 'with stains' or 'with sins'. The riddling statement in 10b that the object is *Ne . . . fracodes gealga* 'not a criminal's gallows' is also ambiguous: not a gallows at all, or the gallows of someone who is not a criminal? The first sense focuses on the status of the tree – it has been horrifically misused – while the second sense focuses on the innocence of the crucified Christ. Since this is a poem, and both senses are compatible, the phrase is rich in meaning.

The opening and closing sections of *The Dream of the Rood* act as a framework to the central account of the crucifixion, but they are also important in introducing and reinforcing themes. A major theme of the poem is the Second Coming of Christ, the belief that at the end of the current age Jesus will return to this earth to judge the living and the dead. This belief was particularly strong in the Middle Ages. There are several allusions to the Second Coming in the opening vision. In 2b, *tō midre nihte*, 'in the middle of the night' or 'at midnight', is the time of day traditionally associated with the Second Coming. Other traditional features of descriptions of the Last Judgement include the shining cross leading the hosts of Christ (4a–6a), the assembled multitudes of angels and men (11–12), and the bleeding tree (20a).

Lines 8–10 and 20–23 are longer than most Old English verse lines, with three stresses per half-line instead of two. These are known as 'hypermetric' verses. They also appear in other poems, but are particularly frequent in *The Dream of the Rood*, giving extra dignity and weight to certain sections of the narrative.

Lines 27–77

In the second section, the Cross gives an eyewitness account of the crucifixion, focusing on its own role as the instrument of execution.

- Where was the tree growing when it was cut down?
- What happened to it then?
- What type of people was it ordered to lift up?

- Who fastened it on the hill?
- What did it see then?
- What could it have done?
- What did it do instead?

Ongan þā word sprecan
'Þæt wæs gēara iū
þæt ic wæs āhē awen
āstyred of stefne mīnum.
geworhton him þǣr tō
  wǣfer-sȳne,
Bǣron mē ðǣr beornas on
  eaxlum,
Gefæstnodon mē þǣr
  fē ondas genōge.
efstan elne mycle,
Þǣr ic þā ne dorste
būgan oððe berstan,
eorðan scē atas.
fē ondas gefyllan,

wudu sēlesta.
(ic þæt gȳta geman)
holtes on ende,
Genāman mē ðǣr strange fē ondas, 30
hē ton mē heora wergas hebban.

oð-ðæt hīe mē on beorg āsetton.

Geseah ic þā Frean man-cynnes

þæt hē mē wolde on gestīgan.
ofer Dryhtnes word 35
þā ic bifian geseah
Ealle ic mihte
'hwæðre ic fæste stōd.'

27 *sēlesta* best
28 *gē ara iū* very long ago; *gȳta* still, yet; *geman* remember
29 *āhē awen* cut down; *holtes* of the forest
30 *āstyred* removed; *stefne* root; *Genāman* seized
31 *geworhton* made ('wrought'); *wǣfer-sȳne* spectacle; *wergas* criminals; *hebban* lift up
32 *beorg* hill; *āsetton* set down
33 *genōge* enough (i.e. many)
34 *efstan* hasten; *elne mycle* with great zeal; *gestīgan* climb
36 *būgan* bow down; *bifian* tremble
37 *scē atas* surfaces
38 *gefyllan* fell, strike down

The death of Christ on the Cross is presented through a mixture of standard and hypermetric verses, perhaps the most moving passage of the poem.

- Identify some of the words and phrases used to describe Christ in these lines.
- Why did Christ mount the gallows?
- What did the Cross do as Christ embraced it?
- Name three things that the Cross did not dare to do.
- What was done with the nails?

- Who or what was drenched with blood?
- What types of words (e.g. nouns, adjectives, verbs) are given prominence in this passage by being placed at the beginnings of phrases or verse units?

Ongyrede hine þā geong hæleð,	þæt wæs God æl-mihtig,
strang ond stīð-mōd.	Gestāh hē on gealgan hēanne, 40
mōdig on manigra gesyhðe,	þā hē wolde man-cyn lȳsan.
Bifode ic þā mē se beorn	Ne dorste ic hwæðre būgan
ymb-clypte.	tō eorðan,
feallan tō foldan scēatum,	ac ic sceolde fæste standan.
Rōd wæs ic ārǣred.	Āhōf ic rīcne Cyning,
heofona Hlāford.	Hyldan mē ne dorste. 45
Þurh-drifan hī mē mid	On mē syndon þā dolg gesīene,
deorcan næglum.	
opene inwid-hlemmas.	Ne dorste ic hira nǣnigum sceððan.
Bysmeredon hīe unc būtū	Eall ic wæs mid blōde bestēmed,
ætgædere.	
begoten of þæs guman sīdan,	siððan hē hæfde his gāst onsended.
Feala ic on þām beorge	gebiden hæbbe 50
wrāðra wyrda.	Geseah ic weruda God
þearle þenian.	Þȳstro hæfdon
bewrigen mid wolcnum	Wealdendes hrǣw,
scīrne scīman.	Sceadu forð ēode,
wann under wolcnum.	Wēop eal gesceaft, 55
cwiðdon cyninges fyll.	Crist wæs on rōde.

39 *Ongyrede* stripped
40 *stīð-mōd* resolute; *gestāh* climbed; *hēanne* high
41 *lȳsan* redeem
42 *Bifode* trembled; *ymb-clypte* embraced (lit. clasped round); *būgan* bow (vb)
43 *scēatum* surfaces
44 *ārǣred* raised up; *āhōf* lifted; *rīcne* powerful
45 *Hyldan* bend
46 *Þurh-drifan* pierced (lit. drove through); *syndon* are; *dolg* wounds; *gesīene* visible
47 *inwid-hlemmas* malicious wounds; *sceððan* injure
48 *Bysmeredon* mocked; *unc* us two; *būtū* both; *ætgædere* together; *bestēmed* drenched
49 *begoten* shed; *guman* man's; *onsended* sent forth
50 *beorge* hill; *gebiden* experienced
51 *wrāðra* cruel; *wyrda* events; *weruda* of hosts
52 *þearle* severely; *þenian* stretched out; *þȳstro* dark shades
53 *bewrigen* covered; *wolcnum* clouds; *hrǣw* corpse
54 *scīrne* bright; *scīman* radiance; *Sceadu* shadow, darkness
55 *wann* dark; *wolcnum* clouds; *Wēop* wept
56 *cwiðdon* lamented

The Cross concludes its account by describing the events subsequent to Christ's death.

- Who removed the body from the Cross?
- What did they do with it?
- What was the tomb made of?
- What finally happened to the Cross?

Hwæðere þær fūse
tō þām æðelinge.
Sāre ic wæs mid sorgum
gedrēfed.
eað-mōd elne mycle.

āhōfon hine of ðām hefian
wīte.
standan stē ame bedrifenne.
Ālēdon hīe ðær lim-wērigne,
Behē oldon hīe ðær heofenes
Dryhten,
mē ðe æfter ðām miclan
gewinne.
beornas on banan gesyhðe.
gesetton hīe ðær-on sigora
Wealdend.
earme on þā æfen-tīde,
mē ðe fram þām mæran
þē odne.
Hwæðere wē ðær grē otende
stōdon on staðole.
hilde-rinca.
fæger feorg-bold.
ealle tō eorðan.
Bedealf ūs man on dē opan
sē aþe.
frē ondas gefrūnon,
gyredon mē

feorran cwōman
Ic þæt eall behē old.
Hnāg ic hwæðre þām secgum
tō handa,
Genāmon hīe þær æl-mihtigne   60
God,
Forlē ton mē þā hilde-rincas

Eall ic wæs mid strælum forwundod.
gestōdon him æt his līces hē afdum.
ond hē hine ðær hwīle reste,

Ongunnon him þā mold-ærn   65
wyrcan
Curfon hīe ðæt of beorhtan stāne,
Ongunnon him þā sorh-lē oð galan,

þā hīe woldon eft sīðian
Reste hē ðær mæte weorode.

gōde hwīle   70
Stefn ūp gewāt
Hræw cōlode,
Þā ūs man fyllan ongan
Þæt wæs egeslic wyrd!
Hwæðre mē þær Dryhtnes þegnas,   75

golde ond seolfre.

57 *fūse* eager ones; *feorran* from afar
59 *sāre* grievously ('sorely'); *gedrēfed* troubled; *Hnāg* bowed down; *secgum* men
60 *eað-mōd* humble; *elne mycle* with great zeal; *Genāmon* seized
61 *āhōfon* lifted; *hefian* oppressive ('heavy'); *wīte* punishment; *Forlēton* left

62   *stēame* with moisture; *bedrifenne* drenched; *strǣlum* arrows; *forwundod* wounded
63   *Ālēdon* laid down
65   *mēðe* weary; *gewinne* battle; *mold-ærn* tomb (lit. earth-building); *wyrcan* to make
66   *banan* slayer's; *Curfon* carved
67   *gesetton* set, placed; *sigora* of victories; *sorh-lēoð* dirge (lit. sorrow-song); *galan* to sing
68   *earme* wretched; *sīðian* depart
69   *mēðe* weary; *mǣran* glorious; *mǣte* small; *weorode* company
70   *grēotende* lamenting; *gōde hwīle* for a good while
71   *staðole* position; *Stefn* voice; *gewāt* departed
72   *Hrǣw* corpse
73   *feorg-bold* body (lit. life-house)
74   *egeslic* dreadful; *wyrd* event
75   *Bedealf* buried; *sēaþe* pit
76   *gefrūnon* heard of
77   *gyredon* adorned

Discussion

This section of the poem again draws on the Old English riddle tradition. Many Old English riddles are written in the first person, using the device of prosopopoeia whereby an inanimate object is personified and given the power of speech. Whereas the riddles use prosopopoeia to disguise the solution, here the same device is used to resolve the theological problem of whether Christ was fully human or fully divine. By making the Cross animate, the poet is able to divide the divine and human aspects of Christ's nature between Christ himself and the Cross. Throughout the account of the crucifixion, the human suffering is transferred to the Cross. The biblical record of Christ's arrest and trial is replaced by a description of the tree being cut down at the edge of the wood and removed from its roots (29–30a), taken away by strong enemies (30b), made into a spectacle (31a), ordered to raise up criminals (31b), carried on men's shoulders until they set it on a hill (32), and fastened in position there by its enemies (33a). By contrast, Christ displays divine free will, voluntarily coming to Calvary (34a), deliberately embracing the cross (42a), and choosing to send forth his spirit (49b). He mounts the gallows bravely in order to save mankind (40b–41). The Cross meanwhile trembles as Christ embraces it (42a), and does not dare to bow to the ground (42b), fall down to the surfaces of the earth (43a), bend (45b), or harm any of its persecutors (47b). The Cross functions as the surrogate body of Christ, as in line 46: *Þurh-drifan hī* <u>*mē*</u> *mid deorcan næglum. On* <u>*mē*</u> *syndon þā dolg gesīene* 'they pierced <u>me</u> with dark nails; on <u>me</u> the wounds are visible' – a role already prefigured in the opening vision with the reference to its *eaxle-gespanne* 'shoulder-span' (9a). Similarly in 48b, the Cross rather than Christ is drenched with blood. Like Christ, it could have destroyed its enemies, but does not: *Ealle ic mihte / fēondas gefyllan, hwæðre ic fæste stōd* 'I could have felled all the enemies, but I stood fast' (37b–38).

The division between the active role of Christ and the passive role of the Cross is reinforced by the language used. From Christ's first appearance in 33b, he is associated with active verbs – *efstan* 'to hasten' (34a), *wolde on gestīgan* 'intended to mount' (34b), *ongyrede hine* 'stripped himself' (39a), *gestāh* 'mounted' (40b), *wolde . . . lȳsan* 'intended to redeem' (41b), *ymb-clypte* 'embraced' (42a) – and with heroic epithets such as *strang ond stīð-mōd* 'strong and resolute' (40a) and *mōdig* 'brave' (41a). In contrast, the verbs associated with the Cross are passive and negative: *ne dorste* 'did not dare' (35a, 45b, 47b), *sceolde . . . standan* 'had to stand' (43b), *wæs . . . ārǣred* 'was erected' (44a), and *wæs . . . bestēmed* 'was made wet' (48b). Unlike other Old English poems, where the main stresses fall on nouns and adjectives, *The Dream of the Rood* gives great prominence to verbs. This is strikingly illustrated in 30–33a, where all but one of the half-lines begin with verbs, many of them verbs of violence directed against the Cross: *āstyred* 'removed', *genāman* 'seized', *geworhton* 'made', *hēton* 'ordered', *bǣron* 'carried', *gefæstnodon* 'fastened'. The alliterative and rhythmic emphasis placed on these verbs helps to create a strong sense of action.

The poem also draws on the Germanic heroic tradition, using the traditional diction of Old English heroic poetry to depict Christ as a warrior lord: *geong hæleð* 'young hero' (39a), *beorn* 'warrior' (42a), and *rīcne Cyning* 'powerful king' (44b). The Cross is depicted as a loyal retainer, using the same *comitatus* imagery that is applied to Byrhtnoth's followers in *The Battle of Maldon*. Like them, it is devoted to its lord: the irony of its position is that it is forced to become the instrument of his death. The disciples who remove Christ's body from the Cross and lay it in a stone tomb are also described as *hilde-rincas* 'warriors' (61b), and as *Dryhtnes þegnas* 'the Lord's retainers' (75b) when they discover the Cross and decorate it with gold and silver after it has been cut down and buried in a deep pit alongside other crosses.

Also drawing on the heroic tradition, the crucifixion is presented metaphorically as a battle. The nails used to fasten Christ to the Cross are described as arrows – *mid strǣlum* 'with arrows' (62b) – and the crucified Christ is described as resting after the *gewinn* 'battle' (65a). The kenning *feorg-bold* 'life-house' used of his body in 73a is directly parallel to *feorh-hūs* in *The Battle of Maldon* 297a, but uses a different word for 'house' as the second element of the compound.

Finally, notice that in 59a, *Sāre ic wæs mid sorgum gedrēfed*, the Cross describes itself in words almost identical to those used by the dreamer of himself in 20b, *Eall ic wæs mid sorgum gedrēfed*: 'I was grievously/all troubled with sorrows.' This is the first of many links between the characters in the poem established through the use of formulaic phrases and verbal repetition.

Lines 78–121

Having completed its account of the crucifixion, the Cross instructs the dreamer how to respond to the vision.

- Name two things that it is time for men throughout the earth and all this glorious creation to do.
- What is the Cross now able to do?
- What type of word is *reord-berend* (89b), and where have you seen it before?
- What types of phrases are *men ofer moldan* (82a) and *heofon-rīces Weard* (91b)?
- Whom did God honour above all womankind?

> Nū ðū miht gehȳran,   hæleð mīn se lēofa,
> þæt ic bealu-wara weorc   gebiden hæbbe,
> sārra sorga.   Is nū sǣl cumen   80
> þæt mē weorðiað   wīde ond sīde
> menn ofer moldan   ond eall þēos mǣre gesceaft,
> gebiddaþ him tō þyssum bēacne.   On mē bearn Godes
> þrōwode hwīle.   For-þan ic þrym-fæst nū
> hlīfige under heofenum,   ond ic hǣlan mæg   85
> ǣghwylcne ānra   þāra þe him bið egesa tō mē.
> Iū ic wæs geworden   wīta heardost,
> lēodum lāðost,   ǣr-þan ic him līfes weg
> rihtne gerȳmde,   reord-berendum.
> Hwæt, mē þā geweorðode   wuldres Ealdor   90
> ofer holm-wudu,   heofon-rīces Weard,
> swylce swā hē his mōdor ēac,   Mārian sylfe,
> æl-mihtig God,   for ealle menn
> geweorðode   ofer eall wīfa cynn.

78 *hæleð mīn se lēofa* my dear man
79 *bealu-wara* of dwellers in evil; *gebiden* experienced
80 *sārra* grievous ('sore'); *sǣl* time
81 *weorðiað* will honour; *wīde ond sīde* far and wide
82 *moldan* earth; *mǣre* glorious
83 *gebiddaþ* will pray
84 *þrōwode* suffered; *þrym-fæst* glorious
85 *hlīfige* tower; *hǣlan* heal, save; *mæg* can
86 *ǣghwylcne* each; *bið* is; *egesa* fear, awe
87 *Iū* long ago; *wæs geworden* became, was made; *wīta* of punishments
88 *lēodum* to people
89 *gerȳmde* opened up; *reord-berendum* to people (lit. voice-bearers)
90 *geweorðode* honoured
91 *holm-wudu* vessel (of salvation) (lit. sea-wood)
92 *swylce swā* just as
94 *geweorðode* honoured

• What does the Cross tell the dreamer to do in lines 95-96?
• What will God do on the Day of Judgement?
• Who will be with him?

Nū ic þē hāte,
þæt ðū þās gesyhðe
onwrēoh wordum
sē ðe æl-mihtig God
for man-cynnes
ond Ādomes
Dē að hē þǣr byrigde.
mid his miclan mihte
Hē ðā on heofenas āstāg.
on þysne middan-geard
on dōm-dæge
æl-mihtig God,
þæt hē þonne wile dēman,
ānra gehwylcum
on þyssum lǣnum
Ne mæg þǣr ǣnig
for þām worde

hæleð mīn se lēofa, 95
secge mannum,
þæt hit is wuldres bēam,
on þrōwode
manegum synnum
eald-gewyrhtum. 100
Hwæðere eft Dryhten ārās
mannum tō helpe.
Hider eft fundaþ
man-cynn sē can
Dryhten sylfa, 105
ond his englas mid,
sē āh dōmes geweald,
swā hē him ǣrur hēr
līfe geearnaþ.
unforht wesan 110
þe se Wealdend cwyð.

95 *hāte* order; *hæleð mīn se lēofa* my dear man
97 *onwrēoh* make known
98 *þrōwode* suffered
100 *eald-gewyrhtum* ancient deeds
101 *byrigde* buried, tasted
103 *āstāg* ascended; *fundaþ* will come
107 *dēman* judge ('deem'); *āh* has; *geweald* power

108   *gehwylcum* each
109   *lǣnum* transitory; *geearnaþ* earns, deserves
110   *mæg* can; *unforht* unafraid; *wesan* to be
111   *cwyð* will say

- What question will God ask in front of the multitude?
- How will people react?
- Through what means can people seek the Kingdom of Heaven?

Frīneð hē for þǣre mǣnige	hwǣr se man sīe,	
sē ðe for Dryhtnes naman	dēaðes wolde	
biteres onbyrigan,	swā hē ǣr on ðām bēame dyde.	
Ac hīe þonne forhtiað,	ond fēa þencaþ	115
hwæt hīe tō Criste	cweðan onginnen.	
Ne þearf ðǣr þonne ǣnig	unforht wesan,	
þe him ǣr in brēostum bereð	bēacna selest,	
ac ðurh ðā rōde sceal	rīce gesēcan	
of eorð-wege	ǣghwylc sāwl,	120
sēo þe mid Wealdende	wunian þenceð."	

112   *frīneð* will ask; *mǣnige* multitude; *sīe* is (subjunctive)
114   *onbyrigan* taste
115   *forhtiað* will be afraid; *fēa* few; *þencaþ* will think
116   *cweðan* to say
117   *þearf* will need; *unforht* unafraid, or possibly 'very afraid'; *wesan* to be
118   *sēlest* best
120   *ǣghwylc* each
121   *sēo þe* which; *wunian* to dwell; *Þenceð* thinks, intends

Discussion

The Cross explains that the purpose of the vision is to prepare mankind for the Second Coming of Christ. The time has now come for men throughout the earth, and all creation, to honour the Cross, and pray to this sign. Because the son of God suffered on it, the Cross towers gloriously under the heavens, and is able to save anyone who is in awe of it. Long ago it was made the severest of punishments, most hateful to men, before it opened up the right way of life to men, honoured above all other trees just as God honoured his mother Mary above all womankind. The Cross tells the dreamer to make the vision known to men, to reveal in words that it is the Cross of glory on which almighty God suffered for the many sins of mankind and the ancient deeds of Adam. The Lord will return to earth with his angels on the Day of Judgement to judge each person according as he shall have deserved in this life. He will ask where the person is who was prepared to taste bitter death for the Lord's name, as he did on the Cross. Everyone will be afraid, and will find it difficult to know what to say, but those who wish to live with God must seek the kingdom (of Heaven) through the Cross.

In this section, the mood of dignified suffering which characterises the account of the crucifixion is replaced by a strong sense of urgency. Notice for instance the repetition of the word *nū* 'now' in 78a, 80b, 84b and 95a, and the use of present-tense verbs referring to present or future time. The slower hypermetric verses no longer appear, and sense units tend to be quite short, creating an effect of rapid movement.

Many poetic techniques are represented within the passage. The compound *holm-wudu* (91a) literally means 'sea-wood', but functions here as a poetic kenning for 'ship', alluding to the Cross's traditional role as a vessel of salvation. The verb *byrigde* (101a) is another example of word-play, punning on the alternative senses 'tasted' and 'buried'. It also forms part of a sequence of imagery relating to the physical senses which began in the opening vision (sight), and continued throughout the Cross's narrative (hearing), and Christ's embrace of the Cross (touch). The image of tasting death reappears in 113b–114a, and is another motif relating to the Second Coming. The phrase *heofon-rīces Weard* 'Guardian of the heavenly kingdom' (91b) is a formula that we have seen before in the first line of *Caedmon's Hymn* (Chapter 6). Within this passage, formulaic repetition is used to link the parallel scenarios in 110 and 117, contrasting the fear felt by all sinners at Judgement Day with the hope inspired by the Cross. Logically, *unforht* in 117b should contrast with *unforht* 'unafraid' in 110b, so it is possible that the second occurrence plays on the alternative sense of the *un-* prefix as an intensifier ('very afraid'), which may also appear in *Wulf and Eadwacer* (Chapter 6).

Vocabulary and formulas are also used to link sections and characters within the poem. The compound *reord-berend* 'voice-bearers' used of mankind in 3a reappears in 89b, an ironic kenning since the only voice heard within the poem is that of the inanimate Cross. The formula *men ofer moldan* 'men throughout the earth' (82a) is repeated from 12a, and the Cross's description of itself as *wuldres bēam* 'beam of glory' (97b) echoes the dreamer's *wuldres trēow* 'tree of glory' (14b). The phrase *elne micle* 'with great zeal' has now been applied to both Christ (34a) and the Cross (60a), and will be applied to the dreamer in the final section of the poem (123a).

Lines 122–155

The Cross has now finished speaking, and the dreamer describes his reaction to the vision.

- What does the dreamer do first?
- Is he sad or happy?
- How does he hope to gain salvation?

Gebæd ic mē þā tō þām bēame	blīðe mōde,
elne mycle,	þǣr ic āna wæs
mǣte werede.	Wæs mōd-sefa
āfȳsed on forð-wege.	Feala ealra gebād 125
langung-hwīla.	Is mē nū līfes hyht
þæt ic þone sige-bēam	sēcan mōte
āna oftor	þonne ealle men,
well weorþian.	Mē is willa tō ðām
mycel on mōde,	ond mīn mund-byrd is 130
geriht tō þǣre rōde.	

122 *Gebæd* prayed
123 *elne mycle* with great zeal
124 *mǣte* small; *werede* company; *mōd-sefa* spirit
125 *āfȳsed* urged; *gebād* experienced
126 *langung-hwīla* times of longing; *hyht* hope
127 *sige-bēam* victory-beam
129 *weorþian* honour (vb)
130 *mund-byrd* hope of protection
131 *geriht* directed

- Does the dreamer have many powerful friends on earth?
- Who or what will fetch the dreamer from this transitory life to the place of great bliss and joy in heaven?
- What image is used to represent heaven?

	Nāh ic rīcra feala
frēonda on foldan,	ac hīe forð heonon
gewiton of worulde drēamum,	sōhton him wuldres Cyning,
lifiaþ nū on heofenum	mid Hēah-fædere,
wuniaþ on wuldre,	ond ic wēne mē 135
daga gehwylce	hwænne mē Dryhtnes rōd,
þe ic hēr on eorðan	ǣr scēawode,

on þysson lǣnan	līfe gefetige
ond mē þonne gebringe	þǣr is blis mycel,
drēam on heofonum,	þǣr is Dryhtnes folc 140
geseted tō symle,	þǣr is singal blis,
ond mē þonne āsette	þǣr ic syþþan mōt
wunian on wuldre,	well mid þām hālgum
drēames brūcan.	Sī mē Dryhten frēond,
sē ðe hēr on eorþan	ǣr þrōwode 145
on þām gealg-trēowe	for guman synnum.

131 *Nāh* do not have (*ne* + *āh*); *rīcra* powerful
133 *gewiton* departed
134 *Hēah-fædere* God (lit. high father)
135 *wuniaþ* dwell; *wēne* look forward
136 *gehwylce* each
137 *scēawode* saw
138 *lǣnan* transitory; *gefetige* will fetch
141 *geseted* set, placed; *symle* banquet; *singal* everlasting
142 *āsette* set
143 *wunian* dwell
144 *brūcan* enjoy; *sī mē Dryhten frēond* may the Lord be a friend to me
145 *þrōwode* suffered
146 *guman* men's

- What two things did Christ give us when he redeemed us?
- What was renewed for those who suffered burning?
- Who was successful on that mission?

Hē ūs onlȳsde	ond ūs līf forgeaf,
heofonlicne hām.	Hiht wæs genīwad
mid blēdum ond mid blisse	þām þe þǣr bryne þolodan.
Se sunu wæs sigor-fæst	on þām sīð-fate, 150
mihtig ond spēdig,	þā hē mid manigeo cōm,
gāsta weorode,	on Godes rīce,
Ān-wealda æl-mihtig,	englum tō blisse
ond eallum ðām hālgum	þām þe on heofonum ǣr
wunedon on wuldre,	þā heora Wealdend cwōm, 155
æl-mihtig God,	þǣr his ēðel wæs.

147 *onlȳsde* redeemed; *forgeaf* gave
148 *Hiht* hope; *genīwad* renewed
149 *blēdum* blessings; *bryne* burning; *þolodan* endured
150 *sigor-fæst* victorious; *sīð-fate* journey
151 *spēdig* successful; *manigeo* multitude

152   *weorode* host
153   *Ān-wealda* Lord (lit. One-ruler)
155   *wunedon* dwelled
156   *ēðel* homeland

Discussion

The final section of the poem completes the vision framework, with the dreamer focusing on the hope of salvation through the Cross. His first reaction is to pray to the Cross with a glad heart (122). No longer merely a spectator, as in the opening vision, or a listener as in the second and third sections, he has now become the central character. An intensely personal sense of involvement is created through the repeated use of first-person pronouns (7 of *ic* 'I', 8 of *mē* 'me', 1 of *mīn* 'my' in 122–146), as the dreamer resolves to devote himself to the Cross. His friends have already left the world, and he looks forward to the time when the Cross will fetch him from this transitory life to eternal joy in heaven – brilliantly presented through the image of the heavenly banquet, linking with references to taste and other physical senses in earlier sections. Present-tense verbs give a sense of immediacy, and the frame of reference broadens in 147 with two emphatic uses of the plural pronoun *ūs* 'us', extending the promise of salvation to all mankind. The dreamer states confidently that Christ redeemed us and gave us life and a heavenly home (147–148a). The poem ends with a triumphant description of Christ rescuing souls from hell-fire, variously interpreted as a reference to the Last Judgement or to the Harrowing of Hell, when Christ descended to Hell after the crucifixion and released righteous pre-Christian souls. The former fits in with a major theme of the poem, but the past tense verbs (e.g. 148b *Hiht wæs genīwad* 'hope was renewed', 150a *Se sunu wæs sigorfæst* 'the son was successful') suggest an event that has already taken place.

Again, these lines are tightly structured, with verbal echoes and parallels, and links with other sections of the poem. Compare for instance the parallel construction of 137 and 145, and notice how the word *blis* 'bliss' is emphasised through repetition in 139b, 141b, 149a and 153b. Both Christ and the dreamer have now been described as *mǣte weorode* 'with small company' (69b, 124a). Since they are in fact each alone, this is another example of 'litotes' or understatement. The same device is represented by the dreamer's statement in 131b–132a that *Nāh ic rīcra feala / frēonda on foldan* 'I do not have many powerful friends on earth': the implication is that he has none.

Glossary of common or familiar words

ac 11, 43, 115, 119, 132   'but'
Ādomes (gs) 100   'Adam'
āna 123, 128   'alone'
ānra (gp) 86, 108   'one'
ārās (s) 101   'arose'
æfen-tīde (as) 68   'evening' ('eventide')
æfter 65   'after'
æl-mihtig (ns) 39, 93, 98, 106, 153, 156; æl-mihtigne (as) 60
   'almighty'
ænig (ns) 110, 117   'anyone'
ær 114, 118, 137, 145, 154, ærur 108   'before, formerly'
ær-þan 88   'before'
æt 8, 63   'at'
æðelinge (ds) 58   'prince'
bæron (p) 32   'carried, bore'
bēacen (ns) 6; (as) 21; bēacne (ds) 83; bēacna (gp) 118   'beacon'
bēam (ns) 97; bēama (gp) 6; bēame (ds) 114, 122   'beam (of light or
   wood)'
bearn (ns) 83   'son'
behēold (s) 25, 58; behēoldon (p) 9, 11, 64   'watched, beheld'
beorhtan (ds) 66   'bright'
beorhtost 6   'brightest'
beorn (ns) 42; beornas (np) 32, 66   'man'
bereð (s) 118   'carries'
berstan 36   'to burst, break'
biteres (gs) 114   'bitter'
blīðe (ds) 122   'blithe'
blis (ns) 139, 141; blisse (ds) 149, 153   'bliss'
blōðe (ds) 48   'blood'
brēostum (ds) 118   'breast'
cōlode (s) 72   'cooled'
cōm (s) 151   'came'
Crist (ns) 56; Criste (ds) 116   'Christ'
cumen (t) 80   'come'
cwōm (s) 155; cwōman (p) 57   'came'
cyning (as) 44, 133; cyninges (gs) 56   'king'
cynn (as) 94   'kind, race'
daga (gp) 136   'days'

dēað (as) 101; dēaðes (gs) 113   'death'

dēopan (ds) 75   'deep'

deorcan (dp) 46   'dark'

dōm-dæge (ds) 105   'Doomsday, Judgement Day'

dōmes (gs) 107   'judgement'

dorste (s) 35, 42, 45, 47   'dared'

drēam (ns) 140; drēames (gs) 144; drēamum (dp) 133   'joy'

dryhten (as) 64; (ns) 101, 105, 144; dryhtnes (gs) 9, 35, 75, 113, 136, 140   'lord'

dyde (s) 114   'did'

ēac 92   'also'

eal (ns) 55; eall (ns) 6, 12, 82; (as) 58, 94; ealle (np) 9, 128; (ap) 37, 74, 93, ealra (gp) 125; eallum (dp) 154   'all'

ealdor (ns) 90   'lord'

eall 20, 48, 62   'all, entirely'

eaxlum 32 (dp)   'shoulders'

eft 68, 101, 103   'afterwards, again'

elne (ds) 34, 60, 123   'courage, zeal'

ende (ds) 29   'end, edge'

engel (as) 9; englas (np) 106; englum (dp) 153   'angel'

ēode (s) 54   'went'

eorðan (gs) 37; (ds) 42, 74, 137, 145   'earth'

eorð-wege (ds) 120   'earthly way'

fæger (ns) 73; fægere (np) 8, 10; fægran (ds) 21   'fair, beautiful'

fæste 38, 43   'firmly' ('fast')

feala (ap) 50, 125, 131   'many'

feallan 43   'to fall'

fēondas (np) 30, 33; (ap) 38   'enemies' ('fiends')

fīfe (np) 8   'five'

folc (ns) 140   'folk, people'

foldan (gs) 8, 43; (ds) 132   'earth'

for 21, 111   'because of'; 93, 112   'in front of'; 99, 113, 146   'for the sake of'

forð 54, 132   'forth, away'

for-þan 84   'therefore'

forð-wege (ds) 125   'departure, way forth'

fram 69   'from'

frean (as) 33   'lord'

frēond (ns) 144; frēondas (np) 76; frēonda (gp) 132   'friend'

fyll (as) 56   'fall'
fyllan 73   'to fell, cut down'
gāst (as) 49; gāstas (np) 11; gāsta (gp) 152   'spirit' ('ghost')
gealga (ns) 10; gealgan (as) 40   'gallows'
gealg-trēowe (ds) 146   'gallows-tree'
gebringe (sj) 139   'bring'
gefæstnodon (p) 33   'fastened'
gehȳran 78   'to hear'
gehȳrde (s) 26   'heard'
geong (ns) 39   'young'
gesāwe (sj) 4   'saw'
gesceaft (ns) 55, 82   'creation'
geseah (s) 14, 21, 33, 36, 51   'saw'
gesēocan 119   'to seek'
gestōdon (p) 63   'stood'
gesyhðe (ds) 21, 41, 66; (as) 96   'sight, vision'
gimmas (np) 7, 16   'gems'
God (ns) 39, 93, 98, 106, 156; (as) 51, 60; Godes (gs) 83, 152   'God'
gōde (as) 70   'good'
gold (as) 18; golde (ds) 7, 16, 77   'gold'
hālgum (dp) 143, 154   'saints' (lit. 'holy (ones)')
hālige (np) 11   'holy'
hām (as) 148   'home'
handa (ds) 59   'hand'
hæbbe (s) 50, 79   'have'
hæfde (s) 49; hæfdon (p) 16, 52   'had'
hæleð (ns) 39, 78, 95   'man, hero'
hē (ns) 34, 40, 41, 49, etc.   'he'
hēafdum (ds) 63   'head'
heardost 87   'hardest'
helpe (ds) 102   'help'
heofona (gp) 45; heofenas (ap) 103; heofenes (gs) 64; heofenum (dp)
    85, 134, 140, 154   'heaven'
heofonlicne (as) 148   'heavenly'
heofon-rīces (gs) 91   'kingdom of heaven'
heonon 132   'from here'
heora (gp) 31, 155   'their'
hēr 108, 137, 145   'here'
hēton (p) 31   'ordered'
hī, hīe (np) 32, 46, 48, 60, 63, 64, 66, 67, 68, 115, 116, 132   'they'

hider 103   'to here, hither'
hilde-rinca (gp) 72; hilde-rincas (np) 61   'warriors'
him (ds) 65, 67, 108, 118   'him, himself'
him (dp) 31, 63, 83, 86, 88, 133   'them, themselves'
hine (as) 11, 61, 64   'him'
hine 39   'himself'
hira (gp) 47   'of them'
his (gs) 49, 63, 92, 102, 106, 156   'his'
hit (ns) 19, 22, 26, 97   'it'
hlāford (as) 45   'lord'
hwænne 136   'when'
hwǣr 112   'where'
hwæt 1, 90   'lo, behold' ('what')
hwæt 2, 116   'what, which'
hwæðre, hwæðere 18, 24, 38, 42, 57, 59, 70, 75, 101   'however, nevertheless'
hwīle (as) 24, 64, 70, 84   'while, time'
hwīlum 22, 23   'sometimes'
ic (ns) 1, 4, 13, 14, 18, 21 etc.   'I'
in 118   'in'
is (s) 80, 97, 126, 129, 130, 139, 140, 141   'is'
langa (as) 24   'long'
lāðost 88   'most hateful' ('loathest')
lǣdan 5   'to lead'
lēofa (ns) 78, 95   'dear' ('love')
lēohte (ds) 5   'light'
līces (gs) 63   'body'
līf (as) 147; līfe (ds) 109, 138; līfes (gs) 88, 126   'life'
lifiaþ (p) 134   'live'
lim-wērigne (as) 63   'limb-weary'
man (ns) 73, 75   'one'
man (ns) 112   'man, person'
man-cyn(n) (as) 41, 104; man-cynnes (gs) 33, 99   'mankind'
manigra (gp) 41; manegum (dp) 99   'many'
mannum (dp) 96, 102   'men'
Mārian (as) 92   'Mary'
meahte(s) 18   'could'
men (np) 12, 82, 128; menn (dp) 93   'men'
mē (as, ds) 2, 4, 30, 31, 32 etc.   'me'
micle (ds) 34, 60; miclan (ds) 65, 102   'great' ('mickle')

mid 7, 14, 16, 20, 22 etc.   'with'
midre (ds) 2   'middle'
miht (s) 78   'can'
mihte (s) 37   'could'
mihte (ds) 102   'might, power'
mihtig (ns) 151   'mighty'
mīn (ns) 78, 95, 130; mīnum (ds) 30   'my' ('mine')
mōde (ds) 122, 130   'mood, spirit'
mōdig 41   'brave'
mōdor (as) 92   'mother'
mōt (s) 142; mōte (sj) 127   'may'
mycel (ns) 130, 139; mycle (ds) 123;   'great' ('mickle')
naman (ds) 113   'name'
nǣnigum (ds) 47   'none' (ne + ǣnig)
ne 10, 35, 42, etc.   'not'
nihte (ds) 2   'night'
nū 78, 80, 84, 95, 126, 134   'now'
of 29, 49, 61, 66, 120, 133   'from'
ofer 91, 94   'above'; 35, 82   'against'; 12, 82   'throughout'
oftor 128   'more often'
on 5, 9, 20, etc.   'in, on, at'
ond 12, 13 etc.   'and'
ongan (s) 19, 27, 73; ongunnon (p) 65, 67   'began'
onginnen (pj) 116   'begin'
opene (np) 47   'open'
oð-ðæt 26, 32   'until'
oððe 36   'or'
reste (ds) 3   'rest(ing place), bed'
reste (s) 64, 69   'rested'
rīce (as) 119; (ds) 152   'kingdom'
rihtne (as) 89   'right'
rōd (ns) 44, 136; rōde (ds) 56, 131; (as) 119   'cross' ('rood')
sāwl (ns) 120   'soul'
sceal (s) 119   'must' ('shall')
sceolde (s) 43   'had to, must' ('should')
scīnan 15   'to shine'
se (ns) 13, 42, 78, 95, 111, 112, 150   'the'
sē (ns) 98, 107, 113, 145   'that, who'
sēcan 104, 127   'to seek'
secgan 1   'to say, relate'

secge (sj) 96 'should say, relate'
seolfre (ds) 77 'silver'
sīdan (ds) 49 'side'
sōhton (p) 133 'sought'
sorga (gp) 80; sorgum (dp) 20, 59 'sorrows'
sprecan 27 'to speak'
standan 43, 62 'to stand'
stōd (s) 38; stōdon (p) 7, 71 'stood'
stāne (ds) 66 'stone'
strang (ns) 40 strange (np) 30 'strong'
sunu (ns) 150 'son'
swā 92, 108, 114 'just as'
sylfa (ns) 105 'himself'
sylfe (as) 92 'herself'
synnum (dp) 13, 99, 146 'sins'
syðþan, siððan, 3, 49 'when'
syþþan 142 'afterwards'
tō 2, 31, 42, 43 etc. 'at, into, to'
trēow (as) 4, 14, 17, 25 'tree'
þā (as) 20, 68, 119; (ap) 27; (np) 46, 61 'the'
þā 33, 35, 39, 65, 67, 73, 90, 103, 122 'then'
þā 36, 41, 42, 68, 151, 155 'when'
þām (ds, dp) 9, 50, 58, 59, 61 etc. 'the'
þāra (gp) 86 'of those'
þās (as) 96 'this'
þǣr 8, 9, 10, 11, 24, 30, 31, 32, 33, 35, 57, 60, 63, 64, 69, 70, 75, 101, 110,
   117, 149 'there'
þǣr 123, 139, 140, 141, 142, 156 'where'
þǣre (ds) 21, 112, 131 'the'
ðǣr-on 67 'therein'
þæs (gs) 49 'of the'
þæt (ns) 6; (as) 18, 21 'the'
þæt, ðæt 28, 39, 58, 66, 74 'it, that'
þæt 4, 19, 26, 29, 34, 79, 81, 96, 97, 107, 127 'that, when'
þe 86, 98, 111, 113, 118, 121, 137, 145, 149, 154 'who, which'
þegnas (np) 75 'retainers'
ðē (as) 95 'you' ('thee')
þēodne (ds) 69 'lord'
þēos (ns) 12, 82 'this'
þone (as) 127 'the'

þonne 128 'than'
þonne 107, 115, 117, 139, 142   'then'
ðū (ns) 78, 96 'you' ('thou')
þurh, ðurh 10, 18, 119 'through'
þysne (as) 104 'this'
þysson (ds) 138; þyssum (ds) 83, 109 'this'
under 55, 85 'under'
ūp 71; uppe 9 'up'
ūs (ap) 73, 75; (ds) 147 'us'
wǣron (p) 8 'were'
wæs (s) 6, 10, 13, 20, etc. 'was'
wē (np) 70 'we'
wealdend (as) 67; (ns) 111, 155; wealdende (ds) 121; wealdendes (gs)
    53 'lord'
weard (ns) 91   'guardian'
weg (as) 88 'way'
well 129, 143 'well'
weorc (as) 79 'work'
wīfa (gp) 94 'women'
wile (s) 107 'wishes, will wish'
willa (ns) 129 'will, desire'
wolde (s) 34, 41, 113; woldon (p) 68 'wished'
word (ap) 27; (as) 35; worde (ds) 111; wordum (dp) 97 'word'
worulde (gs) 133 'world'
wudu (ns) 27 'wood'
wuldre (ds) 135, 143, 155; wuldres (gs) 14, 90, 97, 133 'glory'
wylle (s) 1 'wish'

Concluding Remarks

You have come to the end of this introduction to the literature and language of the Anglo-Saxons. You are now familiar with a range of Old English genres – from historical and religious prose to riddling and epic poetry – and you have gained some direct insight into the cultural origins of the English literary tradition. You should now feel reasonably confident about coping with the language and literary conventions of the Anglo-Saxon people – albeit with the support given in this book. We hope that we have convinced you that there is no substitute for direct access to the original works, or for the often frustrating but frequently illuminating struggle to make sense of the Old English texts themselves. Translations, as we have seen, are always filtered through the concerns and inevitable biases of their translators and their times. By engaging with the original texts, we come face to face with the originators of the world's first truly global language and we learn more about their – and our – habits of thought. Many more advanced textbooks are available, should you wish to travel further along the road to understanding Old English independently of the support provided here. We wish you well on your journey.

Glossary of Technical Terms

This glossary gives brief definitions of the main technical terms used in the linguistic and literary descriptions in *Beginning Old English*. A fuller glossary of linguistic terms with explanations is available at the *Language into Languages Teaching* website: www.arts.gla.ac.uk/ SESLL/EngLang/LILT/frameset.htm.

Accusative: see *Case*.

Active: see *Voice*.

Adjective: a descriptive word that modifies a noun, e.g. 'brave' in 'a brave warrior'. In Old English, adjectives are said to be 'weak' if they are preceded by a determiner like 'the', e.g. 'the brave warriors', and 'strong' if they are not preceded by a determiner, e.g. 'brave warriors'. In Old English, then, weak and strong adjectives have different forms depending on whether or not they are preceded by a determiner.

Adverb: a word that expresses when, how, where, why or to what extent something was done, e.g. 'bravely' in 'they fought bravely' or 'here' in 'it happened here'.

Alliteration: in poetry, the linking together of words through the identical sound of the initial consonants, e.g. 'dull . . . deadly', or 'fiery . . . flame'.

Ambiguity: double meaning.

Anacrusis: the addition of an extra unstressed syllable at the start of a metrically patterned line of verse, to 'lead in' to the verse.

Anapaest: a metrical unit consisting of two unstressed syllables, followed by a stressed syllable.

Ballad: a narrative song or poem, often composed in four-line stanzas, with alternating lines of four beats and three beats per line, rhyming on the second and fourth line.

Case: the particular form of a word that signals its function in a sentence; e.g. the Nominative form 'he' signals that this pronoun is the Subject of its sentence while the Accusative form 'him' signals that it is the Object. Genitives indicate possession (e.g. 'his'), while Datives suggest prepositional meaning (e.g. 'to/with him').

Circumlocution: expressing a concept in an indirect manner, using more words than is necessary.

Clause: a sequence of phrases organised around a verb phrase; for example as a Subject, Verb and Object, or a Subject, Verb and Complement. A subordinate clause acts as a constituent in a larger clause, e.g. 'because he loved her' in 'He married her because he loved her.'

Compound word: a word made up of two other words, e.g. 'gift-giver'.

Conjunction: a grammatical word used to link together words, phrases or clauses, e.g. 'and', 'but', 'if' and 'although'.

Consonant: a sound produced by completely or partially blocking the flow of air from the lungs, e.g. 'p', 'n' and 'f'.

Couplet: in poetry, a pair of consecutively rhyming lines.

Crux: a textual puzzle requiring interpretation or explanation.

Dative: see *Case.*

Declension (also 'Paradigm'): (a) the presentation of the different cases of a noun, and associated adjectives and determiners, usually arranged as Nominative, Accusative, Genitive, Dative; (b) a group of nouns, classified according to their inflexions.

Determiner: words that specify or classify nouns, e.g. 'a(n)', 'the', 'this', 'that', 'my' etc.

Dialect: a language variety characterised by distinctive features of vocabulary and grammar.

Elegy: a mournful or melancholy poem.

Epic: a narrative poem that celebrates a hero's achievements.

Euphemism: the substitution of a more acceptable expression for one that is distasteful or undesirable.

Feminine: see *Gender.*

Foot: in poetry, a unit of metrical verse, consisting of a recurring pattern of stressed and unstressed syllables.

Formula: in Old English poetry, a phrase that is often repeated, largely unchanged, in different contexts.

Gender: the classification of words into three groups, 'masculine', 'feminine' and 'neuter', according to their grammatical behaviour. Today's English follows 'natural' gender based on biological sex (e.g. 'women' are feminine, 'stallions' are masculine and 'computers' are neuter). In Old English, the classification of words as masculine, feminine and neuter is more arbitrary.

Genitive: see *Case*.

Gloss: to explain a word, usually by writing a definition or translation in a text, glossary or dictionary.

Half-line: in Old English poetry, the conventional unit of verse. Each line is made up of two half-lines, usually referred to as the 'a-verse' and 'b-verse', linked by alliteration.

Headstave: the first stressed syllable in the second half-line of Old English poetry.

Heptameter: in poetry, a line made up of seven metrical units, or 'feet'.

Heroic poetry: verse that draws both upon legendary material and upon the 'heroic code', a set of conventions governing the behaviour of warriors in pre-Christian Germanic culture.

Iambic: a metrical unit consisting of an unstressed syllable followed by a stressed syllable.

Imperative: see *Mood*.

Indicative: see *Mood*.

Infinitive: the 'base' form of a verb, e.g. 'to go', or 'to fight'.

Inflexion: the ending of a word that signals its grammatical case, number, tense, etc.

Kenning: in Old English verse, a condensed metaphor, e.g. 'the whale's road' to refer to the sea.

Masculine: see *Gender*.

Measure: in poetry, rhythmical language, 'measured' by metrical units.

Metathesis: the switching of sounds in a word, e.g. 'modren' for 'modern'.

Mood: in grammar, the form of a verb that signals, for example, whether it is stating a fact (indicative mood, e.g. 'fight/fights/fought'), or expressing a hypothesis, or desire (subjunctive mood, e.g. 'save' in 'God save the Queen!') or command (imperative mood, e.g. 'Go!').

Neuter: see *Gender*.

Nominative: see *Case*.

Noun: the kind of word that names things, e.g. 'soldier', 'spear', 'fortress'. A full noun phrase might be made up of a determiner, an adjective and a noun (e.g. 'the brave soldier').

Number: the grammatical signal that shows if a word is singular or plural.

Object: the noun phrase that acts as the goal of the verb, e.g. 'the sleeping warriors' in 'Grendel attacked the sleeping warriors'.

Paradigm: see *Declension*.

Participle: the form of the verb that can be used in combination with 'be' or 'have'. The present participle combines with 'be', e.g. 'is/was *going*', and the past participle combines with 'has', e.g. 'has/had *gone*'.

Passive: see *Voice*.

Pentameter: in poetry, a line made up of five metrical units, or 'feet'.

Person: the form that a verb takes, according to whether the Subject is I/we ('first person'), you ('second person'), or he/she/it/they ('third person').

Plural: see *Number*.

Preposition: a grammatical word like 'to', 'before' or 'with', normally used with a noun phrase to express concepts like location ('to the island'), time ('before the battle') or means ('with an axe').

Pronoun: a word like 'he', 'she', 'it', 'they' etc., used to substitute for a full noun or noun phrase.

Prosopopoeia: in Old English riddles, the convention by which inanimate objects describe themselves in the first person.

Riddle: in Old English poetry, a type of puzzling verse that invites the reader to guess what is being described

Singular: see *Number*.

Stanza: a sequence of lines in poetry, usually linked by rhyme.

Stem: the 'basic' part of a word, that is, the part of a word without prefixes or inflexions, e.g. the stem of 'uncovered' is 'cover'.

Stress: see *Syllable*.

Subject: the noun phrase that acts as the agent of the verb when it is in the active voice, e.g. 'Grendel' in 'Grendel attacked the sleeping warriors'.

Subjunctive: see *Mood*.

Subordinate clause: see *Clause*.

Syllable: a unit of sound, usually consisting of a combination of consonants and vowels, e.g. 'go' has one syllable; 'going' has two syllables. The first syllable of 'going' is the stressed syllable; the second is the unstressed syllable.

Synonyms: words with similar or identical meaning.

Tense: the form of a verb that signals whether it refers to past, present or future.

Tetrameter: in poetry, a line made up of four metrical units, or 'feet'.

Thesis: the unstressed part of a metrical foot.

Trimeter: in poetry, a line made up of three metrical units, or 'feet'.

Unstressed: see *Syllable*.

Unvoiced: of consonants, pronounced without vibration of the vocal cords, e.g. 'th' in 'thin'.

Variation: in Old English poetry, the repetition of an idea in different consecutive phrases, all of which have much the same meaning.

Verb: a word that expresses actions or events. In today's English, main verbs are modified by auxiliary verbs like 'is/has' in 'is going' or 'has gone'. In Old English and today's English, verbs fall into two main classes, (i) strong, or irregular, verbs, which indicate past tense usually by changing the central vowel, e.g. 'swim/swam', and (ii) weak, or regular, verbs, which indicate past tense by adding an inflexion, e.g. 'walk/walked'.

Voice: the form of the verb phrase that indicates whether the Subject is the agent (e.g. 'Beowulf *killed* the dragon' – active voice) or the goal ('Beowulf *was killed* by the dragon' – passive voice).

Voiced: of consonants, pronounced with vibration of the vocal cords, e.g. 'th' in 'this'.

Vowel: a sound produced without blocking the flow of air from the lungs, but altering the shape of the tongue in the mouth. Long vowels have a slightly greater duration, intensity and pitch than short vowels, e.g. in many English accents the vowel in 'cart' is long, while the vowel in 'cat' is short. In most Scottish accents, the stressed vowel in 'agreed' is long, while the vowel in 'greed' is short.

Appendix
Old English Paradigms

For ease of reference, this section sets out the main forms of different types of Old English words. Old English words are generally grouped according to the endings or 'inflexions' they use to signal their grammatical role.

1. Pronouns

The Old English pronoun system looks like this:

	Nominative	Accusative	Genitive	Dative
Singular				
1st person	ic	mē	mīn	mē
2nd person	þū	þē	þīn	þē
3rd person masc.	hē	hine	his	him
3rd person fem.	hēo	hīe	hire	hire
3rd person neut.	hit	hit	his	him
Plural				
1st person	wē	ūs	ūre	ūs
2nd person	gē	ēow	ēower	ēow
3rd person (all genders)	hīe	hīe	hira	him

2. Nouns

There are three main genders of nouns in Old English, each with its own pattern of inflexions:

Masculine nouns (example *cyning* 'king')

	Nominative	Accusative	Genitive	Dative
Singular	cyning	cyning	cyninges	cyninge
Plural	cyningas	cyningas	cyninga	cyningum

Feminine nouns (example *heall* 'hall')

	Nominative	Accusative	Genitive	Dative
Singular	heall	healle	healle	healle
Plural	healla	healla	healla	heallum

Neuter nouns (example *scip* 'ship')

	Nominative	Accusative	Genitive	Dative
Singular	scip	scip	scipes	scipe
Plural	scipu	scipu	scipa	scipum

In addition, there is a group of nouns of all three genders, whose Nominative singular form ends in *-a* (masculine) or *-e* (feminine and neuter). These follow a pattern of inflexions sometimes known as the '*-an* declension' because most of the forms end in *-an*. An alternative term is the 'weak' declension, contrasting with the 'strong' declensions given above.

'*-an* declension' nouns (example *draca* 'dragon')

	Nominative	Accusative	Genitive	Dative
Singular	draca	dracan	dracan	dracan
Plural	dracan	dracan	dracena	dracum

There are some variants on these patterns. For instance, neuter nouns with a 'long' syllable (i.e. either a long vowel, or a short vowel followed by at least two consonants) have no ending in the Nominative and Accusative plural: this is the origin of today's endingless plurals such as *deer* and *sheep*.

Irregular nouns

There are also two groups of nouns that do not follow the main patterns. The first are nouns of relationship: OE *fæder* 'father', *mōdor* 'mother', *brōþor* 'brother', *dohtor* 'daughter' and *sweostor* 'sister'. These often take no inflexional endings except for Genitive plural *-a* and Dative plural *-um*.

The second is a group of nouns which undergo a vowel change rather than adding an inflexional ending. The declension is illustrated by OE *tōþ* 'tooth':

	Nominative	Accusative	Genitive	Dative
Singular	tōþ	tōþ	tēþ	tēþ
Plural	tēþ	tēþ	tōþa	tōþum

It is from declensions such as this that today's irregular plurals such as *foot/feet, goose/geese* and *tooth/teeth* derive. There were more nouns of this type in Old English, including OE *bōc* 'book', but most of them have now adopted the standard *-s* plural, as with *book/books* (instead of *book/beek*).

3. Determiners

The declensions for the determiners *se* 'the' and *þes* 'this' are as follows:

	Nominative	Accusative	Genitive	Dative
Singular				
masculine	se	þone	þæs	þæm
feminine	sēo	þā	þǣre	þǣre
neuter	þæt	þæt	þæs	þæm
Plural (all genders)	þā	þā	þāra	þæm
Singular				
masculine	þes	þisne	þisses	þissum
feminine	þēos	þās	þisse	þisse
neuter	þis	þis	þisses	þissum
Plural (all genders)	þās	þās	þissa	þissum

4. Adjectives

Adjectives are gathered into one of two groups or 'declensions', depending on whether or not they are preceded by a determiner. The pattern of inflexions for adjectives preceded by a determiner is known as the 'weak' declension:

Weak adjectives (example: *gōd* 'good')

	Nominative	Accusative	Genitive	Dative
Singular				
masculine	gōda	gōdan	gōdan	gōdan
feminine	gōde	gōdan	gōdan	gōdan
neuter	gōde	gōde	gōdan	gōdan
Plural (all genders)	gōdan	gōdan	gōdra	gōdum

The pattern of inflexions for adjectives which are **not** preceded by a determiner is known as the 'strong' declension:

Strong adjectives (example: *gōd* 'good')

	Nominative	Accusative	Genitive	Dative
Singular				
masculine	gōd	gōdne	gōdes	gōdum
feminine	gōd	gōde	gōdre	gōdre
neuter	gōd	gōd	gōdes	gōdum
Plural				
masculine	gōde	gōde	gōdra	gōdum
feminine	gōde	gōde	gōdra	gōdum
neuter	gōd	gōd	gōdra	gōdum

5. Verbs

The following table gives the main variations in the indicative forms and participles of regular ('weak') and irregular ('strong') verbs, as well as for the irregular verb *to be*. Weak verbs are exemplified by *wunian* 'to live, dwell', while strong verbs are exemplified by *feohtan* 'to fight'.

	Weak	Strong	Irregular
Infinitive	wunian	feohtan	bēon
Present participle	wuniende	feohtende	wesende
Singular			
1st person	wunie	feohte	eom
2nd person	wunast	feohtest	eart
3rd person	wunaþ	fieht	is
Plural (all)	wuniaþ	feohtaþ	sind(on)
Past participle	gewunod	gefohten	gebēon
Singular			
1st person	wunode	feaht	wæs
2nd person	wunodest	fuhte	wǣre
3rd person	wunode	feaht	wæs
Plural (all)	wunodon	fuhton	wǣron

The following table gives the main variations in the subjunctive and imperative forms of weak and strong verbs, as well as for the irregular verb *to be*.

	Weak	Strong	Irregular
Infinitive	wunian	feohtan	bēon
Present			
Singular (all)	wunie	feohte	sīe
Plural (all)	wunien	feohten	sīen
Past			
Singular (all)	wunode	fuhte	wǣre
Plural (all)	wunoden	fuhten	wǣren
Imperative singular	wuna	feoht	bēo
Imperative plural	wuniaþ	feohtaþ	bēoþ

Further Reading

The following books and websites are recommended if you wish to take your study of Old English and Anglo-Saxon culture further.

History and Culture

Blair, Peter Hunter (2003), *An Introduction to Anglo-Saxon England*, 3rd edn (Cambridge: Cambridge University Press).

Campbell, James (ed.) (1991), *The Anglo-Saxons* (Harmondsworth: Penguin).

Lapidge, Michael, Blair, John, Keynes, Simon and Scragg, Donald (eds) (1999), *The Blackwell Encyclopaedia of Anglo-Saxon England* (Oxford: Blackwell).

Sawyer, P. H. (1998), *From Roman Britain to Norman England*, 2nd edn (London: Routledge).

Webster, Leslie and Backhouse, Janet (eds) (1991), *The Making of England: Anglo-Saxon Art and Culture, AD 600–900* (London: British Museum Press).

Wilson, David M. (1984), *Anglo-Saxon Art from the Seventh Century to the Norman Conquest* (London: Thames & Hudson).

Literature

Aertsen, Henk and Bremmer, Rolf H. (eds) (1994), *Companion to Old English Poetry* (Amsterdam: VU University Press).

Alexander, Michael (2002), *A History of Old English Literature* (Peterborough, Ont.: Broadview Press).

Fulk, R. D. and Cain, Christopher, M. (2002), *A History of Old English Literature* (Oxford: Blackwell).

Godden, Malcolm and Lapidge, Michael (eds) (1991), *The Cambridge Companion to Old English Literature* (Cambridge: Cambridge University Press).
Greenfield, Stanley B. and Calder, Daniel G. (1986), *A New Critical History of Old English Literature* (New York: New York University Press).
Pulsiano, Phillip and Treharne, Elaine (eds) (2001), *A Companion to Anglo-Saxon Literature* (Oxford: Blackwell).

Language, Textbooks and Readers

Baker, Peter S. (2003), *Introduction to Old English* (Oxford: Blackwell).
Marsden, Richard (2004), *The Cambridge Old English Reader* (Cambridge: Cambridge University Press).
McCully, Chris and Hilles, Sharon (2004), *The Earliest English: An Introduction to Old English Language* (Harlow: Longman Pearson).
Mitchell, Bruce (1995), *An Invitation to Old English and Anglo-Saxon England* (Oxford: Blackwell).
Mitchell, Bruce and Robinson, Fred (2001), *A Guide to Old English*, 6th edn (Oxford: Blackwell).
Smith, Jeremy J. (2005), *Essentials of Early English*, 2nd edn (London: Routledge).
Sweet's Anglo-Saxon Primer (1953), 9th edn, revised by Norman Davis (Oxford: Clarendon Press).
Sweet's Anglo-Saxon Reader in Prose and Verse (1975), 15th edn, revised by Dorothy Whitelock (Oxford: Oxford University Press).
Treharne, Elaine (ed.) (2003), *Old and Middle English, c.890–c.1400: An Anthology*, 2nd edn (Oxford: Blackwell).

Translations

Bradley, S. A. J. (1982), *Anglo-Saxon Poetry* (London: Dent).
Crossley-Holland, Kevin (2002) *The Anglo-Saxon World*, new edn (Woodbridge: Boydell).
Heaney, Seamus (2002), *Beowulf: A Verse Translation* (New York: W. W. Norton).
Swanton, Michael (1993), *Anglo-Saxon Prose* (London: Dent).

Websites

http://www.doe.utoronto.ca
http://www.arts.gla.ac.uk/SESLL/EngLang/ugrad/OE/Homepage.html
http://www.ucalgary.ca/UofC/eduweb/engl401/site.htm
http://www.engl.virginia.edu/OE/
http://www.georgetown.edu/faculty/ballc/englisc/instant-oe.html

Index

145/24